LORD
DURHAM'S
MISSION
TO
CANADA

THE CARLETON LIBRARY

A series of Canadian reprints and new collections of source material relating to Canada, issued under the editorial supervision of the Institute of Canadian Studies of Carleton University, Ottawa.

LORD DURHAM'S MISSION TO CANADA

❦ ❦ ❦

AN ABRIDGEMENT OF
LORD DURHAM:
A BIOGRAPHY OF
JOHN GEORGE LAMBTON,
FIRST EARL OF DURHAM
BY
CHESTER NEW

❦ ❦ ❦

EDITED AND INTRODUCED BY
H. W. McCREADY

The Carleton Library No. 8 / McClelland and Stewart Limited

© *McClelland and Stewart Limited, 1963*

Reprinted 1965 and 1968

By permission of the Oxford
University Press and Mr. G. C. New

Chester W. New, *Lord Durham*:
A biography, of John George Lambton,
first Earl of Durham, was first
published by the Clarendon Press,
Oxford, in 1929

The Canadian Publishers
McClelland and Stewart Limited
25 Hollinger Road, Toronto 16

Design: Frank Newfeld

PRINTED AND BOUND IN CANADA
BY
T. H. BEST PRINTING CO. LIMITED

CONTENTS

Preface to the Carleton Library Edition
page viii

Introduction
The Career of Lord Durham to 1838
page ix

I The Canadian Situation

Lower Canada; Papineau; the British Party;
the Rebellion of 1837; Upper Canada; the
Family Compact and the movement against it;
the conception of Responsible Government;
the Baldwins; Sir Francis Bond Head; the
Rebellion of 1837 and its aftermath.

page 15

II Preparing for Canada

Durham's appointment; debates in Parliament;
Durham's instructions and powers; his study
of the Canadian question and of representations made to him; Tory attack; Durham's
staff appointments.

page 41

III A Good Beginning

Durham's arrival in Quebec; initial arrangements; protest to Washington; friction with
the authorities in London; the problem of the
political prisoners; Bermuda Ordinance.

page 62

Preface to the
Carleton Library Edition

Professor Chester W. New's *Lord Durham: A biography of John George Lambton, first Earl of Durham* was published in 1929, and although long out-of-print and in heavy demand for many years, it has never been re-issued. No substitute has been available for the major figure and phase of Canadian history with which it deals. Immediately upon its appearance, New's biography superseded the only earlier account of Lord Durham's life, that of Stuart J. Reid, published in 1907. Nor has any work published since 1929 challenged New's definitive interpretation of Durham's career.

Professor New was a most industrious and persistent researcher, and the fact that his work was based throughout upon extensive and intensive study of the primary sources, especially personal papers, parliamentary reports, and newspapers, in all the principal private and public repositories of Britain and Canada, will be evident to every reader. It will also be noted that Professor New had a conception of the biographer's task that was some distance removed from that of Lytton Strachey. "My business," he wrote in his 1929 preface, "has been primarily to describe and interpret, and not to praise or blame. I have conceived of the task of the biographer as simply to set the stage and permit the central figure, his colleagues, friends, and opponents, to speak and act for themselves." It has been the judgement of British and Canadian historians that Professor New admirably fulfilled his conception of the biographer's rôle.

Lord Durham's Mission to Canada comprises chapters 16-23 of the original biography. In addition to the earlier chapters on Durham's career in England, a final one, "The Last Months," has also been omitted. Professor New's original preface has been left out, together with an appendix exploring the authorship of the Durham *Report*. The chapters reprinted here are the part that centre upon Durham's mission to Canada and his famous *Report* – that section of the book most necessary to students of Canadian history.

Introduction
The Career of Lord Durham to 1838

The essential features of the brief but distinguished public career of John George Lambton, first Earl of Durham, are readily set forth. He was born on April 12, 1792, the eldest son of William Henry Lambton, a well-to-do, North-of-England landlord and colliery-owner, to whom he succeeded at the tender age of seven. To his father – who had been Member of Parliament for the City of Durham in the Whig interest – as well as to his guardians and his tutor, Lambton owed the Foxite Radical Tradition which was his most distinguishing feature in a public career devoted to politics. His father had been one of the small Whig remnant that remained loyal to Charles James Fox throughout the dark days of the Anti-Jacobin reaction in the 1790's and had been among the founders of the Society of the Friends of the People. His tutor, Dr William Beddoes, had been fired out of Oxford because of his sympathies with the French Revolution. His guardians and relatives were of the same persuasion, and Foxite influences were uppermost in the family circle. Neither Eton (1805-8), nor the 10th Dragoons (1809-11), nor a Gretna Green marriage with Lord Cholmondeley's natural daughter, Henrietta, tamed this strain in Lambton's make-up. Indeed, it may be regarded as formative and fundamental to his entire career.

Lambton entered the House of Commons in September 1813 at the age of twenty-one, and represented the County of Durham as a Whig from that date until he was raised to the House of Lords as Baron Durham in 1828. Promptly upon his entry into Parliament he associated himself with liberal and radical causes and quickly gained notoriety as a critic of the Tory administration of the day and as an advocate of Progressive legislation. He supported Catholic Emancipation, advocated the removal of all legal disabilities from Dissenters, and took up the case of Queen Caroline with gusto. It was, however, as an early champion of Parliamentary reform that Lambton made his mark on the Whig Party, on Parliament, and on the country. It was this enthusiasm, in particular, that earned him the sobriquet "Radical Jack," and made him the darling of the reform agitation of the 1820's and 30's. His first major public step in this direction was taken in December 1819 when he announced in the House of Commons that he would shortly introduce a bill for the reform of Parliament. Lambton's declaration was to prove a milestone not only in his political career, but in the history of the Whig Party as well. "It was the first open sign of Whig support for Parliamentary change since the days when Lambton's father had helped to initiate the reform proposals of the Friends of the People, more than twenty years before."

The trial of Queen Caroline pushed all else aside for the next several months and it was not until the spring of 1821 that Lambton found an opportunity to keep his promise. His motion of April 17 calling on the House of Commons to go into Committee of the Whole in order to consider the state of popular representation was easily beaten in a thin House by a skilful manœuvre led by George Canning, but enough had been done to associate Lambton with redistribution, secret ballot, abolition of rotten boroughs, extension of the suffrage, and short Parliaments. It established him as a Radical, indeed a leader of the Radicals, within the Whig Party, forged an alliance between him and Hobhouse, Burdett, Place, and Whitbread, and identified the Whigs with radical Parliamentary Reform once again. His Bill of 1821 was, indeed, to prove a detailed anticipation of the famous measure of 1832.

Lambton's activities were not confined to Parliament or to its reform. He also revealed, in these early years of his public career, a lively interest in a number of philanthropic endeavours. He supported the "march of mind," as Brougham called the advance of popular education, subscribing to the Mechanic's Institute movement and to the University of London. He gave particular attention to the conditions of work in the mines and exerted himself to improve the lot of workers in his own collieries. Humphrey Davy's safety lamp was developed with Lambton's encouragement and support and as the result of experiments conducted in his coal mines. Lambton also organized and subsidized an ambitious benefit society for his miners; he provided them with libraries and schools and strove in every respect to prove himself a model employer.

Lambton had but a minor rôle in the political history of the 1820's. He was absent for a year repairing his health, never sound at the best of times, and he seems to have had little influence upon events at other times. His removal to the House of Lords as Baron Durham in 1828 was not, however, intended as a retirement from politics. His position of leadership in the Radical cause continued to be recognized, and his influence upon the Whig leader, Lord Grey, whose son-in-law he had become by his second marriage in 1816, continued to grow. Thus when the Grey government was formed in November 1830 it was natural that this early "Chartist" should find a place in it as Lord Privy Seal, and it was almost inevitable that he should be named with Lord John Russell, Lord Duncannon, and Sir James Graham to the Cabinet Committee charged with responsibility for drafting the Bill to reform Parliament. Durham's appointment to the Committee was a recognition of the fact that he had long occupied an advanced position on the question – while men, such as Grey, had remained hostile or indifferent – a position to which events had at length driven the Whig Party. The result was to establish Durham as a major figure in great affairs of state. He was much the most radical of the four who drafted the government's Bill; the ballot and the democratic implications of the measure were of his making. In the ensuing, long-drawn-out crisis Durham led the defence of the government's proposals in the House of Lords, and he was one of the earliest proponents of the policy of overcoming the Lords' opposition, not by compromise, but by a wholesale creation of new peers. The failure of the cabinet and the Prime Minister to move as fast or as far as Durham wished on these matters brought him to the verge of resignation by the end of 1831. His continued support was of the utmost importance to the Grey government and to the success of the Reform Bill, for he was able to hold Radical opinion behind the government in the House of Commons and in the country as no other member of the administration could. Radicals like Francis Place knew that Durham trusted the people, that he was completely in sympathy with the democratic movement, and that he would work to secure the most liberal changes in the electoral system that circumstances would permit. An aristocrat and son-in-law to Lord Grey, yet applauded by Francis Place! His position was unique indeed. He emerged as the popular hero of the reform agitation: the Whig leader from whom, indeed, still more was to be expected, for Durham made no protestations about "finality."

Once the struggle for the Reform of Parliament was won – Durham was, fittingly enough, one of the Royal Commissioners by whom the royal assent was signified in the House of Lords on June 7, 1832 – Durham's career entered upon an entirely novel and unexpected course. The last eight years of his life were to find him away from Britain much of the time on a series of special missions overseas. It was probably far from accidental that "Radical Jack" found himself thus consigned to honourable exile. Both Lord Grey and his successor, Lord Melbourne, together with other members of the government had come to think of Durham as a dangerous colleague. They feared his radical enthusiasms and his lack of tact and restraint, and they were anxious to occupy his talents in situations that would separate him from his popular following in the country, in the rank and file of the Whig Party and in the House of Commons. The first of his special assignments, that of Ambassador Extraordinary to the court of the Tsar in St Petersburg, took him out of England from July to October 1832. His task was to endeavour to negotiate a peaceful settlement of a situation in the Low Countries which appeared likely at that time to lead to trouble, if not war, between Russia and Britain. The Belgians had recently gained their independence, but the Dutch continued to hold Antwerp. They were encouraged by the Russians in doing so. The English democrat and the autocrat of all the Russians hit it off surprisingly well, and Durham was able to report to his government the assurances of the Tsar that his aid to the Dutch would not take an active form. Belgian independence could therefore be completed without fear of intervention.

Durham's return to England in October 1832 was followed by a deterioration of his relations with his fellow Whigs. Personal issues – in particular a bitter and lasting quarrel with Brougham which originated in suspicions of his treachery to Lord Grey – and disagreements on policy, led to Durham's resignation from the cabinet and to his nourishing pretensions to the party leadership itself. The latter endeavour proved unrewarding and he therefore accepted from Melbourne a second appointment abroad, this time as Minister Plenipotentiary and Ambassador Extraordinary to Russia. He stayed in St Petersburg for more than two years on this occasion, returning to England in the summer of 1837. It was shortly after his return that Melbourne asked him to undertake another special mission on behalf of the government, this time to report on the situation in British North America. Durham refused. But the news of the two rebellions, which reached London at the end of the year, led Melbourne to approach Durham again and enabled him this time to secure his consent (January 15, 1838).

It can scarcely be claimed that Melbourne had secured an expert for the Canadian mission, for Durham was as innocent of all knowledge of his new subject as the proud British tradition of the virtuous amateur requires. In any case, what Melbourne had in mind in pressing Durham into service was the need of rallying the radical peer and his following to the support of the insecure Whig government, since Canadian policy and problems had lately become a potent weapon of Radical attack upon them. Durham as High Commissioner in British North America with responsibility for recommending new policies would serve to keep the Radicals in line and strengthen the tottering Melbourne administration. It would be safer for the Whig government, moreover, if this enthusiastic improver were to expend some of his zeal at a safe distance on the other side of the Atlantic. Durham hesitated for two weeks and then, reluctantly and with a sense of patriotic sacrifice, he gave way and assumed responsibility for investigating the entire Canadian situation.

The man who in this manner and by this path came to set foot on Canadian soil on May 29, 1838, was a remarkable personality. He had been a life-long rebel himself so that a comparison with Lord Byron is by no means far-fetched. With chronic ill-health there was combined in him unusual physical energy and a spirit of magnificent if wayward ambition. He had in young manhood acquired many of the interests of the Regency buck and these never altogether left him. He was passionately fond of horse-racing and of hunting and shooting, and he indulged handsomely a taste for extravagant hospitality for which his social position and family fortune afforded him the means. Much more serious traits were his aristocratic arrogance, his vanity and petulance, and – worst of all – the violence of his outbursts of temper. Undoubtedly there was a close connection between his recurring bouts of irritability and bad temper on the one hand and the rise and fall of his vitality, the occurrence and recurrence of the sieges of migraine headaches which attacked him throughout his entire career. From his early twenties until his premature death at the age of forty-eight there was scarcely a month entirely free of the latter, and scarcely a single year after he passed thirty failed to bring him a breakdown in health of some kind and of some proportions. He was, nevertheless, distinguished among his contemporaries by his "marked independence of spirit, his courage, – recognized by friends and enemies alike and only criticized at times because there was too much of it, – the keen quality of his mind and his remarkable ability to analyse a situation and realize and describe its biggest and broadest aspects, are all intimately related to his political career and illustrated in other pages of this book."

In retrospect it appears that Durham's career reached its climax with the presentation of his famous Report. With that, his great work was done. Within eighteen months he was dead, a casualty, so Canadians have always been inclined to believe, in the struggle for responsible government. He had been unusually well while at work on the Report, but the spring and summer of 1839 saw him decline sharply and he had to spend several months at Cannes exhausted and in very bad health. He was, moreover, bitterly disappointed in the Melbourne government, though his last weeks found him formally reconciled with all the ministers and even with his old enemy Brougham. Only belatedly was it discovered that Durham was suffering from consumption – the disease that had taken his father, his first wife, and four of his children. He died on July 28, 1840. There is a tradition that shortly before his death he said, "Canada will one day do justice to my memory." Probably Canada did occupy Durham's thoughts at the end, and one of the children who was summoned to his death-bed was shortly to arrive there as Lady Elgin, wife of the Governor General who put Durham's principles into full effect.

H. W. MCCREADY
McMaster University
September, 1963

CHAPTER I The Canadian Situation

The situation that awaited Lord Durham in Canada was the most critical in its history. The purpose of this chapter is simply to analyse that situation and thus provide the setting for his administration and his contributions to Canadian history. No attempt will be made to outline the events of every administration from the days of the conquest. Much of that will be taken for granted or must be sought elsewhere.

In both Lower and Upper Canada the population was divided into two clearly-defined sections whose antagonism for years had been bitter and apparently irreconcilable. While similar in many respects, the situations were so different as to render separate treatment necessary.

The clash in Lower Canada was economic, racial, and constitutional. The conquering British armies had found on the banks of the St. Lawrence an agricultural population which from generation to generation had lived its happy, contented, unchanging life isolated from the rest of the world. Fears of many sorts which the conquest aroused in their hearts were discovered to be unwarranted. They continued to enjoy their religion without let or hindrance; their happy social life still centred around the parish church; the same laws governed their civil relations, protected their property, and ensured their inheritances; their mother-tongue was preserved to them and shared the official honours with that of the conquerors. The real menace came not from the new political power, but from the establishment in their midst of a different type of life. A group of bustling Anglo-Saxon merchants, heirs of generations of commercialism, worshippers of what commercialism considered progress, threatened the good old life. The old province must be reshaped to serve their ends, the old ways must be broken down in the interests of every improvement that would facilitate modern business. All the way through the history of the province, from 1763 to 1837, this conflict between agriculturists of a particularly conservative stamp and mercantilism of an aggressive type can be discerned.

If there had been no racial difference this economic clash would have been inevitable in its character and serious in its consequences, but it was intensified by the fact that the agricultural interest was French and the more important mercantile interests were in the hands of the English-speaking traders. The old ways were defended with all that pride of race – not only the French blood but a peculiar pride in his Canadianism – which characterized the French-Canadian, while the more matter-of-fact Anglo-Saxon chafed at the unprogressive attitude of a conquered people that had the presumption to believe that it could thwart the march of progress which the British race had carried to the ends of the earth. Becoming more and more impatient at the way their economic aims were thwarted, the 'British party' rang the changes on the racial issue. This was a British country; it should be made British in fact as well as in name. There were murmurings that too much had been done for the French by the British Government and that much would have to be undone; the French must be forced to adapt themselves to English institutions. The British minority assumed with an easy insolence that the country belonged to them. The French suspected in every move of the British party a challenge to their ancestral institutions, and their devotion to these waxed stronger and more unconquerable in proportion to the impatience of their antagonists. Yet through it all the French-Canadians were loyal to the British Government and grateful for its generosity, and if these years saw a growing antipathy to their British neighbours in Canada they also saw a growing respect for the British Crown and a devotion to British ideals of government.

The Constitutional Act of 1791 had set up in each province a constitution under which the executive function was exercised by a Governor appointed by the Crown, assisted by an Executive Council also appointed by the Crown but always on the nomination of the Governor, and the Legislature consisted of a Legislative Council nominated in the same manner and a Legislative Assembly elected on a broad popular franchise. Naturally the British mercantile interests captured and retained control of the two Councils, and the French agricultural interests dominated the Assembly. To suppose, however, as so many writers have done, that the political and constitutional struggle which resulted was only a form under which a racial rivalry fought itself out is to ignore the history of the American colonies, where a similar form of government had prevailed, and that of Upper Canada, in both of which cases no such racial lines were drawn and yet constitutional conflicts of the first magnitude were precipitated. If all Lower Canadians had been of the same race, the system of government would have produced a politico-constitutional clash which would have had the most serious consequences. The British Government learned singularly little, so far as colonial policy was concerned, from the American Revolution. Misunderstanding the cause of that movement to be a dispute over taxation, it was scrupulously careful in that field; but the political history of both Lower and Upper Canada in the period preceding Lord Durham's Report is to a remarkable extent a repetition of that of the American colonies. An English Executive in conflict with colonial Assemblies, well-meaning Governors tied up by instructions from London which were the result of ignorance rather than tyranny, colonial legislatures increasingly resentful of overseas restrictions on their legislation, the Assembly seeking to get its way through the control of appropriations, conflicts over a suggested Civil List, the refusal to vote supplies, the exaggerated importance and undisciplined ambitions of demagogues who constituted themselves tribunes of the people – they had been the staples of political warfare in the colonial days on the Atlantic sea-board, and here they recurred in the history of the Canadas. Some better constitutional way had to be discovered. The eyes of Downing Street were blind to this fact. Lord Durham was to see it clearly and point the way to stable government and a united Empire.

In Louis Joseph Papineau the French party in the Assembly possessed a leader of remarkable personal magnetism and oratorical power. Probably no Canadian leader has ever exercised such an influence over the electorate. Ardent and uncompromising in temperament, his speeches were frequently violent, exaggerated, bitter, and unfair. There is much in them that proves distasteful to the modern reader, removed as he is from the emotions of that time. But one cannot read his private letters without admiration for a kindly and generous humanity and those finer qualities of mind and heart that were frequently obscured in the heat of battle. He was something of a demagogue, but in devotion to his country he was quite sincere. A bad system, fostered and intensified by a wealth of British ignorance, developed in his high-strung temperament a violent antipathy to things as they were. With all his faults he was, in the best sense of the term, a great Canadian. Under a better system he might have developed into a constructive statesman.

As it was, the satisfactions of official service and power were closed to him, and the only outlet for his political instincts and ambition lay in the career of a perpetual leader of opposition, irresponsible and undisciplined. Steeped in democratic theory, he was conscious of the enthusiastic support for nearly a quarter of a century of a people who were so far from being sovereign that their will was constantly and contemptuously thwarted. He grasped for the only means of power that lay within his reach, that of obstructing and paralysing the efforts of those who sought to govern in the interests of a minority. Throughout the greater part of that period, minor government appointments in this French province were almost monopolized by Englishmen, and the more important offices were held by Englishmen and a few Frenchmen, who, it was believed, were selected on account of the ease with which they could be detached from the interests of the majority and controlled by the British minority. It is true that in the height of his career Papineau was offered a seat in the Executive Council. He has been blamed for refusing it, but he believed that he would be constantly overborne in the house of his antagonists and that he would have surrendered substance for a shadow.

The most powerful weapon within the reach of Papineau and his Assembly majority was control of the revenues, but in the earlier years the Government had enough revenue within its own control to enable it to defy the Assembly. Changes in the British political situation were to some extent reflected in Canada. When British Toryism was modified by the liberalism of the Canningites a series of reforms was initiated in the Canadas. The recommendations of the committee of 1828 were for a time neglected, but ultimately most of them were acted on. With the accession of the Whigs to power in 1830 a more generous era of conciliation began. A fair share of new appointments was given to French-Canadians, the Councils were improved, and the impossible old system was patched up almost as well as it could be. The Assembly was offered control of all but the casual and territorial revenues on condition of its voting a very limited Civil List for the life of the sovereign. It refused to comply with the condition. When the British Government generously granted the Assembly all but the casual and territorial revenues unconditionally it maintained a recalcitrant attitude; it appeared to many to be refusing the hand of conciliation by making no move toward a Civil List. For this conduct

Papineau and his followers have been severely criticized by the most eminent French-Canadian historians. But it is difficult to see how such a settlement, well-intentioned though it was on the part of the Colonial Office, could have afforded any permanent satisfaction. Under such a system the representatives of the people would have been able to create deadlocks by refusing supplies, but they would not have been able to exercise any positive power; the local oligarchy would not be dislodged so long as the salaries of the principal officials were guaranteed by a permanent Civil List. Papineau and his Assembly majority held out for control of the whole provincial revenue, and agitated for an elective Legislative Council which would give them complete control of the Legislature. In so doing, they were clearly following American models – as is suggested also by Papineau's leadership of the Assembly from the Speaker's chair. Nor were these the only respects in which the policies and suggestions of Papineau and his followers were determined by the political procedure of the United States. Here, as in the upper province, the constitutional influence of the neighbouring republic was strong.

The famous Ninety-two Resolutions of 1834 bristled with American conceptions of government. By that time the adoption of this extreme policy had lost Papineau the support of Neilson, Cuvillier, and other moderates who went over to the camp where the watchword was the defence of the constitution. But the ensuing election gave Papineau a stronger popular majority than ever, which strengthened his confidence that he could force the British Government to concede his terms. For four years before 1837 either no supplies were voted by the Assembly or they were voted under conditions that caused the Legislative Council to throw out the bill. Salaries of all sorts were lamentably in arrears, the greatest distress prevailed among employees of the Government, and public services were disorganized. The British Government was clamorously urged by the 'British party' to take drastic action.

The British (mercantile) party had talked for years of the 'tyranny' of the Assembly, and certainly in the heat of the struggle that Assembly – like the British Parliament in the days of the Stuarts – had frequently used what power it had in a tyrannical manner. Now in 1835 and 1836 the word 'tyranny' assumed a grim reality, and the British party developed a desperate mood. No sympathy with the aspirations of the French agricultural population and the thwarted ambitions of their political leaders, no disgust at the alliance of a petty oligarchy with the big business interests, can blind one's eyes to the very real grievances of the British mercantile population as a whole. In the early days they had been forced to do business under a French legal system because a most reasonable compromise had been refused them (under circumstances, however, which had been most trying to the British Government and their Canadian Governor). The Assembly majority would not vote money for improvements in communication which were essential to the development of trade. When they sought to invest their profits in land they were confronted with hindrances of all sorts created or fostered by the agricultural population who did not want them on the land. For years the absence of Registry Offices made it impossible for them to secure clear titles, and the provision for the registration of mortgages was still exasperatingly unsatisfactory. And now this 'anti-commercial' party, as they called it, was paralysing the Government and establishing with a considerable degree of success what they considered a French ascendancy in a British province. They saw the Whig Government in England pursuing toward that party a conciliatory policy which they believed to be hopeless, and the Governor, Lord Gosford, openly and extravagantly courting the support of the French leaders.

Two illustrations may inform us of the feelings that were frankly voiced by many of the British party during these years, 1835 and 1836. Mr. T. H. Stayner, Deputy Postmaster-General, described by one of Lord Durham's Commissioners as 'probably the largest landholder in the two Canadas',[1] was by no means an irresponsible hot-head, although he felt himself persecuted by post-office investigations. He wrote from Quebec, December 3, 1835, to the Hon. John Macaulay, who was about to become a member of the Legislative Council of Upper Canada:

The conviction is fast forcing itself upon the minds of the English that the crisis is at hand when blows must be come to and the question be decided whether they are to be slaves or freemen. They feel at the same time that they cannot fight the impending battle without support. Some flatter themselves with the idea that the people of Upper Canada will be able to aid them in the contest, others that their hope is in the neighbouring States. I have very little doubt that a convention will be held before the winter is over to make preparation for an event that will effectually open the minds of the people of England to convince them when too late that an imbecile and truckling Government, in pandering to the violence and tyranny of a cruel French faction, have not only alienated the affections of their own true and loyal offspring, but lost to the Empire the finest jewel in the Imperial diadem! I should attempt in vain to describe the savage fierceness *with which those of English origin now begin to speak on this subject. They are to a man disgusted with their prospects and ardently desirous of any change that may relieve them of the odious tyranny which now rules the country.*[2]

On the 16th of the same month the following statement was made editorially by the *Montreal Gazette*:

The Americans prior to their Revolution for grievances of a lighter character addressed themselves patiently and calmly to the Imperial Parliament, and when it turned a deaf ear to their complaints, they appealed to arms, and the result to them was success. They acted in the spirit of their fathers, and the Constitutionalists of Lower Canada are animated by feelings equally powerful and honourable. They are fully resolved, let the consequences be what they may, to uphold and preserve the inheritance bequeathed to them by their ancestors.

When rebellion came two years later it was not from the British population, but from the more impatient among the French. The game was turned against them by the action of the British Government in the Russell Resolutions of March 1837, one of which empowered the Governor to use money out of the provincial revenues other than casual and territorial without any vote by the Assembly. This checkmated Papineau, spread a spirit of desperation among his more ardent followers, and lent colour for the first time to charges of British tyranny. Up to this point the struggle had been against the despotism of a local oligarchy, and the only sin on the part of the British Government had been that of ignorance. Now a quarrel with England was developed, and every attempt was made to create parallels with the situation in the American colonies preceding the Revolution. The use of the people's money without the consent of their representatives was compared with taxation without representation, British goods were boycotted, and the vocabulary of the

American Revolution was reflected in the names of such organizations as the Sons of Liberty. Papineau discountenanced anything in the way of violence, but among his supporters there developed drilling, military display, a considerable amount of sedition, and some treasonable language. At the same time many of the 'British party' were anxious to see rebellion break out in order that its suppression might give them control of the situation, and some of them seem to have conspired to provoke it. Whether or not Gosford and Colborne fell into their designs, it was their attempt to arrest Papineau that precipitated the rebellion. Papineau himself had never advised rebellion, and up to this point had used all his influence against it, in the face of the inflammatory utterances of the Nelsons and O'Callaghan. He took no part in the fighting. He cannot in any reasonable sense of the term be considered the leader of the Lower Canada Rebellion. Its leaders were Dr. Wolfred Nelson, O'Callaghan, T. S. Brown, Girod, and Chénier, only one of whom was a French-Canadian by birth. The movement was confined to the Montreal district, about two thousand men were involved and it was easily suppressed. A serious situation might have developed, however, had it not been for the stalwart loyalty of *Le Canadien*, the most influential French newspaper, and the Catholic Church. The bishops made every possible effort to check the movement, and the priests with hardly an exception exerted their influence against it. The heartless destruction of property and burning of villages which followed the defeat of the rebels was for the most part, no doubt, the work not of the regular troops but of loyalists who had been terrorized in the preceding months and were seeking vengeance. But even those who realized this believed that it might have been prevented, and it created throughout the province a bitter and sulky feeling against Colborne and the British authorities. The rebellion had only intensified the difficulties of a situation for which neither Downing Street nor Lower Canada had been able to discover any adequate remedy and which was now submitted to the consideration of Lord Durham.

It would seem at first sight as though the situation in Upper Canada called for very little attention in a life of Lord Durham. While he was nominally Governor-General, the administration of the upper province was actually in the hands of its Lieutenant-Governor, Sir George Arthur. Lord Durham not only had very little to do with it, but his stay in Canada was cut short before he could thoroughly inform himself in regard to it, and the section devoted to Upper Canada is unquestionably the weakest part of his Report. It must be borne in mind, however, that all the most important recommendations of the Report applied to the Upper province as well as to the Lower, that they initiated a new era in Upper Canada, and that Lord Durham grasped the main factors of the situation there with sufficient clearness and vigour to point the way to the removal of the principal difficulties. Again, it has been generally supposed that the principle of Responsible Government, the application of which he successfully recommended to the British Government, was first developed as a leading policy of the Reformers of Upper Canada. That assumption calls for consideration in the following pages.

In a province the entire population of which was of British descent there was of course no racial clash. While some of the discontent was caused by economic factors, there was no clear line of economic cleavage between the political parties. The constitution, however, was the same as that of Lower Canada, and its ineptitudes caused similar results. The governors fell into the hands of a local oligarchy which controlled the Executive and Legislative Councils. A Reform party was organized in opposition to this group, and when the former secured a majority in the Assembly there ensued a conflict between the governing bodies quite similar to that in Lower Canada. The principal difference lay in the fact that in Upper Canada the office-holders were supported by a party powerful enough at times to win elections and secure a temporary majority in the Assembly. Reform of the councils, complete Assembly control of the provincial revenues, exclusion of judges from the councils, were leading policies of the Upper Canada Reformers as they were of the Papineau party in Lower Canada. If the former were divided on the question of making the Legislative Council elective, so were the latter, and the immediate followers of Mackenzie supported that proposal as ardently as those of Papineau. Democratic sentiment was widespread in both provinces and at war with oligarchy. In both an effective democracy was impossible until Lord Durham's powers of analysis and vision were applied to the situation. Before that, the colonies were not trusted with the full British system of government, and in Upper as in Lower Canada, there was some tendency to turn to American conceptions. Bidwell led the Reform party in the Assembly from the Speaker's chair, the American principle of an elective

Upper House was vigorously though not universally advocated by the Reformers, and a minority among them were in favour of pushing the elective principle to such extremes as the election of sheriffs and judges. This drift toward American ideas was checked when Lord Durham turned the tide into the channel of the full British system.

The 'Family Compact' was the analogue of the 'Chateau Clique' in the lower province. No well-informed Canadian needs to be reminded that the 'family' feature of it was exaggerated. It may, however, be necessary to point out that its leading members were able if somewhat narrow-minded men, and that their administration was on the whole a capable one; that they were no more addicted to graft than many of the provincial governments of later days; and that while the Gourlay case shows the depths of injustice to which they were willing to resort in self-defence, their despotism was of such a nature that it came to be considered intolerable only because a large section of the Canadian people would be satisfied with nothing short of popular government. In their appointments to office they were rigidly exclusive, and the ranks of Reform were swelled and its leadership provided to some extent by thwarted ambition.

The sources of democracy in Upper Canada are to be found in the natural conditions of a new country and in the ideals and aspirations which its settlers brought from the United States and Great Britain. In Great Britain aristocratic traditions had centuries behind them, and in the United States they had some claims to recognition, but those of the Anglo-Saxon race who made their way into the woods west of the Ottawa and north of the Great Lakes and into the little towns on the water front, to win from nature a heritage of their own creation, were not likely to tolerate suggestions of aristocracy, social, political, or religious, which in the conditions in which they lived must necessarily bear the tinsel of an artificiality which they despised above all things. The essence of their character was self-reliance, the most prominent trait of their descendants to the present day − a self-reliance stimulated by the climate in which they lived and the necessities of their social life. Toward everything that smacked of special privilege and of honours and powers that were not the natural rewards of vigour and stamina they displayed a Canadian sensitiveness that the inhabitants of the older civilizations have not been able fully to appreciate even to this day. They had no time to think about abstract theories of government, but the broad conception of democracy which had found expression in American institutions and was to flame up in the English struggle for Parliamentary Reform found among them a natural habitat.

Most of the earliest settlers were Americans. Rather than take part in a rebellion or to countenance a breach in the British Empire, they had found their way to the northern wilds that were still British. But they had been rooted and grounded in American conceptions of democracy and American institutions. If any way had been discovered of reconciling imperial unity and American self-government they would have welcomed it, and they did not leave their desire for self-government behind them when they entered Canada. By the Constitutional Act of 1791 they were granted an elective legislative assembly similar to those of their former home. But the British Government continued to encroach in the legislative field, and the Executive was, as in the American colonies, nominally British and actually oligarchic. Democracy and self-government were both checked half-way, and the sons and grandsons of the United Empire Loyalists were not the least restive in the growing colony. Then came Americans who were not Loyalists, but who, attracted to Canadian farm lands, immigrated from the United States in large numbers in the period between the American Revolution and the Canadian Rebellion. They became good Canadians in the sense that most of them were loyal to their new allegiance and took a pride in their new country that was of substantial importance in the development of Canadian nationalism. But they, like the Loyalists, brought with them an attachment to the institutions, social, political, and religious, of the American colonies and the early United States, the influence of which on Canadian life has received too little attention from Canadian historians. Most of them were not the 'republicans' that English and Canadian Tories accused them of being, for they believed that the institutions to which they were attached could be successfully operated under a monarchy, but they were thorough-going democrats.

The other source of immigration was the British Isles. Following the Napoleonic Wars thousands left the 'Old Country' to seek their fortunes in Canada, and this stream rapidly became the main channel. They left a country seething with unrest and more than once on the verge of revolt. They were the children of discontent, and although conditions were better in the new world, it was difficult to cure them; they must have their discontent there too. At home they had, in the midst of dissatisfaction, seen a new light – Reform. They came, nearly all of them, from the lower and middle classes, and most of them were ardent supporters of that Parliamentary Reform which promised an effective democracy in Great Britain, and whose hope among the seats of the mighty during this whole period was – Lord Durham. It is significant that the years when this movement was at its height were those of the largest proportionate British immigration, and that many of these new settlers came from the north of England and Scotland where the Reform sentiment was strongest and where Lord Durham was most popular.

In Canada they were to enjoy the extended franchise which they had sought at home, but in spite of that they found Toryism in the saddle as it was in Great Britain before 1830. The Government was oligarchic in spite of a representative Assembly, and that oligarchy and its friends thought of democracy precisely as did the ruling class at home. The Governors, all of whom came from that ruling class, regarded the discouragement and suppression of democracy at all costs as the most sacred obligation of their office. So Reformers in England became Reformers in Canada. This was not true of all of them and the fact that the oligarchy, misnamed the Family Compact, received as much support as it did can probably best be explained by the skill with which its leaders misrepresented the settlers from the United States to the immigrants from England, the divisions which were fomented between earlier and later settlers, the power of patronage which was entirely in the hands of the Compact, and the impatience of sturdy practical farmers with political agitators who were able to achieve so little in the way of reform when they were in a majority in the Assembly. The forces of democracy were too strong to be very long denied, but the great breach in the wall of oligarchy through which democracy was to enter the citadel was to be made by the same hand as in the Mother Country. Lord Durham's Report formed the Canadian counterpart of the Great Reform Bill.

The movement against the Family Compact was strengthened by religious feeling. The oligarchy was largely Anglican, and sought to secure to the Church of England the privileges of an established church. The Governors believed it to be their business to promote the Church of England in the interests of loyalty and the suppression of democracy. But the Anglicans were in a minority in Upper Canada. Among the American conceptions referred to above, none has been more vital than that of the separation of Church and State, and while the Americans were bringing with them that predilection, the English immigrants, most of whom were Dissenters, transferred to Canada the struggle to abolish their legal disabilities. In this, as in the Reform struggle, Lord Durham had been their outstanding champion among the ruling class.

To-day one may view that religious struggle in a detached frame of mind, but a hundred years ago feelings were whipped to a white heat. It was intensified and dramatized by two leaders of powerful personality. John Strachan was a convert to the Church of England from Presbyterianism; Egerton Ryerson, the Goliath of the Dissenters, had been refused ordination in the Church of England. Both made valuable contributions to Canadian progress, notably in the field of education. Since the Dissenters were more numerous, and their cause proved to be the victorious one, the virtues of Ryerson and the demerits of Strachan have been well impressed upon Canadian history-books. In their own day each was regarded by his supporters as a dauntless champion of righteousness, and by his opponents as a tricky ecclesiastical politician. The struggle for and against Anglican control was waged over legal restrictions (such as the disability of Dissenting ministers to perform the marriage ceremony), the schools, the university, and government grants, but it centred in the Clergy Reserves, those reservations of a fixed proportion of public lands for the support of a 'Protestant clergy'. The success of the Church of England in securing the bulk of the Clergy Reserves was regarded as the crowning sin of the Anglican oligarchy. In point of fact, the Church of England made very little out of them financially, but men goaded by what they considered injustice and irritated by the handicap which the Reserves placed upon the economic development of the province, insisted on regarding them as sources of untold wealth. The Clergy Reserves were undoubtedly the main cause of discontent in the province and the greatest single provocative of the Rebellion of 1837. But, as in the case of the more directly political conflict, the Family Compact party was aided by divisions in the ranks of its opponents, and realized the value of the control of patronage. A few years before the Rebellion, Ryerson and the bulk of the Methodists, the strongest religious body, swung away from the Reformers. Their explanation was that they distrusted extreme views and feared disloyalty, while their opponents pretended to find the cause in recent substantial government grants to the Methodist Church. The issue split the Methodist force itself, as many of them, particularly outstanding laymen, stood for a refusal of all government support to a religious body, and for absolute separation of Church and State.

As far as the discontent in Upper Canada was economic in origin, it had to do mainly with the land. The oligarchy had been guilty of gross favouritism in the granting of land, and the whole system was unsatisfactory. The presence of large blocks of uncultivated Crown and Clergy Reserves in each township was a barrier to communication and impeded all community interests. Roads were bad, and there was little improvement in sight. Large tracts of land, much of it on the water-front, were kept vacant for speculative purposes. Everything conspired to handicap those holding land in the back-lying districts, where the feeling of dissatisfaction was most marked. It was believed that the Family Compact had no concern for these grievances and that its interests were bound up with their perpetuation. On the other hand the Tories supported the more extensive public works that were essential to the development of trade, while the Reformers assumed toward them a parsimonious and unprogressive attitude that was particularly unfortunate when there was a Reform majority in the Assembly. In the period immediately preceding the Rebellion a financial depression stimulated the discontent, and the Rebellion itself not only caused further economic distress but cast a gloom that brought men to the verge of despair. It was for a stricken country that Lord Durham was called to prescribe.

Lord Durham's Report was to be the great healing measure. Its prescriptions were to be many and important, but the one that went to the heart of the situation was that principle which was to destroy oligarchy and make democracy effective, thus enabling the people to work out their own salvation – the principle that has come to be known as Responsible Government. When we employ that term in relation to present-day constitutional practice, we include most, if not all, of those conventions which govern the relations between the Crown, its Ministers, and Parliament. Some of those conventions were non-existent in 1838; that difference we may reserve for the discussion of the Report. But the most vital and central elements of Responsible Government were already established in British practice. The King's public acts were countersigned by Ministers who assumed individual responsibility for them, legal as well as moral, and the King's Ministers were collectively responsible to the majority of the House of Commons in a manner so direct and effective that they must resign as a body – or appeal to the electorate – when it became apparent that they had lost the support of that majority. It was particularly this latter collective responsibility to the Assembly, the Canadian counterpart of the House of Commons, which was designated as Responsible Government in the period between Lord Durham's Report and the administration of Lord Elgin, and the establishment of which has been considered the key-stone of Canadian political liberty.

In the best Canadian historical literature it is constantly assumed that this principle was a leading policy of the Upper Canada Reformers for some time before the Rebellion of 1837. Examining this in the light of the correspondence, newspapers, and pamphlets of the period, one cannot go very far without realizing that he is confronted with a problem in terminology.

The term 'responsible government' was frequently employed by the Reformers. But it was used in a number of different senses, and scarcely ever in the sense indicated above – the Responsible Government of the 40's and the core of that of the present day. If we remind ourselves of the various ways in which the word 'responsible' is used in everyday parlance, we can understand better their employment of the term. The Reformers of pre-rebellion days did not start with a constitutional theory; few of them understood either the theory or practice of the British constitution. They started with facts. Their government was an *irresponsible* one in every common meaning of that term. Most of the offices through which the Government was administered were practically life appointments, made and continued without any reference to public sentiment. Their occupants had no sense of responsibility. They were accountable for their conduct to no one in Canada but the Governor whom they usually controlled. Their responsibility to the Colonial Office was, except on rare occasions, a dead letter. In their policies they need make no concessions to public opinion, and no matter how unpopular they might become, their tenure of office was still secure. Their rendering of financial accounts was unsatisfactory, and they were under no obligation to explain and justify their administrative transactions to either the people or the people's representatives. Some of the Governors took the position that the Assembly had no right even to discuss the executive side of government. In their sphere, the legislative, Reform Assemblies could achieve little, because their measures were thrown out by the Legislative Council, itself an irresponsible body made up for the most part of these same irresponsible officials. Government was thoroughly irresponsible in character.

The Reformers insisted that it should be made responsible. They wanted 'a responsible government' – frequently they employed the expression: 'a cheap and responsible government'. But how was this to be secured? Many suggestions were made and to each of them the term 'responsible government' was applied. The Governor should appoint men who were the objects of popular esteem and he should dismiss individual officials who were unpopular; that was 'responsible government'. The Legislative Council should be made elective; that was 'responsible government'. It was even suggested that the Executive Council and most of the offices of state should be elective, and some extremists wanted an elective Governor. A common demand was that responsibility should be effected by the appointment of a court of impeachment independent of the Legislative Council. Sometimes the demand for 'responsible government' meant 'turn the rascals out and let good men in', and sometimes it meant simply disgust with the present order of things and delight in a phrase that was a good round mouthful. The prevalence of the form 'responsible to the *people*' is an indication that the agitation was not for Responsible Government in the later sense of the term. Occasionally responsibility to the *people's representatives* was demanded, but when the context is studied it may be seen that, in almost every case, that only meant a general accountability to the Assembly for their conduct.

But Responsible Government in the more precise sense in which that term was later employed was occasionally advocated in this period. This advocacy, never thrust into the forefront of political discussion, was nearly always associated with the names of William Warren Baldwin and Robert Baldwin. In 1828, a group of prominent citizens led by the older Baldwin petitioned the British Parliament to remove from office the advisers of the Governor when they lost the confidence of the people, and to provide satisfactory means for their impeachment. This looks like responsible government as it was advocated quite generally at that time – the removal of an official when he became unpopular and the opportunity of punishing him through impeachment. In that sense it was probably understood by most of those present. But William Warren Baldwin's letter to the Duke of Wellington, which accompanied this petition, is substantially a request for Responsible Government in the later sense of the term. It suggests 'a provincial ministry responsible to the provincial parliament and removable from office by His Majesty's representative at his pleasure and especially when they lost the confidence of the people as expressed by their representatives in the assembly', and that all acts of the Governor should be countersigned by one of these ministers. In the *Upper Canada Herald* of October 14, 1829, reference is made to a pamphlet which suggested that the Executive Council should be made up of heads of departments, and 'resignation of office must follow the loss of a parliamentary majority'.[3] This too was probably the work of one of the Baldwins or of that small circle of friends who alone understood what they were aiming at.

Certainly Responsible Government of this type was never a leading tenet of the Upper Canada Reformers in the period before the Rebellion. One searches for it in vain in the speeches, resolutions, and election appeals until the year 1834, and while a few traces of it can be found then, it was not an issue in the election of that year; and when 'a responsible government' found a place among the listed policies of the Reformers, it was worded in the vaguest and most general terms. The Reformers won the election of 1834, but no trace of the Baldwin doctrine can be found in the address in reply to the Governor's speech when the Assembly convened in the following January. The request was there made that 'the favours and patronage of His Majesty' should be 'indiscriminately bestowed on persons of worth and talent who enjoy the confidence of the people *without regard to their political* or religious *opinions* and Your Excellency's Councils filled with moderate, wise, and discreet individuals who are understood to respect and be influenced by the public voice'. The phrase is not mentioned, but this is probably what 'a responsible government' meant to most of the Reformers in that assembly.

But a trace of the Baldwin idea (Responsible Government in its ultimate connotation)[4] can be discovered a few months later. As chairman of the Committee on Grievances, William Lyon Mackenzie was given full opportunity for his favourite occupation. Nothing was overlooked, and the grievances discovered were legion. Several hundred stock questions were put to the witnesses examined by the Committee, and among them was this one: 'Would not the British constitutional system, by which the head of the government is obliged to choose his counsellors and principal officers from men possessing the confidence of the popular branch of the legislature, be more suitable to the wants and wishes of the country, if adopted in Upper Canada, than the present irresponsible form of government?' This was very indefinite, fell far short of the Baldwin expositions, and was calculated to elicit a favourable reply from many who did not understand and had never advocated what came to be known as Responsible Government. Few of the witnesses showed any appreciation of the significance of the application of the British system. Considering his point of view, the most intelligent answer was that of Archdeacon Strachan: 'I do not believe that the government is an irresponsible one; the rest of the question is too vague to permit of a definite answer.' But a sufficient number of favourable answers was received to permit the committee in its report to group the witnesses into three classes – first, those who believed that the Government was well enough as it was; second, those who 'desire a responsible ministry – some heads of departments well paid, to direct the government, to prepare bills and most of the business of the session, and to hold office or lose it according as they may happen to be in minority or majority in the House of Assembly'; third, those who 'contend for elective institutions'. The report stressed the necessity of an elective Legislative Council, the principal demand of the Reformers throughout this period, and the sympathies of the Committee were clearly with this third class. This Seventh Grievance Report was never adopted by the Assembly, but on April 15, 1835, five days after its presentation, the Assembly passed a petition to the King which dealt mainly with the Legislative Council, but which in its closing words expressed approval of the principle of His Majesty 'graciously consulting the wishes of your faithful people as expressed by their representatives in the choice of responsible advisers', which was sufficiently indefinite for the majority to vote for it.

In the following year, 1836, Robert Baldwin had a splendid opportunity to urge upon the Governor the view held by himself and his father. Sir Francis Head, the new Governor, sought to reform the Government by retaining in his Executive Council three not unpopular Tories, and appointing to act with them three generally esteemed Reformers, one of whom was Robert Baldwin. That was in exact accordance with the Reformers' address of the preceding session. It was selecting as advisers 'persons of worth and talent who enjoy the confidence of the people without regard to their political opinions', and Mackenzie and other Reformers rejoiced that a 'responsible government' had been established.[5] But it was very far from the Baldwin conception. Baldwin at first insisted that since the Reformers were in a majority in the Assembly, the remaining Tory counsellors should be dismissed and their places filled by Reformers. He probably also urged on Head the permanent adoption of a rule that the Council must collectively have the support of the majority of the Assembly. But since the Governor would not consent, he waived the insistence on the immediate application of his principle and accepted office.

The issue which developed a few days later between Head and his Council was not over the Baldwin principle of Responsible Government except in so far as the latter included the necessity of the Governor consulting his Council. Of the dependence of the Executive on a majority in the Assembly there is not a trace in the Council's protest to the Governor.[6] They simply claimed that in accordance with the Constitutional Act the Governor was obliged to consult them in regard to the *whole* administration of the province. In so doing they took an entirely false position, and Sir Francis Head and the lawyers of the Family Compact, who now rallied to his support, had an easy task in proving that the Constitutional Act only required that the Governor consult his Executive Council in certain specific matters, while in other respects he was free to ask their advice when he felt that he needed it. So pliable, however, was the *term* 'responsible government' that both sides claimed to be contending for it. The Council insisted on being consulted in order that they might be fairly held responsible to public opinion. The Governor represented them as seeking to secure for themselves and their friends the patronage which he proposed to distribute impartially, and appealed to the country against 'the family domination of an irresponsible Cabinet', and to the farmers particularly against 'the irresponsible domination of a Toronto ministry'. After the Executive Council had resigned and the Governor had appointed others in their place, the Toronto city council, pressing one meaning of the term 'responsible government', protested to the Governor that these new appointees did not 'possess the public confidence'. Head, always more astute than his opponents, replied that the best proof that one of these men possessed the public confidence lay in the fact that the very body from whom this address emanated had a few weeks before elected him Mayor of Toronto.[7] Even the few who understood and believed in the Baldwin conception of Responsible Government refused to advocate it boldly, and the only clear references to it during this struggle are occasional warnings on the lips of Tory speakers. Robert Baldwin claimed at a later date that Responsible Government, as he championed it, was approved by a resolution of the Assembly shortly after the resignation of himself and his colleagues. But that resolution, dealing in the main with a request for information from the Governor, simply declared 'the appointment of a responsible Executive Council to advise Your Excellency on the affairs of the province to be one of the most happy and wise features in the Constitution'; it was carried by a vote of 55 to 2. The Tories declared during the debate that they and the Governor would welcome the fullest publication of facts and that they considered that the Council was and always had been 'responsible'. The speech of Peter Perry, who moved the resolution, shows clearly that his idea of a responsible Executive was quite different from that of Baldwin; and Hagerman, who led the debate for the Tories, while insisting that they had always had a responsible executive, declared that he would vote for the resolution on the precise understanding that he refused to discuss any question of principle until they had the facts before them and knew what they were talking about. For Robert Baldwin to use that resolution to support his clear-cut advocacy and exposition of Responsible Government in his letter to the British Government was misleading – to the British Government at the time, to Lord Durham in the preparation of his Report, and indirectly to later historians.[8]

The Governor who unfurled the British flag on Government House, and directly appealed to the electors in the most fervid language to support the King's Representative and the British connexion, has been regarded as something of a clown on the stage of Canadian history, and his victory over the Reformers in the election of 1836 has been ascribed to an unscrupulous use of the Government patronage and to the support of Ryerson and the Methodists. Both patronage and the Methodists played their part. But Head can be acquitted of the flagrant dishonesty with which he was charged; and Ryerson had deserted the Reformers before the election of two years before, although he took a more active part against them at this time. The whole story has been regarded too much in the light of a later time when Canada is no longer a colony and when, therefore, British connexion is not in serious danger. Head possessed two gifts which he employed with remarkable success — the gift of language and that of popular appeal. The leaders of a democratic party found themselves confronted by a governor determined to do his own ruling irrespective of party, in the interests of the whole people and with their approval, who had a natural bent for the art of demagoguery and who could beat them at their own game.

Whether or not they pulled the wrong man out of bed that morning in Kent to confront him with the astounding news that he had been appointed Governor of Canada, this obscure poor-law commissioner, pitchforked without adequate political knowledge into one of the most difficult situations in political history by a government which cared little about colonies, deserves more sympathy than he has ever received. He had no solution for the difficulties; no one had till Durham came. The one he suggested was well-meaning. He was more liberal than any of his predecessors, less interested in politicians, and more interested in the common people. He took the people into his confidence as no previous governor had done. It was perhaps a skilful satellite of his, or even his own fine pen, that introduced into an address from backwoodsmen the statement that when they went to their shanties at night they thought of him as their friend, but in the enthusiasm of the moment they may well have adopted the sentiment as their own; they were sick of politics and sought only the impartiality which he promised them. As long as he could talk and write and promise, and his administration was not yet tested, he was brilliant. He fought with the courage which always wins men, in behalf of a sentiment in which they believed. He was regarded in those early days of his régime by thousands of Canadians — thousands even who had been consistent Reformers — with a deep admiration, which it should not be so difficult for us to understand. He sincerely believed that he was fighting for British connexion and British institutions, and perhaps he was. The programme with which the Reformers confronted him — elective Legislative Council, control of all revenues by the Assembly, the British Government to keep its hands completely off colonial legislation – was an American programme. 'Responsible government' was mentioned occasionally in the varied senses indicated above, but it was usually responsibility 'to the people', and direct responsibility to the people was the American idea of government. To Head, the Reformers either consciously or unconsciously were making for independence and American annexation. The Reform newspapers advocated an elective Legislative Council as the great desideratum, and if the bulk of the people could then have been converted to it – to say nothing of a number of other American institutions that were advocated – the retention of a British Canada would have been much more difficult. Head – ignorant, prejudiced, blatant as he was – was not altogether wrong in his instincts. The people, though discontented and anxious for popular government, were devoted to British institutions, and there is a striking contrast between the failure of the Reformers in the election of 1836 and the overwhelming popularity of Lord Durham's Report, recommending as it did a system that was as thoroughly *British* as it was democratic.

The Governor had behind him in this election the best brains of the Family Compact, who foresaw that in a few months he would be in their power; and the Reform leaders played into his hands. They permitted the battle to begin over what he could easily represent as a scramble after patronage. On the eve of the election he enlightened the public as to the way in which they were abusing the patronage already in their hands as leaders of the Assembly. Local improvements were controlled by commissioners appointed by the Assembly. The Governor published the list of commissioners. Nearly all the names were those of Reform members of the Assembly; Bidwell was a repeater, Peter Perry's name occurred no less than six times, and various family relationships were involved.[9] These were the men who were attempting to capture from the Governor the main patronage of the province; that was the meaning of their insistence on being consulted on *all* the affairs of the province and their objection to his making appointments on his own initiative. He represented himself on the other hand as the guardian of the people's interests, who would save them alike from the Family Compact and from these hypocritical self-seeking agitators. The Reform leaders took up an untenable position on the Constitutional Act, and this enhanced the moral strength of Head's position. Just before the dissolution of the

Assembly, Bidwell, the leader of the party, in his capacity as Speaker, laid before that body a letter from Papineau which said, 'the state of society all over continental America requires that the forms of its government should approximate nearer to that selected under propitious circumstances and after mature deliberation by the wise statesmen of the neighbouring Union', and urged a stalwart opposition to British oppression. Nothing could have given more convincing colour to Head's flag-waving. Mackenzie and Peter Perry attacked the Governor in terms that justified his statement that 'in no part of the civilized world would such language be tolerated', and were so insulting that they must have turned votes against them even in a day when open criticism of governors was a popular practice. It was easy for Head to make men believe that he was being vilified simply because he was doing his duty like a man. Whether or not the Assembly's refusal of supplies was a mistake in itself, it rocked a financial boat that was in heavy seas; it did this in the interests of a course that was as badly presented as it was conceived; and gave an air of sincerity and a convincing force to Head's 'bread and butter' appeals.

The defeat of the Reformers sent Robert Baldwin to England, and placed that stalwart champion of self-government in the inconsistent position of complaining to the Home Government against a Governor who had been sustained by a popular majority. Lord Glenelg, the Colonial Secretary, refused to grant him a personal interview, and as a consequence Baldwin wrote him a letter which gave a clear statement of the Responsible Government which was ultimately to prevail – government by a Cabinet occupying the same position in relation to the Governor and Legislature as did the British Cabinet to the King and Parliament, and holding or resigning office on the same conditions – the letter which at a later date probably suggested to Lord Durham the ideas that revolutionized the British Empire. But neither Glenelg nor any of his colleagues could rise to an imperial vision, and they would have none of Baldwin's suggestions. This letter of Robert Baldwin's, as well as his father's letter to the Duke of Wellington, probably misled the British Government into believing that whenever the Canadian Reformers spoke about 'responsible government' they meant what Baldwin meant, and that his suggestions represented a general demand in the Canadas. This error is reflected in the official reports of the period and in the Russell Resolutions.

In the meantime things went from bad to worse in Upper Canada. It was soon apparent that though Head could win an election, he could not govern. No one could have governed the province successfully under that old system, but few could have done as badly as he. His policy proved to be an impossible one, Family Compact rule came back again, the country was caught in a financial depression, and discontent smouldered and flared as never before. The situation seemed hopeless. Mackenzie, embittered by the defeat of the Reformers, became wilder in his talk, and the heightened disaffection turned his thoughts definitely toward rebellion. Mackenzie's chief lieutenants were drawn from that minority group which he had led within the Reform party. The main body of Reformers held aloof. No doubt many more were ready to take up arms than were represented in the fiasco of Yonge Street and the western risings, but the number of potential rebels constituted a small proportion of the population. On the placid surface of the British mind, however, the news of rebellion in both the Canadas broke like a bombshell, and in the excitement of the moment the extent of the disaffection was vastly exaggerated. The sensational news came to England in many a distorted form — including American newspapers which, with the dash and enterprise that characterized them even at that early date, reported that the city of Toronto had been captured by the rebels, the Governor and all the officials imprisoned, and many buildings consigned to the flames.[10]

The principal results of the rebellion were that it placed a colony for the time being in the centre of the stage in Great Britain and brought Lord Durham to Canada.

With the leader of the rebellion Lord Durham had nothing to do except to prevent his return to the province. But the post-rebellion situation cannot be understood until we disabuse our minds of two popular fallacies in regard to William Lyon Mackenzie — that he had been the leader of the Reform Party in Upper Canada, and that he and his rebels fought for Responsible Government. The recognized leader of the Reformers during the whole period in which Mackenzie was a member of the Assembly was Marshall Spring Bidwell. Mackenzie did the most talking both inside and outside of Parliament, and by his good and bad qualities alike got himself into the centre of the most riotous scenes of the period; as a result he was frequently a popular hero, but his popularity waxed and waned with bewildering rapidity. It was stated by a Reform speaker after the rebellion that although the Reformers were in a majority in the Parliament of 1835-6, Mackenzie voted in a minority more frequently than in a majority. An examination of the Journals of the House shows that that was not true, but that he did vote in a minority on a number of occasions. This was not because he voted with the Tories but because he brought in motions of which most of the Reform members disapproved. He was generally supported by a group of extremists of which he was the leader. Their names recur among those most prominent in the rebellion. They followed him to the end; they were 'his own true blues'.

As for the rebels fighting for Responsible Government, it should be clear at first sight that the constitution issued by Mackenzie was built up directly on that of the United States and was quite inconsistent with Responsible Government. Immediately before the rebellion he had been summarizing and holding up for the emulation of the people of Upper Canada various American state constitutions. A complete review of his newspaper articles, letters, and published speeches would show that while he occasionally employed the term 'responsible government' he did so infrequently, and that on almost every occasion he used it either in a very general sense or in one of the senses noted above *other* than Responsible Government as it came to be known in later Canadian history and constitutional practice. One of the means by which Mackenzie hoped to secure 'a responsible government' was the election of the Legislative Council, to which he sometimes added the election of the Governor; another was control of the revenue by the Assembly. We have already noted the attitude of the Seventh Grievance Report of which Mackenzie was the chief author and the fact that he rejoiced at the establishment of what he considered responsible government by Sir Francis Head. On the other hand there are a few recorded statements of Mackenzie's in which he did refer to the desirability of the Executive Council being made responsible to the majority of the Assembly in such a manner that they should resign when they lost that majority. These are sufficient to show that the idea advocated by the Baldwins entered his mind at times as one of a number of desirable changes; but he was never a consistent advocate of it, and neither he nor any of the Reform leaders placed it in the forefront of the battle. He did not show any clear appreciation of its significance; in his letters to Neilson[11] he revealed an uncertain knowledge of the working of the British system of cabinet government; and in the years immediately preceding the rebellion he made no mention of it. None of his fellow-rebels advocated Responsible Government in its true connotation.

Mackenzie was not a constructive political thinker, but he was of the stuff of which good leaders of revolt are made. Always on the track of wrong-doing, he sometimes saw evil where it did not exist, he was frequently violent, abusive, and even wild in his language, but he was a man of rugged independence, high principles, stalwart courage, indefatigable industry, a fiery hatred of oppression and injustice in every form, and a passionate love of liberty. He was heroically unselfish, and he suffered more for his convictions than any public man of his time. He led a revolt against conditions under which men who loved freedom could never be content. For his zeal and public spirit, frequently mistaken as it was, Canadians of succeeding generations must be sincerely grateful. He laid the axe to the root of the tree. He made possible the constructive period which followed the rebellion and Lord Durham's Report.

While discontent was rife in each province, the relation between the provinces was far from satisfactory. The ocean ports were in Lower Canada, and geography made of Upper and Lower Canada an economic unit which politics had divided. The British Government devised various means of affording Upper Canada a share of the customs duties collected at the ports of the lower province, but one arrangement after another proved unsatisfactory. Upper Canada spent large sums on waterways in the interest of interprovincial trade which were rendered nugatory by the failure of Lower Canada adequately to improve its means of communication. But although economically desirable, the union of the two provinces was opposed by various groups on political grounds. The British merchants of Lower Canada strongly favoured it. It was probably in their interests that a union bill, credited to Edward Ellice, was introduced into the British Parliament in 1822, but in the face of protests from Canada and opposition from home it was withdrawn. It contained provisions that were unjust to the French-Canadians and thus increased the bitterness with which they opposed any suggestion of a union of Upper and Lower Canada.

There has been a tendency to speak of Self Government and

Responsible Government as though they meant the same thing. Self Government in Canada – that is the control by Canada of her own affairs – was attained largely through the establishment of Responsible Government as a result of Lord Durham's Report, but it is necessary to keep the two ideas distinct. Responsible Government made executive Self Government possible; there had already been a considerable measure of legislative Self Government. The latter was a heritage from the American colonies. The British Government made an honest effort to afford the Canadian Assemblies something like legislative autonomy, but Canadians of all parties became increasingly sensitive to occasional interferences by the Home authorities in this sphere of government. These manifestations were part of a growing desire to control their own affairs, executive and legislative alike. Canada was approaching the situation of the American colonies on the eve of the Revolution. That break had come because no constitutional scheme was forthcoming that could retain a healthy nationalism within the larger circle of Empire. It has frequently been said that if a Lord Durham's Report had been possible in 1775 the American Revolution would not have taken place. But there was no Lord Durham at that time and, what is more important, there was no possible receptivity in the British Government to a Lord Durham's Report. An oligarchy dominated by rotten boroughs could not be expected to appreciate either American democracy or the American desire for self-government. But in the intervening years, largely through Durham's efforts, the oligarchy had been destroyed and the foundation of a democratic Britain had been established. So the two movements were united in his person. He came to Canada to complete his life-work by laying the foundations of a new Empire which in the freedom, pride, and enthusiasm that self-government brings would gird that new Britain whose face he had set toward a sane democracy.

✿ ✿ ✿

CHAPTER II Preparing for Canada

After some hesitation, and an urgent personal appeal from the Queen, Lord Durham accepted appointment as High Commissioner of British North America, January 15, 1838. On the same day he wrote to Lord Grey:

> *I have stipulated with Melbourne that it is to be a temporary mission. I am not to be stinted in powers or in money and am to have unstinted appointment of all civil officers whom I may think necessary for the efficient execution of my duties. The undertaking is a fearfully arduous one and nothing but the extreme emergency of the case could induce me to make such a sacrifice both public and private. . . . I hope my absence will not be extended beyond the autumn of next year.*[1]

At the same time Lady Durham wrote to her mother: 'There is quite enough in such an undertaking to make one very unhappy', and on the next day:

> *Lambton is becoming so excited, that I hardly dare appear before him with a grave face, and yet . . . it is impossible I should not feel many a bitter pang and many a heavy anxiety. . . . I would not move a finger to help the Government. But when one is told that one may be the means of doing so much good and of preventing great bloodshed in an unhappy country, then I think it is difficult to refuse one's best exertions, and if the thing succeeds I shall rejoice on this account, but not at all for the sake of the Government. I feel a wicked wish to say this to all of them and have done so to Mr. Ellice and Mr. Ponsonby, but I suppose even if I have the opportunity, that I may as well hold my tongue with the others.*[2]

There are words in Melbourne's reply to Durham's letter of acceptance which, in view of what happened later, assume a grim significance: 'I can assure you that I consider you as making a great sacrifice for the chance of doing an essential service to the country. As far as I am concerned, and I think I can answer for all my colleagues, you will receive the firmest and most unflinching support.'[3]

On the 17th Lord John Russell introduced the measure which suspended the constitution of Lower Canada until November 1840, and provided for a Special Council, – five members to constitute a quorum – with the advice and consent of the majority of which the Governor should be empowered to make any laws or ordinances within the powers of the suspended legislature. A number of the Radicals opposed the measure at first in spite of their enthusiastic appreciation of the appointment of Lord Durham, but their opposition dwindled as the bill proceeded until on the last division only eight votes were recorded against it. The Tories supported the second reading, but promised amendments in committee. Under pressure from Peel and at the suggestion of Ellice, Russell withdrew a pre-amble on whose maintenance Lord Durham had attempted to insist. It related to a conference of representative men of the two provinces which the Governor was to summon to secure advice with a view to government improvements, and reminds us of Lord Durham's care at the time of the preparation of the Reform Bill to be thoroughly informed in regard to the sentiments and desires of the people and of the popular leaders. As we shall see, Lord Durham chose another way of securing the opinions of the Canadian people.

The debates on this measure were for the most part trite and monotonous, and reflected a most superficial knowledge of the Canadian situation. Most of the Radical speakers gave expres-sion to the desire of that party for an immediate separation of Canada from Great Britain, while nearly all of the other speakers regarded such a separation as being inevitable in the course of time, but insisted that the time had not yet come. The latter number included Russell. Not a single speaker ventured to predict or hope for a permanent connexion. There was no criticism of Durham's appointment, most of the speeches expressed hearty approval of it, and the Radicals pronounced enthusiastic encomiums on his capacity and integrity. Peel and Warburton threw out the suggestion of a federation of all the British North American provinces. Charles Buller startled the pious attitude of some of the members toward the rebels by insisting that the Government should 'set a memorable example by not shedding one drop of blood'.

In the Lords, Brougham attacked the Government with an impetuosity, a fierceness of invective, and acerbity of sarcasm which even he had rarely equalled. Rightly or wrongly his hearers felt that his speeches were coloured by his personal quarrel with Melbourne. Those who anticipated a renewal at this time of Brougham's feud with Durham were disappointed. He mentioned Durham's name only once, and then in an obviously sincere reference to his patriotism in undertaking the mission. Brougham rang the changes on the hesitancies, delays, and inconsistencies of the Government's conduct in relation to Canada.

If you will have dominions in every clime, if you will rule subjects by millions on opposite sides of this globe . . . I stop not to inquire, nor do I raise the question, whether to the distant millions, over whom you thus assume dominion, this mighty or remote sceptre be a blessing or a curse. But of one thing I am absolutely certain, that, at all events, this resolution to retain so vast an empire imposes on you the paramount duty of wakefulness over its concerns. It prescribes the condition that you shall be alive to its administration – that you shall not slumber over it, neither sleep, nor like the sluggard fold the hands to sleep.

In another passage he said that when compared with Melbourne and Glenelg 'King John or Richard Cromwell became wise, politic, and vigorous rulers'. In a later speech he did not 'set any high value upon such a possession as Canada'. 'In a national way I really hold those colonies to be worth nothing'. The only important question was the mode in which a separation, sooner or later inevitable, was to take place. In the present instance, British pride would have to satisfy itself by the suppression of the rebellion and the re-establishment of authority. After that was done, there should be 'an estimate calmly made of the profit and loss which result from our North American domain. I am well assured that we shall find there very little worth the cost they have entailed on us in men, in money and in injury to our trade; nay, that their separation will be even now a positive gain, so it be effected on friendly terms and succeeded by an amicable intercourse'. The contrast between Brougham's attitude to the Empire and that of Durham must be borne in mind when we come to a consideration of the crisis of the following summer.

Melbourne took Brougham's first attack patiently, satisfying himself with a reference to his speech as 'a most laboured and extreme concentration of bitterness'. But on the next occasion, the easy-going Prime Minister launched a counter-attack that was permeated with personal feeling. He favoured the House with a passionate history of the personal quarrel between himself and Brougham. Brougham leaped to his feet and, with a dramatic gesture toward Melbourne, cried out, 'I hurl my defiance at his head! I repeat it. I hurl at his head this defiance. I defy him to point out any, the slightest indication of any one part of my political conduct having even for one instant been affected in any manner by feelings of a private or personal nature.'

Lord Durham was reminded in these days of his own quarrel with Brougham, of a mutual antipathy of long standing between himself and Melbourne, and of the fact that the Tories hated him as their most deadly foe. In a short speech, which was his only contribution to the debate, he urged in the most tactful and persuasive manner that they should all rise above such considerations for the sake of the larger interests involved. He had undertaken this task only after the greatest reluctance. If, however, he could open the way to better government and renewed prosperity in Canada, he should deem no personal sacrifice too great for such a result. 'I feel, however, that I can only accomplish it by the most cordial and energetic support, a support which I am sure I shall obtain, of my noble friends, the members of Her Majesty's Cabinet; by the co-operation of the Imperial Parliament; and, permit me to say, by the generous forbearance of the noble lords opposite, to whom I have always been politically opposed.'

Early in February Lord Durham as Deputy Grand Master of England presided at a Masonic Festival in honour of the Grand Master, the Duke of Sussex. He referred to his approaching mission to Canada and 'hoped he should ever be guided by the principles which adorned the craft. He hoped that he should ever recollect that the main characteristics of Masonry were charity and forgiveness to all mankind.'[4]

Lord Durham's instructions and commissions differed materially from those of previous Governors. Like them he was to administer Lower Canada and to be Governor-in-Chief of Upper and Lower Canada, New Brunswick, Nova Scotia, and Prince Edward Island, but it was intended that his powers in relation to these latter provinces should be much less formal than those of his predecessors. He was to be, in a full sense of the term, Governor-General of all the British North American provinces, including Newfoundland. He had a great task of investigation as well as of administration, and was appointed 'High Commissioner for the adjustment of certain important questions depending in the provinces of Lower and Upper Canada respecting the form and future government of the said provinces'. It was recognized that these problems were related to problems in the other provinces.

While visiting any province he was to assume full administration of its government. 'It will be the duty of each Lieutenant-Governor to enter into a free and confidential correspondence with your Lordship on every topic on which you may invite such communications, and to obey every instruction not in itself unlawful which you may address to him; but it will be desirable to limit such correspondence to questions of general and permanent interest.' He was also given an absolute power of pardon in cases of treason without any necessity of waiting 'till the royal pleasure should be known'.

In effect, Lord Durham was to exercise dictatorial power in Lower Canada, was to exercise supervision at will over the government of the other provinces, and as High Commissioner was to shape and recommend a new system of government. No man before or since has been sent to America with such vast powers and such important duties. In his instructions there was little to guide him and little to restrict him. As Sir Charles Lucas has said, 'it would be difficult to find a more futile set of instructions to a strong man setting out on a difficult mission, but they had the merit of leaving him a wide discretion'.

During the months that intervened between his appointment and his sailing for Canada, Durham, who always studied closely any question with which he had to deal, was informing himself in regard to Canada, and was being informed by various voluntary communications from interested and disinterested parties. Letters, petitions, and newspapers streamed in to him directly or through the Colonial Office from British merchants interested in the Canada trade, such as Gould and Gillespie, who had for some time conducted an efficient bureau of information for the Colonial Office in their own interests. Through these and similar communications from Moffatt and Badgley, Canadian merchants who had come to London at this time with the purpose of getting the ear of the English Government, Durham received very extensive *ex parte* information in regard to the grievances of the British party and the measures they advocated, with a special emphasis on the union of Upper and Lower Canada, the sins of the French, and the necessity of destroying French pride and making Canada 'British in its laws, language, custom and feelings'.[5] One of the letters communicated to Lord Durham in this manner was from Archdeacon Strachan. Among other things he described his feelings at the time of the Upper Canada Rebellion. He could not understand why he was only third on the rebels' list of those to be hanged. 'The Governor had precedence, but why in this career of honor the Chief Justice [John Beverley Robinson] should have been placed before me I have yet to learn.' The reason, no doubt, why the letter was forwarded to Durham was that it contained the following statement: 'One thing must never be lost sight of, whether the measure be a union of the two provinces or a federal union of all the British North American Colonies, and that is, a representation possessing British principles and feeling must be secured.'[6]

In a lengthy memorandum addressed to Durham by Moffatt and Badgley, April 9, they advocated the following aims and measures – a fixed Civil List, improvement of the compositions of the Councils, the independence of the judiciary, a provincial tribunal for the trial of impeachments, a general and efficient system of elementary education supported by contributions of the inhabitants, the improvement of the St. Lawrence waterways, an adequate system of registration for incumbrances on real estate, abolition of feudal tenure, incorporation of the cities of Montreal and Quebec, improvement of the jury law, rearrangement of the electoral constituencies of Lower Canada to afford adequate representation to the British population, 'losing the French population in the great Anglo-Saxon family established through North America', and a legislative union of Upper and Lower Canada.[7]

Roebuck, who had been the agent in London of the Lower Canada Assembly, made no such effort to bring the French point of view before Durham's attention, nor did any of his Radical friends.[8] Durham could learn much of it, however, if he had the patience to wade through their verbose pamphlets and speeches. 'Bear' Ellice apparently turned over to Durham two letters which he received at this time from the French-Canadian leader Lafontaine, who was in Paris. Writing on March 15, Lafontaine told Ellice that the appointment of Lord Durham had awakened in him the hope of a better future and that he had written to Canada to that effect. He hoped that a general amnesty would be proclaimed. Lord Durham 'may expect as soon as his appointment is known a thousand injuries at the hands of the Tory press of that country, on account of the liberal sentiments which he has always declared. And if he is not on his guard against the intrigues of the Quebec officials (of which I should, however, in justice, except Mr. Daly, the provincial secretary) I venture to say, judging by the past, that his administration will run the greatest risks, exposed to the atmosphere of that *entourage*, of which almost all of our governors have sooner or later become the victims'.[9] As we shall see, Durham followed this advice, and when he arrived in Canada got rid of all the old official group with the exception of Daly. In his letter of the 17th Lafontaine declared that the French-Canadians must be treated as equals and that there must be no favouritism. Lord Durham would succeed if he appointed an entirely new Council and dominated it, but if he retained the old material he would accomplish nothing.[10] Again Durham followed Lafontaine's advice.

Ellice himself might be expected to attempt in a tactful manner to influence Durham in the interests of the Canadian merchants. He saw a good bit of Durham during these months,[11] consequently his statement to Lafontaine that 'I do not know his opinions and write without conversation or communication with him'[12] is an astonishing one. Ellice, however, gave Durham a copy of the letter in which it was made.

Lord Durham distrusted the statements of the British merchants, and was anxious to get the other side of the story. Noticing that Roebuck held aloof from him, he instructed some one to tell Roebuck that he believed Lord Durham would be pleased to have him call on him. Roebuck was strongly prejudiced against Durham. He was the only one of the Radical leaders who had not responded enthusiastically to his appointment, and at this time he was hand in glove with Brougham. He replied to this hint: 'If Lord Durham desires to see me and receive what information I can give, the plain proper mode is to request me to wait on him.' Lord Durham then made the direct request. Our knowledge of what occurred at the interview is dependent entirely on Roebuck's account of it:

Lord Durham assumed that I, together with all the rest of the world, must be exceedingly interested in his career as Governor-General of Canada. . . . He proposed to me, without circumlocution, that I should forthwith leave England, transport myself through the United States, and take up a position somewhere near the frontiers of Canada, but not within them, and put myself into a secret correspondence with him. To this extravagant proposal, dictated by an over-weening self-estimation, I gave a peremptory refusal.

Roebuck offered, however, to give any information at his disposal, and at Durham's request, promised to put it in writing.[13]

The result was Roebuck's plan for the government of Canada, on which Lord Durham's first proposals in Canada were very closely modelled. It was a plan for a federal union of British North America. In each provincial government there was to be a Governor, an Executive Council of not more than five, and an Assembly. The salaries of the Governor and Executive Councillors were to be fixed by the legislature for a period of six years. There was to be no Legislative Council, but the Executive Council should have the power of amending but not rejecting bills sent up from the Assembly. The Assembly was to be elected by ballot for a term of three years and have control of all provincial revenues. In the federal government, the Governor and Executive Council should have the same powers as in the provincial governments. The members of the federal Assembly were to be elected by the provincial Assemblies, each province to have five members and one additional member for every 50,000 population. The following was to be the principle of the division of powers: 'The general government has no powers not expressly conferred on it; the local governments have all powers not expressly taken away.' Provision was to be made for a supreme court to adjudicate on constitutional questions arising out of the federal relationships and for the impeachment of judges and other officials. 'Montreal, by common consent, seems to be the spot which ought to be selected for a general government.' The plan also contains reminders that there is a great need of municipal government and that 'the whole judiciary of Lower Canada needs complete revision'. While this was intended as a plan for a federation of all the provinces, that might not be possible, and Durham was advised to 'form a plan for the federal union of Upper and Lower Canada – make this *imperative,* and allow the other provinces to join if they think fit'.[14]

According to Roebuck, Durham told him that he approved of the scheme and that he would propose it for adoption. He did so in a modified form, but, as we shall see, was forced by circumstances to abandon it. The idea of a federation of all the provinces came to Durham from many quarters, and was approved by Ellice and Howick.[15] The Canada merchants provided him very industriously with arguments against it, including a memorandum entitled 'Heads of objections to a Federative Union', drawn up by Andrew Stuart.[16] This federation idea appealed strongly to Durham with his remarkable receptivity for sweeping conceptions and his determination to translate the ideal into the practical if there was any possible way to do so. This attitude, which developed with the passing weeks and was strengthened by his observations in Canada, is thus described by Charles Buller, his Chief Secretary:

The plan appeared [to Lord Durham] to offer a chance of putting an end to existing discussions, of overwhelming the enemies of British connexion in the Canadas by the unanimous loyalty of the Lower Provinces, of extinguishing the pretensions of French nationality, and at the same time of leaving each different community in possession of its own laws and of the power of managing its own local affairs. The plan had in Lord Durham's eyes the still greater merit of combining these large and richly endowed Provinces for common purposes of improvement, of forming out of these divided and feeble elements a single community with vigour as well as singleness of action, and of thus raising upon the northern frontier of the United States a rival union of British Colonies, which might ere long, by the development of its vast internal resources, form a counterbalancing power on the American Continent.[17]

According to Buller, Durham went out to Canada with very few prejudices. But he indicates that while he himself, owing, no doubt, to his close Radical affiliations, was very favourable to and sympathetic with the French-Canadians, he felt that Lord Durham 'had too strong a feeling against them on account of their recent insurrection'. Buller believed that the rebellion was due to 'the deplorable imbecility of our colonial policy', but 'Lord Durham from the first took a far sounder view of the matter: he saw what narrow and mischievous spirit worked at the bottom of all the acts of the French-Canadians; and while he was prepared to do the individuals full justice, and justice with mercy, he had made up his mind that no quarter should be shown to the absurd pretensions of race, and that he must throw himself on the support of the British feelings, and aim at making Canada thoroughly British'.[18] In this, as in much that he later wrote in his Report, we can discern the fact that Lord Durham was influenced, quite naturally, by the view so commonly held at this time among the upper class in England that the French-Canadians were a disloyal and lamentably inferior people who could never fit in to the providential scheme of things until in some mysterious manner they were made into Englishmen. As we have seen, however, he went out with every intention of being fair to them, of showing no favour to the English, and of developing a scheme of government with which they would be satisfied.

Among the many representations made to Durham, there is not the slightest trace of Responsible Government or of an extensive measure of Self Government. Furthermore, most of these suggestions – including that of Roebuck – were quite incompatible with the epoch-making recommendations on these subjects which he made in his Report. Nor is there any reflection of them in his own letters and speeches or in Buller's account of these days. There is not the slightest evidence that he went to Canada with these ideas in his mind.

The date of Durham's departure for Canada was delayed unnecessarily. Even if it were considered inadvisable for him to go via New York, the St. Lawrence navigation was open for some time before his arrival. The delay was unfortunate and, in any case, Durham, who could have hastened his departure, must bear most of the responsibility. He may have been influenced by the desire to secure as much information as possible before he launched out on his difficult task, by considerations of health and of his exaggerated conception of the Canadian climate, or by his desire to have time to develop adequately his magnificent and almost regal establishment. In his sketch of the mission, Buller wrote: 'I think that Lord Durham's first object should have been that of commencing his work with promptitude. The delay took off the bloom of the Mission; the insurrection was to all appearance wholly suppressed before we started; the danger began to be thought less urgent; and the general impression of the necessity for great powers and unusual measures was gradually weakened.'[19]

The Tories showed a real concern over Canada so long as British rule in that country was imperilled by rebellion, which was a hard-fisted fact that they could understand. In those circumstances their true blue loyalty asserted itself; Canada, for the moment, was of some importance, and they refused to impede the Government in its patriotic mission of repression. But as soon as news from Canada assured them that the rebellion was a thing of the past, that this 'jewel' was still safely set in the British 'crown', they were free to play politics again. The Government was once more imperilled by a Tory-Radical alliance which could operate most successfully on the basis of the Canadian question. And the Tories had the further motive of crippling the man whose power in England they most feared. To force Lord Durham to resign would be a great victory for them from every point of view. Sensitiveness and temper were his vulnerable points, and insult was a most effective weapon.

After some rumbling of the guns, the campaign began in force on April 2, when Lord Chandos moved a resolution in the House of Commons declaring that the establishment of the Governor-General should be provided and conducted with every degree of economy consistent with the due remuneration of the persons whose employment was necessary, and proposing that the expenditure of Lord Gosford should be considered a precedent. Every member of the House who understood anything of the situation must have known that the motion was, in view of Lord Durham's extraordinary duties and the suspension of the constitution – not to consider the bare rooms in which Gosford had lived at Quebec – as absurd as it was insulting. Yet the Tories fought for it as ardently as though Bonaparte had come back to life and was pounding at the gates of London. Much of the talk about the number of Lord Durham's grooms and servants, the horses, the family plate, and the expensive furniture he was taking to Canada was irrelevant to the resolution because they were paid for out of Lord Durham's private purse, as was also the salary of his secretary, but they were the better calculated for that reason to rouse the disgust of the proud and angry earl, who had refused to accept any salary for himself. And then there was the scandal of his aides-de-camp! He was taking out eight of them, four paid and four unpaid (that is, paid by Lord Durham himself). Lord Chandos said that he had never on any occasion heard of a man who required so many aides-de-camp. The Duke of Wellington when in command of the allied armies had had at times only four and never more than six. Lord John Russell replied that they were needed to carry confidential communications between the Governor-General and the Lieutenant-Governors, but he added that the number was rather to be considered in reference to the dignity and rank of the person to whom they were attached than to the active services they rendered. Sir Robert Peel shrewdly insinuated that the Government was allowing Lord Durham to fix the amount of expenditure. The resolution was defeated by a majority of two. It was a small division to which the Opposition 'brought their halt and their blind' in a house that was far from full, but it was a warning to the Government of the delicate position in which it stood.

The Tory newspapers continued to ring the changes on the elaborate character of the establishment. The *Morning Chronicle*, on the other side, suggested that an effective headline would be 'The Butter-Boat Question'.

The Times *is evidently coming to close quarters with the Lord High Commissioner, and in a day or two we shall have his stock of shirts and stockings or peradventure a night-cap question on the tapis. . . . The legal adviser and the aides-de-camp and lieutenants too many to any degree, and plates, dishes and butter-boats, and pots and pans might sail away and welcome, provided only Lord Durham would stay behind in disgust.*[20]

Lord Durham had stipulated that he should have a free hand in regard to appointments. And he proceeded to secure the most capable men. Scores of letters reached him during these weeks from influential people and intimate friends who had relatives with an eye on Durham's liberal salaries. To all of these he replied with uniform politeness and firmness that he was very sorry that he could do nothing for them. Durham had insight as well as courage in this respect, and for the first time in her history Canada was served by Great Britain with the best brains available.

Charles Buller was appointed Chief Secretary. He was one of the best known and most popular of the Radical members of Parliament. As the outstanding wit of the House of Commons, he was always sure of a good hearing, but it was felt by many who knew him best that his reputation in this respect overshadowed the credit that was due to him for the possession of more substantial qualities. He had an acute, resourceful mind. He was somewhat lacking in aggressiveness. He had the qualities of a good follower rather than a leader. He lent his fine mind readily to others, and his thought was more brilliant than it was tenacious. Behind an indolent, easy-going manner, he gave evidence of remarkable capacity for industry and application. His name was frequently associated with that of Macaulay as a shining light of the younger generation.

He was the son of an official in the East India Company, and entered Parliament in 1830. His family was closely associated with a number of rotten boroughs, and at the time of the Reform Bill his liberal tendencies placed him in a position very similar to that of the hero of Mr. Stanley Weyman's well-known novel of that period. He not only displayed the courage of his convictions; he associated himself with the most pronounced Radicals, became a member of the Executive of the National Political Union, and presided at some of the most important meetings of that body. It seems probable that some of his ardent admiration for Lord Durham was associated with the latter's leadership of the Reform movement both during and after the Reform Bill struggle.

In the spring of 1838 he was thirty-one years of age. He was even-tempered, amiable, friendly, kind-hearted with a strain of tenderness, but manly and straightforward in his own quiet playful way. There were hours when he was serious enough and sober to the point of tension, but those were the hours he hid from the world. He appeared to many who knew him well as one who found life a continuous entertainment. 'Charles Buller was there,' wrote Hobhouse in his diary. 'A little girl, Stanley's daughter, not seven years old, said to him, "You are always joking. I do not ever know whether what you say is true". This is quite the character of the man. The child is right.'[21] A contemporary journalistic sketch gives us the following account of his parliamentary manner:

His style of speaking is rather the conversational than that elevated manner which has become associated with our ideas of oratory. He stands at the table of the House, and addresses the ministerial benches as if the occupiers were his very dear and familiar friends, to whom he was telling some very good story, in which they themselves figure as the principal personages. . . . There he stands, turning their fallacies inside out, and piercing a solemn pomposity with a keen, sharp rally, which not only throws the Opposition into a united and corporate fit of laughter, but not seldom makes the victims of his playful satire join in the laugh against themselves. It is delightful to see him transfixing a fallacy with the point of an epigram or putting his opponent into a parenthesis.[22]

When, ten years after his appointment by Lord Durham, Charles Buller was cut off in his prime, and Macaulay said: 'I could almost weep for him,' Carlyle wrote for the *Examiner* the following epitaph on his former pupil:

A very beautiful soul has been suddenly summoned from among us; one of the clearest intellects and most aerial activities

*in England has been unexpectedly called away.... His luminous
sincere intellect laid bare to him in all its abject incoherency
the thing that was untrue; which thenceforth became for him a
thing that was untenable, that it was perilous and scandalous to
attempt maintaining.... The essence of his mind was clearness,
healthy purity, incompatibility with fraud in any of its forms.
What he accomplished therefore, great or little, was all to be
added to the sum of good; none of it to be deducted.... To hear
him, the most serious of men might think within himself, 'How
beautiful is human gaiety too.'... His wit, moreover, was ever
the ally of wisdom, not of folly, or unkindness, or injustice; no
soul was ever hurt by it.... This man was true to his friends,
true to his convictions, and true without effort, as the magnet to
the north. Weak health marked out his limits.... He was not
the man to grapple, in its dark and deadly dens, with the
Lernaean coil of social hydras, perhaps not under any circumstances, but he did what he could; faithfully himself did something, nay something truly considerable. And in his* patience
*with the more that by him and his strength could not be done,
let us grant that there was something of the beautiful too!...
He has fallen at this point of the march, an honourable soldier,
and has left us here to fight along without him. Whatever in
him was true and valiant endures for evermore — beyond all
memory or record.*[23]

Next to Charles Buller, the most important man associated
with Lord Durham's mission to Canada was Edward Gibbon
Wakefield. Regarded in that day as something of a faddist and
shunned on account of the scandals associated with his private
life, Wakefield is recognized to-day as the most capable expert
on the economic side of colonial problems in the England of
that period. With his unerring judgement of men, Durham
recognized that fact and determined to take Wakefield to
Canada, no matter what any one might say about it.

Wakefield came of a family intensely interested in social
problems. Elizabeth Fry was his cousin. His father had been a
writer on economic and social subjects as well as a farmer and
a land-agent, a friend of Francis Place, and a student of popular education, social statistics, and lunatic asylums. Gibbon
Wakefield manifested throughout his life a generous interest in
promoting the welfare of humanity, especially among the more
destitute classes, for which he blithely sacrificed both time and

money. This trait was strangely blended in his character with a predilection for methods that were devious, a desire to over-reach no matter what degree of trickery was resorted to, and a cool and sometimes heartless disdain for the moral code. He was a better man than he was generally believed to be, but his contemporaries cannot be blamed for feeling that they could not tell which element would assume the ascendancy in any particular situation. Lord Durham was freed from such fears because he knew that he could count on Wakefield's personal devotion to him.

Early in life, Wakefield had eloped with a ward in Chancery. 'Two carriages simultaneously left Tunbridge Wells, driving in opposite directions, one containing Edward Gibbon Wakefield and Eliza Pattle, the other two persons dressed to represent them. The uncles followed the wrong one.'[24] The bride brought Wakefield a substantial fortune, most of which he managed to lose after her death a few years later. In 1826 the readers of the English press were regaled for months with the Turner case. Gibbon Wakefield (with the aid of his brother) concocted a story which induced a young girl in a boarding school, daughter of a wealthy manufacturer, to leave the school with him although he was a total stranger to her, and later to contract a nominal marriage with him, having been informed that it was suggested by her father's solicitor as the only means of saving her father from financial ruin. The conspirators, however, failed to realize their profits. Gibbon Wakefield was arrested in France, brought back to England for trial, and sentenced to three years imprisonment in Newgate. The marriage was dissolved by a special Act of Parliament.

When his prison term was over, Wakefield found himself a social outcast, but he pursued through various anonymous and indirect paths his self-appointed task of organizing systematic emigration for an overcrowded England and economically regenerating the colonial empire. His theoretic bases were laid down in his first book, written in prison, and entitled, *A Letter from Sydney*. The public accepted it as a genuine message from a country which Wakefield had never seen and as emanating from a colonist advising a prospective settler; Wakefield's name did not appear. The fundamental Wakefield ideas were – that cheap land was the bane of the colonies, large tracts were appropriated, and the labour supply was inadequate; public lands should be sold at fixed and reasonable prices, and the

Government should use a large proportion of the money so obtained in providing for systematic emigration to the colonies; if there were no cheap land available the immigrant labourer would have to work on the land of others until by his thrift he was able to pay the reasonable price for land of his own; land, capital, and labour would thus be yoked together to produce a prosperous community.

In 1830 Wakefield organized a Colonization Society with the object of developing systematic emigration. Torrens, Grote, and other Radicals were prominent members, and Wakefield's own name was kept very much in the background. At the instance of the Society – Wakefield directing operations from behind the scenes – the Government in 1831, owing largely to the enlightenment and open-mindedness of Lord Howick, at that time Under-Secretary for the Colonies, applied several of Wakefield's principles to the granting of land in New South Wales. In 1833 Wakefield organized the 'South Australia Association', of which Buller was one of the directors. 'At that time', as Wakefield said, 'the country now known as South Australia was a nameless desert about which nothing was known by the public or the Government.'[25] Wakefield and Buller traced its boundaries with a pencil on a map. South Australia was then constituted by Act of Parliament, Wakefield's principles of sale and emigration were applied and the introduction of convicts forbidden. Wakefield himself was pushed aside on account of his prison record; dissatisfied with the price fixed for land sales, he withdrew from the project. He then turned his attention to New Zealand, and in May 1837 organized the New Zealand Association to promote emigration to that country. Buller and Molesworth were among the directors, Wakefield's name was again left in the background, and when a few weeks later Lord Durham returned from Russia, his earlier interest in New Zealand was appealed to and he was induced to become Chairman of the Association. Wakefield was probably influenced by the fact that all of his friends belonged to the political group who desired to see Lord Durham Prime Minister. When that day came, New Zealand would get its chance.[26] It was probably on account of New Zealand business that Wakefield's sailing for Canada was delayed, and he went out a few weeks later than Lord Durham. Durham intended to give full recognition to this social outcast who had done so much for the British Empire and who might do much more in the future. When he arrived in Canada, Wakefield was to be appointed Commissioner of Crown Lands and Emigration, but he did not propose to inform the Government of that fact until the appointment was made.

Lord Durham selected for his Military Secretary, Colonel Couper, who, in addition to other splendid qualifications, had the advantage of having served in Canada under Sir James Kempt, one of the most popular of Canadian Governors. The need of municipal government in Canada was realized by Durham to some extent before he left England, and he determined to institute an investigation and secure a thorough-going report of the situation. For this purpose he selected William Kennedy, the editor of the *Hull Advertiser* and owner of several other newspapers, with whom he had been associated in the election of 1834, and who had done signal service in connexion with municipal reform in England. In the latter connexion Joseph Parkes had described him as 'a very shrewd and clever fellow'. He was apparently conversant with the municipal institutions of the United States as well as those of Great Britain.[27] Although Kennedy's name has been hitherto unknown to Canadian historians, he made a signal contribution to our history. The report which he prepared in collaboration with Adam Thom was the basis for Poulett Thomson's municipal establishments in Upper and Lower Canada.

In two of his selections, Turton and Ellice, Lord Durham was influenced by friendship and sentiment, although in these cases also the men possessed qualifications of a superior character. Edward Ellice, Jr., son of 'Bear' Ellice, was appointed private secretary. He was a young man of ability, a member of Parliament, and well acquainted with Canada. During the week in which Durham was thinking over the Canada proposal, 'Bear' Ellice, in a glow of paternal pride, had written him as follows: 'If you do go to Canada, don't say anything about a secretary, till you see whether or not we could persuade Edward to go with you. He would be a great comfort to Lady Durham' (who, in her letters to her mother from Canada, betrayed a decided dislike for him). 'And he has more intelligence and knowledge of the world than any person you could pick up.'[28]

We now come to an appointment which was most unfortunate in its results, although it affords another illustration of Durham's generosity and courage. The Turton appointment requires careful consideration because it caused the first serious break between Durham and the Melbourne Government and did a great deal to pave the way for the final one. When the Dictator's estimates were discovered to include provision for a 'legal adviser', members of Parliament professed to be unable to understand why that should be necessary when there was a Solicitor-General and Attorney-General in Lower Canada. But Durham had determined to have as little as possible to do with the old officials. Several of the most important of the grievances which the British merchants had reported to him were closely connected with questions of law, not to mention the fact that they were clamouring for a complete change in the legal system of the province. Roebuck, the late agent of the French-Canadians, had urged upon him the fact that 'the whole judiciary of Lower Canada needs complete revision'. Durham would not have such work done by any one who had been involved in the political disputes of the province. He wanted a first-class English lawyer. His selection was Thomas Turton, who had already served him in a legal capacity, notably in the drafting of his Reform Bill of 1821. He had known him all his life and he had complete confidence in him.

But Turton, like Wakefield, had a 'past'. The really ugly details of the Turton case were also matters of common knowledge. Mrs. Turton had successfully sued her husband for divorce, naming her sister as co-respondent. It had created almost as great a sensation as the Turner case. Turton had been Durham's friend since the days when they were school-mates, and, as Charles Buller said, Durham, like Canning, never abandoned a friend. He showed the greatest kindness to Turton at the time of his personal trouble, and later he made every effort to give him that 'second chance' to which he believed he was entitled. Certainly if any man ever expiated his sins by sincere repentance, every possible effort at restitution, remorse, and a better life, Turton did.[29] He had lived a most exemplary life in India for fifteen years, but although he had been elected a churchwarden of the Cathedral Church of Calcutta, he was apparently not received in the best society. Lord Durham tried to get him into Parliament, but Kennedy persuaded him that it would be impossible.[30] Now Durham felt that he had matters in his own hands and he was determined to give Turton his chance.

Turton and Buller both stated later that Durham was encouraged in this step by two members of the Government, that E. J. Stanley made the original suggestion to Durham, and that when Turton hesitated about accepting, Hobhouse promised that he would be appointed to the first Indian judgeship that fell vacant after his return to India.[31] Lord Durham, however, made the selection and secured Turton's consent without consulting either the Prime Minister or the Colonial Secretary. The Government had promised Durham a free hand in the matter of appointments, but it had not anticipated that he would make appointments which were calculated to be detrimental to its interests without consultation. When Melbourne heard of what was going on, he wrote to Durham, April 9: 'Turton's was not a common case. It will injure both you and the Government. . . . If you have gone to this extent with him, I do not see what can be done, but I am afraid of the effects.' But he changed his mind and began to press for a reversal. 'If the appointment is to be got rid of, the sooner and more quietly it is done the better. . . . Your mission and consequently the public service will suffer from such an appointment.'[32] In the face of this strong feeling on Melbourne's part, Durham assumed a singularly high-handed attitude.

On the 12th, Ellice wrote to Durham: 'I had a very satisfactory conversation with Ld. Melbourne last night, after you were gone, and have no doubt this affair will be arranged as you desire, when you return[33] or before you sail. He felt the manner in which you had given way as far as it was possible for you to concede to their wishes and admitted the [illegible] distinction that could be made between his going with you in one capacity or the other.'[34] Before Lord Durham sailed, he and Lord Melbourne arrived at a distinct understanding that while Turton was not to receive any appointment from the British Government, Durham was to be free not only to use him in any unofficial capacity, but also to appoint him to office in Canada on his own responsibility if he should consider it desirable to do so.[35]

Durham's statement of the matter was never contradicted by the Melbourne Government or any member of it, and it is confirmed by Ellice, who was extremely frank in his letters to Durham, particularly when an opening was afforded for adverse criticism. Ellice regretted the whole Turton affair, but he said on this point, in a letter which pre-dated any of Durham's statements:

My construction of your intention was, – that you would act on your own responsibility on your arrival, in making such appointments as the circumstances of the colony, at the time of making them, should justify, and that if you saw no objection to appointing Turton, that you would act in his case on the same principle as on all others.[36]

Lord Durham's original intention had been that Turton should receive a large salary, but after the trouble arose over his appointment, Turton refused to accept Durham's offer to pay the salary himself and insisted on receiving no remuneration whatever. And so it came about that the services of three of the four men who made the largest contribution to the Durham mission, whose ultimate success constituted it the most important by far in the history of our Empire, did not cost the British Government one shilling. Durham, Wakefield, and Turton received nothing, and Durham paid the salary of his own secretary and some ten thousand pounds beside in one way or another. One was a wealthy man and the others were in comfortable circumstances, but the spirit of these men, who, under the inspiring genius of their leader, laboured to save Canada and lay the foundation of a new type of Empire, may well serve as a constant inspiration in the face of the call which patriotism makes in the days of peace.

By the middle of April everything was ready, but 'Mr. Ralph', that bluff and genial uncle who had been his guardian and lifelong friend, lay seriously ill in the North; Durham postponed the sailing, took the long journey to Lambton, arrived at eleven o'clock one night and left at four the next day, went to Windsor for a last audience with the Queen, and sailed from Portsmouth on the 24th.

The affectionate pen of Charles Buller described the scene.

I had got on board about an hour before Lord Durham came. . . . I had just got over my difficulties, when the steamer bringing Lord Durham and his family came alongside. All the parade of naval reception was of course exhibited on the occasion; the marines were drawn up, and the officers, with the captain at their head, were on the deck, when Lord Durham, who had been very ill the night before, came looking very pale, and wrapped in a large cloak, with Lady Durham and his children around him. Painful thoughts arose within me at the sight of a man so distinguished leaving his country with his whole family for what, though an honourable, was still a painful exile, and a duty of arduous responsibility; and when on a sudden the band struck up its loud and slow strain, the sudden excitement brought the tears at once into my eyes.[37]

❁ ❁ ❁

Gales and head-winds, now and then a day or two of calm, then more stormy weather and head-winds! The elements might have been reflecting the life-experience of the man of destiny whom the 'Hastings' was taking to Canada. And Durham was 'wearied with it, being impatient to arrive'. But 'he was tolerably well' and looked 'a great deal better than he had done for some time'. He had only one of his bad attacks in his head. He and Buller worked hard, studying documents, discussing the problems of the mission; now and then their talk slipped back to the battles of other days and the Reform Bill period and *its* problems. To break the monotony Buller and Turton organized private theatricals and a mock trial. At last they saw the rocks of Anticosti and the bleak coast of the Gulf, then more weary days, then the grandeur and beauty of the St. Lawrence, and on the 27th of May they dropped anchor off Quebec, 'amid a whole fleet of men-of-war under the very guns of the magnificent fortress'.[1]

They did not land until the 29th. In the meantime Durham received visitors and studied the newspapers. The first batch of newspapers which had come on board a few days before informed him of the unfavourable attitude of the British merchants, in regard to which he had been warned before leaving England. The more violent among them were loud in their criticisms of both the British and Canadian Governments, and at a recent meeting in Montreal several of the speakers had stated that they had little to hope for from a man of Lord Durham's radical views. Lord Durham must have noted the contrast between this and the attitude of the leading French-Canadian paper. *Le Canadien* called attention – as it had been doing for some time – to the liberal character of Lord Durham and his secretaries. It pointed out that the great leader of the Reform movement in Great Britain had brought with him to Canada men who had been active in the same cause and the lawyer who had drafted his Reform Bill of 1821.

We may be sure that if the Home Government had been ill-disposed toward us, it would not have sent us the most liberal men to set our affairs in order. . . . It is here that the ill-will is, here the abuses, here the projects of oppression; in the Mother

Country there is only ignorance and perhaps a little prejudice. Very well, let us enlighten this ignorance and dispel these prejudices; here is our opportunity.[2]

Durham made an imposing and business-like beginning. The display so essential to him was everywhere in evidence. Never had a Governor arrived in such magnificence and with such a retinue. The amount of baggage – which it took two days to land – bewildered the inhabitants. Clad in a gorgeous uniform with silver embroidery, wearing the collar of the Bath, and mounted on a fine white horse, Lord Durham rode through the cheering crowds to the Castle of St. Louis. There he showed his mettle. After taking the oath of office, he refused to do what every other Governor had done; he would not continue the appointments of the old Executive Councillors. He then ordered that without delay the names of all political prisoners should be laid before him with the depositions on which they had been committed and all available information on every case, and that similar returns should be made in regard to those against whom warrants had been sworn but who had succeeded in fleeing from justice. On the same day he issued an impressive proclamation, of which the following were the most significant passages:

The honest and conscientious advocates of reform and of the amelioration of defective institutions will receive from me, without distinction of party, race, or politics, that assistance and encouragement which their patriotism has a right to command from all who desire to strengthen and consolidate the connexion between the parent State and these important colonies; but the disturbers of the public peace, the violators of the law, the enemies of the Crown and of the British Empire will find in me an uncompromising opponent, determined to put in force against them all the powers, civil and military, with which I have been invested. . . . I invite from you the most free, unreserved communications. I beg you to consider me as a friend and arbitrator – ready at all times to listen to your wishes, complaints, and grievances, and fully determined to act with the strictest impartiality. If you, on your side, will abjure all party and sectarian animosities, and unite with me in the blessed work of peace and harmony, I feel sure that I can lay the foundation of such a system of government as will protect the rights and interests of all classes, allay all dissensions, and permanently establish, under Divine Providence, the wealth, greatness, and

*prosperity, of which such inexhaustible elements are to be found
in these fertile countries.*

In place of the old Executive Councillors, to whom he wrote
a very tactful letter,[3] he appointed Buller, Turton, Colonel
Couper, and Routh, the Commissioner-General, from his own
staff, and Daly – whose retention Lafontaine had advised.
(Turton had already been appointed one of his secretaries on
the very day Lord Durham landed.) These acts were greeted
with acclamation by both parties. *Le Canadien* and *Le Populaire*
were most enthusiastic. The former, in dilating on the high
hopes these actions created, made a happy quotation from Lord
Durham's reform speech of 1821. It also noted the fact that the
political prisoners had been granted permission to walk about
in the prison courtyard. 'It seems that the atmosphere has
changed since the arrival of Lord Durham, and that a refreshing
breeze has reached even the most unfortunate.'[4] The majority
of the English population were as pleased with the proclamation
as the French, and they had no regrets for the old Council.
They had supported the official clique only for the sake of
protection against what they had considered the tyranny of the
Assembly, and they were not sorry now to see it broken. The
Montreal *Transcript* said: 'The days of reform have indeed
dawned upon this colony, and we rejoice in its brightened
prospects. . . . We duly appreciate the motive as well as the
policy which has actuated the Earl of Durham in dismissing the
previously existing councils. Every part of the old constitutional
fabric was rotten.'[5] And yet Lord Durham was to find that these
actions which met with such hearty approval in Canada were
criticized in England as being 'high-handed', tyrannical, and
anything else that English party politics could readily invent
and the common English ignorance in regard to Canada could
more readily believe.

His next act displayed the same vigour and astuteness, and
met with a similar approval. A few hours after he landed in
Quebec, early in the morning of May 30, a Canadian steamer,
called the *Sir Robert Peel*, was attacked at Wells Island on the
American side of the St. Lawrence, where it had stopped to take
on wood, by a group of pirates under the leadership of the
notorious Bill Johnson – mostly Americans, but co-operating
with the Canadian rebels then in the United States. The passen-
gers were forced to leave the boat, a considerable sum of money

was seized and the steamer was burned. It was felt in Canada that this was no isolated outrage. For months the safety of Canadian citizens had been threatened by the conspiracies of Canadian rebel-refugees in the United States and their American sympathizers. These men had secured arms, held meetings, announced their intention of invading Canada, all with the greatest openness. Scarcely any preventive measures were taken, and while the more educated classes in the United States were not sympathetic, in many places 'influential citizens' as well as a considerable proportion of the lower orders had countenanced these proceedings. Immediately the news reached Quebec Lord Durham issued a proclamation offering a reward of £1,000 for information that would lead to the conviction in the United States courts of the perpetrators of this outrage, and assuring the people of Canada that adequate measures would be taken for the defence of the frontier.[6]

He decided at the same time to send a special mission to Washington to remonstrate with the United States Government. For this he selected Lady Durham's brother, Colonel Charles Grey, who had come to Canada as an officer of the 71st. The selection was a happy one. He was the most tactful member of the Grey family. And Lord Grey's son would be sure of a good reception in Washington.

Durham gave Charles Grey the following written instructions:

I have directed Mr. Fox to request an interview for you with the President of the United States. You will be pleased to express to him my feelings of sincere respect for him and his country: and assure him that, in the discharge of my duty as Governor-General of British North America, I shall be most anxious to cultivate relations of amity and cordiality with the Government of the United States. You will acquaint him that I feel persuaded that he will view the outrage at Wells Island with feelings of as much indignation as myself, and that I can confidently rely on the most prompt and efficacious means being taken by the American authorities to bring the perpetrators of this heinous offence to condign punishment. At the same time you will make him understand that something is required from the United States government; that the redress of this particular outrage must also be accompanied by measures for the prevention in future of similar crimes. The British frontier cannot be

*left exposed to these perpetual attacks and this constant irrita-
tion: and I have a right to call on the American government to
fulfil the most sacred of all duties, the due observance of the
faith of treaties and the strictest maintenance of the rights of
friendly powers. I earnestly hope that the executive power on
the American side will be effectively and promptly employed.
In justice to those of His Majesty's subjects, the insecurity of
whose lives and properties, in consequence of these repeated
attacks proceeding from the United States, is daily and hourly
represented to me, I make this communication. In all circumstances, and at all hazards, I must afford them protection, and it
will give me the sincerest pleasure to find that my task is rendered
easier by the co-operation of the American government.*[7]

In his dispatch to Stephen Fox, the British Minister at
Washington, Durham employed stronger language: 'I am convinced that the government of the United States will feel it due
to their national honour to prevent the repetition of offences,
the longer continuance of which, and of the impunity with
which they have been hitherto perpetrated, is a disgrace to all
civilized governments.'[8]

As a result of this mission, the United States government
instituted a patrol of the frontier waters by a number of
steamers carrying fifty soldiers each under the command of
officers of the army or navy and a thorough search of the
Thousand Islands on the American side. The Commander-in-
Chief of the United States Army was ordered to take charge of
operations, with instructions also to concentrate the regular
forces at certain points, and to use 'every exertion to detect the
unlawful combinations against the peace of a neighbouring and
friendly power'. The Secretary-at-War's instructions to the
Commander-in-Chief contained the following sentence:

*From the respect for the laws, hitherto so signally evinced by
citizens of the United States on all occasions, it is apprehended
that the border inhabitants of the northern frontiers are not
generally acquainted with the enactments which may render
their conduct penal; you will, therefore, on your arrival at the
frontier, cause to be published and widely circulated copies of
the laws of the United States.*[9]

Lord Durham on his part arranged for an immediate increase
of the naval forces on the lakes and upper St. Lawrence under
Captain Sandom.[10]

The British Minister at Washington reported to the British Government on June 24 that Colonel Grey's mission had been very successful. The President and his Government were 'more sincere in their desire to suppress border disturbances and more alive to the danger which exists that a continuance of the piratical conduct of the citizens may involve the two countries irrevocably in war'. He went on to advocate further military reinforcements for Canada. 'It is by a formidable and an imposing, and by what careless lookers-on will reckon perhaps a superfluous display of military force in Canada that the best chance will be obtained of . . . saving the English and American peoples from . . . a general war'.[11] Stephen Fox may have been too pessimistic in regard to the chances of war breaking out. Certainly he hardly wrote a letter in this period in which he did not refer to the outbreak of war as being inevitable unless this or that measure was taken immediately.

On the day before Stephen Fox wrote this from Washington, Durham sent off a very similar dispatch to Glenelg. The maintenance of strong military and naval forces in Canada was of the first importance if good relations with the United States were to be secured.

The cord must not be relaxed until the final settlement of the affairs of these provinces has taken place. . . . The sight of our efficient means of protecting the tranquillity of our colonies and the interests of His Majesty's subjects will go a great way towards removing those vague expectations of discussion and dissension amongst ourselves from which the unscrupulous and enterprising portion of the Americans anticipated increased profit to themselves and additional power to their country. I must, therefore, earnestly request your Lordship to keep up the amount of our naval and military force to the fullest possible extent during the present year.[12]

Durham was not too confident of the ability of the American federal government, no matter how active it became, to prevent the conspiracies of the Canadian rebel-exiles in the United States. Its powers were limited, and co-operation with the state governments was difficult. But he believed that one of the most important results of Charles Grey's mission would be an impressive display of co-operation between Washington and Quebec. 'This unnatural excitement on the frontiers . . . has been kept up in a great measure by the rumours which have been circulated of the bad faith and real wishes of the United

States government, and nothing can so much tend to allay it as a public, unanswerable act of combined vigour, evincing the good understanding existing between the military authorities of both nations.' Although a certain element of the American frontier population seemed to be out of hand, 'all the accounts I receive concur in reporting that ninety-nine out of a hundred of the respectable and influential citizens, whatever may be their politics, unite in condemning the conduct of the frontier population and in deprecating the idea of a war with England'.[13]

It was extremely fortunate that the governor who afterwards did so much to establish better relations with the American people by his friendliness and cordiality toward them should have at the outset impressed them with his firmness and business-like character. At the same time, to the Canadian people of all classes, both in Upper and Lower Canada, Durham's actions in this as in other matters betokened the coming of a new era. None of Durham's predecessors had talked business in this manner to the American government and none had secured such results.

At the same time he was very busy with other problems – municipal government, seigniorial tenure, registry offices, police establishments, and the routine of administration. Lady Durham recorded in her journal that 'from the moment of his arrival he devoted himself unremittingly to business' and 'that he would scarcely ever find leisure for the air and exercise which were so necessary to his health'.[14] For a few days in the second week he was ill and running a high temperature, but by the 11th day he was at it again as hard as ever.[15]

In the midst of this successful beginning and energetic application to his problems came the first of a series of harassing communications from the British Government. He learned that he had not been three days gone on his mission of conciliation and reconstruction before the Tories had dug up the Turton scandal. On the 27th Lord Winchilsea inquired in the House of Lords if this Mr. Turton, who was to be Lord Durham's legal adviser, was the same Mr. Turton – and so on. Lord Melbourne replied that no legal adviser had been appointed. On the 30th the noble defender of British honour came at Melbourne again with the assertion that Mr. Turton had certainly accompanied the Earl of Durham to Canada, and three definite questions – had a public situation of any sort been offered to him, had he received any promise of an appointment on his arrival in Canada, were any part of his expenses to be paid for by the public? Instead of answering these questions in a straightforward manner the Prime Minister apparently decided to bluff and play for time, in the confidence that Durham would not take any action before word could reach him. So he coolly made the following statement:

I say, first of all, that no situation whatever was offered by Her Majesty's Government to the gentleman to whom the noble earl has alluded; and next that he has gone out to Canada, if he has gone out at all, which I do not mean to deny, without any appointment, without any prospect of an appointment, and without any intention on the part of the Government, or on the part of my noble friend, the Earl of Durham, to appoint him to any public situation whatever.

Then Melbourne lost no time in rushing off the following to Durham:

My Dear Durham,

I write this in great anxiety and in hopes that it may reach you soon and in time entirely to preclude any hasty and indiscreet step. If I had not been able to say that Mr. Turton had gone out without any appointment and without any prospect of an appointment I am confident that we should have had motions made and carried in both Houses of Parliament to cancel the appointment and to remove Mr. Turton from it – as it is [illegible] by me that there is no intention either on the part of the government or on yours to appoint Mr. Turton to any public situation in the colony, you must bear me out in this and must by no means put him forward in any manner. As it is, his having gone out at all [illegible] very great sensation and you must expect personally much animadversion upon this account. Beware of scamps and rogues . . . whatever their ability may be.

If you touch G. W. with a pair of tongs it is utter destruction, depend upon it – T. D. [Tommy Duncombe] is not so bad, but he is one of the same genus and can do nothing but harm – If you do not disembarrass yourself of all these sorts of [illegible] they will pull down your public character and reduce it to nothing even were it ten times as high as it is. . . .[16]

This letter was clever enough from Melbourne's point of view, but there was hardly a word in the fine moral lecture at which Durham's gorge would not rise. It would have been bad enough in any case, but following fast on the heels of what Durham regarded as a weak and treacherous misrepresentation of facts on Melbourne's part, it must have sent him into a towering rage. And he had appointed Turton. And there would probably be more lies at home – and he, off in Canada, would make a most appropriate scapegoat.

Melbourne was in a most anxious state of mind, and three days after writing his first letter he wrote again repeating the substance of the former letter for fear it might 'have been delayed in its course or have missed its destination'. He advised Durham to send Turton 'home again'. 'A report is got abroad of Gibbon Wakefield having gone out to you and, joined to the affair of Turton, makes a great sensation. At all events keep clear of him.'[17]

Glenelg also took his part in the letter-writing. He has heard that Wakefield has gone to Canada. If that is so, he is not to receive any official appointment. The Government has no objection to his unofficial employment on Crown lands and emigration, in which he may be very useful.[18] 'The feeling is even stronger with respect to Mr. T – n than we had anticipated, and indeed so strong as to prove that there is but one course to pursue. In fact the Government are pledged that the gentleman shall not hold any appointment in Canada.'[19] This writing of 'T – n' as Glenelg would have written 'D – n' or 'H – l' was not calculated to appease Durham's indignation.

When these letters reached Canada Turton offered to resign. In his letter of resignation he expressed regret that his presence should have created embarrassment for Durham. When one member of the Government had suggested his appointment and another had offered an Indian promotion to induce him to accept it, he had anticipated no difficulties. He had come to Canada at a very considerable financial sacrifice.

It is with the utmost surprise after your Lordship had waived my direct appointment from Ministers on the parliamentary establishment, that I now find them expressing a desire that I should not be appointed by your Lordship to any important office in this colony. [He prefers, however, to resign rather than place Lord Durham in the position of appearing to force him on a reluctant Ministry.] May I add that the estimation in which you are pleased to hold my services, and your opinion of my fitness to hold those appointments, will ever be amongst the proudest of my recollections. As you have known me well for a long course of years, I cannot but feel that your confidence in me and in my capacity to serve my country more than counterbalances the censure of those who unhappily know little of me but from circumstances which I must always deeply deplore. To me, my Lord, it will always be a heartfelt solace to the hour of my death.[20]

Durham refused point-blank to accept this resignation. A week later, on June 15, he wrote to both Melbourne and Glenelg. He stated in both letters that he had appointed Turton to a secretaryship, but that no salary would be required from either the British or Canadian governments. Having made this appointment before their letters had reached him, he would not withdraw it. In the letter to the Colonial Secretary he stated that he would give Wakefield no official appointment.

If you, the Government at home, only support me and show a good front to the Tory marplots in England, I will answer for handing over to you in a few months all the North American provinces in a state of loyalty and contentment. If you cannot do this, but show the slightest want of confidence in me, you will do well immediately to replace me by another whom you can consistently support, for nothing can be so fatal to British supremacy here as an appearance of dissension and want of concord in the authorities of the State, colonial and metropolitan.

He reminded the Prime Minister that it had been distinctly understood that he was to be at liberty to appoint Turton on his own responsibility after his arrival in Canada. He had intended to appoint him to his Special Council or to the Judicature Commission, but would not do so now. He had already been of inestimable service.

The proceedings about him in England have created general disgust here, and the most strict people in the Province have gone out of their way to be civil to mark their sense of them. . . . As for Mr. Wakefield, your letter arrived before him, and I have therefore been able, without compromising my own character and independence, to comply with your desire. He holds no employment or official situation whatever, nor will his name appear before the public at all. 'Oh, no! we never mention him; his name is never heard.' Really, if it were not very inconvenient, all this would be very ludicrous. But I am placed in a very painful situation. I am called to perform an almost superhuman task. You provide me with no – or at least inadequate – means from yourselves, and you then interfere with the arrangements I make to supply myself with the best talent I can find. . . . [In Canada] they believe in my good intentions towards all, and in my having support from home. See you to that; I will provide for the remainder. The colonies are saved to England, as far as I am concerned, but you must be firm. Don't interfere with me while I am at work. After it is done, impeach me if you will. I court the fullest responsibility, but leave me the unfettered exercise of my own judgement in the meantime.[21]

On June 18 he appointed a Commission of Inquiry on Crown Lands and Emigration for all the British North American provinces. The Commission was also given power to make temporary regulations in each province. At the same time a circular dispatch – prepared by Buller – was sent to all Lieutenant-Governors urging them so far as possible to abstain from alienating Crown lands in the meantime.[22] Charles Buller was appointed Commissioner, but Wakefield did most of the work and was assisted by R. D. Hanson and C. F. Head, Assistant-Commissioners, and H. Petrie, Secretary.[23]

This was the first of Lord Durham's sub-commissions. That on Education was appointed on July 14, with Arthur Buller, brother of Charles Buller, brought from England for this purpose, as Commissioner, and C. Dunkin as Secretary. The Commission on Municipal Institutions was appointed August 25, with Charles Buller as Commissioner, and in this case the work was done by the Assistant-Commissioners, William Kennedy and Adam Thom. Turton was at work framing a suitable Registry Bill, Charles Buller was engaged in a similar task in regard to the commutation of feudal tenure on the Island of Montreal, and Turton and Arthur Buller were making a careful study of the whole legal and judicial system. There is every reason to believe that within a year Lord Durham would have removed all real grievances, satisfied every reasonable demand, and established adequate systems of municipal government and education in both Upper and Lower Canada – in addition to his epoch-making work of reconstructing the government of Canada and the character of the British Empire – if Downing Street had left him alone and the British Parliament could have refrained from using Canada as a football for British politics.

But the trouble which was being prepared for Durham in England, while it reduced many of his designs to the form of bases for future legislation, also clarified his vision and nerved his courage to outline that new system under which the forces that destroyed his authority should never be let loose again, but Canadian policies for all time to come should be controlled by Canadian politics.

At the end of June he had two months and a half before the storm broke. During the closing days of that month he gave the cities of Lower Canada their first police system worthy of the name, a reform which was permanent and had a marked influence on the organization of the police in Upper Canada. Quebec and Montreal had had nothing better heretofore than an old-style 'watch', and conditions had been deplorable. Gosford and Colborne had been taking steps to devise something better. Durham's energy took the matter up where they left it, and in a short time gave both cities a thoroughly organized and efficient system along the lines of Sir Robert Peel's 'new police' in London. Within a few years Toronto, Kingston, and other Canadian cities adopted the same system.[24]

Ever since his arrival Durham had been grappling with that most delicate problem, the disposal of the Lower Canada political prisoners. Following the Rebellion wholesale arrests had been made. Colborne had released 326 prisoners, and of the 161 who remained he believed that 72 had been deeply implicated.[25] Lafontaine had suggested to Ellice a general amnesty. The French generally pretended to hope that that would be the line Durham, with his generosity and breadth of mind, would take. But it is difficult to believe that they really expected it. On the other hand the influential firm of Gillespie and Moffatt had informed Glenelg that the British in Lower Canada would be satisfied with the banishment of a few of the most serious offenders, so long as the place of confinement was far enough away.[26] Glenelg had come to feel strongly, and Durham agreed with him, that there should be no executions, but that some form of punishment should be imposed upon a few. The main difficulty lay in the means of securing a conviction. The Lower Canada law officers had reported that convictions could not be secured even in the clearest cases in the ordinary courts of law if juries were selected in a regular manner, because French-Canadian jurymen would vote for acquittal.

Lord Glenelg had acquainted Lord Durham with this difficulty on the eve of the latter's departure from England. Yet at the same time he enjoined him not to employ any special tribunal. 'By the verdicts of the ordinary juries the fate of the prisoners must be decided.' He was to follow Glenelg's instructions to Colborne, which were enclosed. These suggested that the greater number of prisoners should be released, leaving only those whose offences could not be overlooked. 'Even among these there will be distinctions to be made. Some might perhaps be safely arraigned and permitted to plead guilty, if they should be willing to adopt this course upon an assurance that the judgement recorded against them should not be executed, if they would voluntarily withdraw from His Majesty's domains in British North America and continue absent.' Of the others, it was suggested that a few against whom the strongest cases could be made, and who would be supported by a smaller amount of popular sympathy, should be placed on trial first. If they were convicted other cases could be proceeded with. If they were acquitted, the others would have to be detained and dealt with in some more effective manner.[27]

Durham must have smiled when he read these instructions. Of those who were presumably most guilty, the guiltiest of all were to be put on trial with the chances a hundred to one for their acquittal. Then after they went scot free, those who were less guilty were to be kept in prison until some irregular device could be invented to secure their adequate punishment. Apart from its absurd injustice, such a course would subject his government to humiliating defeat, the triumphant scorn of the rebellious and the wrath of the loyal, all the old feelings would be stirred up by the trial, and the worst difficulties would still be ahead. It could not have taken him long to decide against that. But his instructions insisted that he punish some and that they should not be tried except by the ordinary courts. The problem was not an easy one. He was not forbidden to pack the juries, a device that had been frequently resorted to in Canada in the past; but he was the last in the world to pack a jury. Charles Buller and Turton, after studying the situation, suggested that the leaders should be punished by an *ex post facto* law, but Durham vetoed that as being un-British. After a careful review of the cases, since the number to be punished had been left to his discretion, he selected eight as the most culpable. He decided to secure from them a confession of guilt and, on the basis of that, pass an ordinance banishing them to Bermuda and pardoning the others. Glenelg had suggested something similar to this, but very different in its application; Glenelg's proposal applied to only one group of those to be punished, and the banishment would leave them free in the United States, which would be most inadvisable. Durham's solution was more lenient and more masterly than anything suggested by Glenelg, and at the same time satisfied all the necessities of the case.

Buller went to Montreal to consult with the leaders of the 'British party' and to negotiate with the eight. The British leaders in Montreal proved much more amenable to Buller's persuasive power than the bloodthirsty statements of their press would have led one to expect. They all expressed approval of the proposal except Moffatt, who favoured trial by a special commission. Buller had approached the eight prisoners concerned through John Simpson, Roebuck's step-father, who was collector of customs at Coteau-du-Lac. The proposal was quite acceptable to them. In their first statement, after asserting that if Lord Durham had come sooner there would have been no rebellion, and that they did not rebel against Her Majesty's person and government but against colonial misgovernment, they said, 'if there be guilt in high aspirations we confess our guilt and plead guilty'. That did not satisfy Buller, and he sent Simpson back. Their sceond statement, signed on June 26, contained the following passages:

> My lord, we have some reason to apprehend that the expressions used by us in a letter addressed to your lordship on the 18th instant may appear vague and ambiguous. Our intention, my lord, was distinctly to avow that in the pursuit of objects dear to the great mass of our population we took a part that has eventuated in a charge of high treason. We professed our willingness to plead guilty, whereby to avoid the necessity of a trial; and thus to give as far as in our power tranquillity to the country. . . . We again place ourselves at your lordship's discretion and pray that the peace of the country may not be endangered by a trial.

This was accepted.[28]

The ordinance was enacted two days later, June 28, the coronation day of Queen Victoria. It will be remembered that Durham had been given the power to legislate with the consent of a Special Council to be appointed by himself and to consist of not less than five members. He now appointed this body with the following members: Buller, Couper, Charles Grey (all members of his staff), Vice-Admiral Paget, Major-General Macdonnell. They ratified the ordinance as a matter of form. This action, severely criticized in England, afforded general satisfaction in Canada. It was in harmony with Durham's policy of not associating with his government the members of either of the Canadian parties until old sores were healed, necessary reforms adopted, and a revised system of government organized.

The ordinance banished these eight prisoners to Bermuda, where they were to be subjected 'to such restraint . . . as may be needful to prevent their return to this province'. It also declared that if any of them or any of sixteen specified individuals (including Papineau, O'Callaghan, and Brown), against whom warrants had been issued and who had fled from justice, should return to the province without the permission of the Governor, they should be declared guilty of high treason 'and shall, on conviction of being so found at large or coming within the said province without such permission as aforesaid, suffer death accordingly'. Durham and his Special Council were here defining a new crime; that is, they were enacting a criminal law. They believed they had power to do so since full legislative authority had been placed in their hands. This was accompanied by a proclamation in the name of the Queen that in view of this ordinance no further proceedings would be taken against those charged with complicity in the rebellion, and that on giving security for their future good conduct they should all be released and allowed to return to their homes. The ordinance exempted from the amnesty the murderers of Weir and Chartrand.[29]

On the same day Lord Durham wrote a personal letter to Queen Victoria, in which, after offering his congratulations on the occasion of her coronation, he said:

Unable as I am, in the execution of your Majesty's service, personally to tender my homage, and assist in the ceremonies of this day in England, I can only console myself by laying at your Majesty's feet, from America, the best tribute of loyal respect and devotion which I can offer. . . . I have been able to do this [the amnesty] in your Majesty's name without danger, because I have in my own done all that sound policy required in the way of punishment and security. Not one drop of blood has been shed. The guilty have received justice, the misguided

*mercy; but at the same time, security is afforded to the loyal
and peaceable subjects of this hitherto distracted province.* . . .[30]

In his letter to Melbourne of the same date he said: 'It is a
great weight off my mind, and a great gratification to find that
the proceedings I have adopted have been approved by all
parties – Sir J. Colborne and all the English party, the Canadians, and all the French party. . . . I hope you will send
directions to the Governor of Bermuda to treat the prisoners
with all due leniency.' Neither this letter nor his dispatch to
Glenelg of the following day[31] goes much beyond bare statements of what he had done. There is some cogent argument as
to why he had not given them a jury trial or sent them to a
penal colony, but there is no explanation of his selection of the
Council, not a word about the prisoners' statement except the
fact that they had confessed, and a general lack of background.
He failed to put the Ministers in a position to answer questions
in Parliament. A masterly solution of a problem was followed
by negligence.

The exiles sailed for Bermuda in the *Vestal* July 3. It was
said that Buller sent them extra articles of comfort for their trip
and that they drank Lord Durham's health. They had given
Durham their parole not to attempt to escape from the *Vestal*
or from Bermuda, and Durham instructed Admiral Paget to
assure the Governor of Bermuda that their parole could be
relied upon and to urge him to show them all possible leniency
and consideration. They reached Bermuda July 24.[32]

When Durham told Melbourne that *all* the British party and
all the French approved of his ordinance he fell into that habit
of exaggeration to which he was so prone. A meeting of French
extremists at St. Roch passed a series of violent resolutions,
and the *Montreal Herald* used this as it did every action of
Durham's as a handle for attack. But certainly the majority of
both parties were very well pleased with it and regarded it as a
most satisfactory and statesmanlike solution of the difficulty.
Of the newspapers, the *Montreal Herald* alone was antagonistic,
the *Montreal Gazette* and *Montreal Transcript* had little to say
one way or the other, the *Montreal Courier*, the *Quebec
Mercury*, and the *Quebec Gazette* expressed decided approval,
and *Le Canadien* and *Le Populaire* were enthusiastic. *Le
Canadien* of July 2 stated that the measure would be acceptable
to all liberals, lauded Durham's generosity, and drew a pointed

contrast between his treatment of the rebels and that of the government of Upper Canada, with its executions and confiscations of property. As Dr. Chapais has pointed out,[33] the outspoken and censorious *Le Fantasque* was loud in its praise of the measure and, in its issue of July 12, said: 'In short, all the acts of the Governor have been marked with the stamp of precision, skill, firmness, and independence', which afforded a welcome contrast to those of his predecessors. Such statements and the whole situation here adverted to should be kept carefully in mind in view of the outcry a month later in England over the wrongs of the French-Canadians, the poor misused victims of the Dictator's high-handed and tyrannical methods.

An aspect of the reception of the ordinance, almost as important, was its effect in the United States. The danger spot in the Canadian rebellion had always been the attitude of the Americans. Lord Durham's ordinance of June 28 was the great turning-point. It was natural that Americans should have seen in the Canadian rebellion a repetition of their own revolutionary struggle and have invested the 'patriots' with all their substantial grievances of those days, and the Government of Great Britain with all the tyranny of their legendary George III. But the Yankee, for all his prejudices, had keen eyes, and when he saw a British governor, who had been resolute enough to talk to Uncle Jonathan as Durham had a few weeks before, treat the leaders of a serious revolt against the British Crown in this fashion, he adjusted his perspective appreciably and showed a disposition to re-think this question of British tyranny so far as the Canadians were concerned. As Buller described it:

All parties agreed in extolling it as a noble, wise, and liberal act. The very newspapers that had been previously most violent in assailing the British Government changed their tone for a while. And the revulsion of feeling throughout the Union was general and permanent. From that hour the feelings of national jealousy and political sympathy gave way to that of admiration of Lord Durham. From that hour the disaffected in Canada ceased to derive any aid from the public opinion of our neighbours, and among our difficulties we had no longer to contend with the chance of war with the United States.[34]

At the same time Lord and Lady Durham were carrying on an elaborate and successful social programme. Lord Durham's first levee and Lady Durham's first drawing-room were held

early in June. The latter was said to be unique in that it was
conducted precisely on the plan in use at the Court of St. James.
At the upper end of the supper room on a buffet covered with
maroon-coloured cloth was a splendid display of family plate
and Lord Durham's racing trophies.[35] Describing the occasion
in a letter to her mother, Lady Durham said:

> The ladies had all done their best in dressing and were
> smarter than I expected, but seemed in a great fright. That they
> are also when they come to dinner, particularly with Lambton,
> though he does all he can to put them at their ease. I cannot help
> telling you that the one he took out to dinner the other day, who
> had been given him as the highest person present, ate jelly with
> her knife.

Lady Durham also observed that the French ladies were
pleasanter and better mannered than the English.[36]

But more remarkable than levees, drawing-rooms, and balls
was their daily hospitality. While they were at Quebec they had
never less than twenty-three at dinner and sometimes as many
as forty-four. 'So little', wrote Lady Durham, 'were we ever in
private that I never once saw him dine out of uniform, from
the day we landed till that on which we re-embarked to return
home.' In his invitations Lord Durham broke through the
charmed circle of the official group and invited representative
people from all sections of the population. He broke the social
monopoly of the official clique as decidedly as he had crushed
their political power. They never forgave him. Their accusations
that he treated them discourteously were not without prejudice.
It is possible, however, that when they took it upon themselves
to remonstrate with him, they met with an impatient response.[37]

Never had the old city of Quebec seen such regal splendour
as marked every public act of Lord and Lady Durham. When
Lady Durham went driving, she was always accompanied by a
string of outriders, and when Lord Durham rode out for exercise it was never without a scarlet-coated retinue of imposing
proportions.

On July 4 they were ready to begin a tour of Upper Canada.
'During this time', said Lady Durham, 'he was generally well
in health and in good spirits, pleased with the prospect of
success.'[38]

❂ ❂ ❂

Lord Durham had not yet visited Montreal, and as it lay in his course to the Upper Province he included it in his tour. He arrived there July 5 and landed July 6. Montreal was the stronghold of the ultra section of the 'British party'. Their toryism had prejudiced them against Durham at the outset. There was a feeling on the part of Durham and his staff that, though the leaders had consented to the Bermuda ordinance, their followers were in a discontented mood. Charles Grey wrote to his father:

He met with really a most enthusiastic reception, and I am happy to say that his coming has been attended, as I was always sure it would, with the best possible effect. His answer to the address, both the formal one and the little speech he made after it, and, still more, his civility to the leading men of the English party, and his open manner with them, have completely gained them, and they seem now disposed to place as much confidence in him as they before appeared to feel the contrary.[1]

In his addresses he emphasized the maintenance of the British connexion, the development of the vast resources of Canada, and the union of all parties to achieve common aims. As he appeared in public day after day his receptions became more enthusiastic in character, and on the 9th Lady Durham could write to her mother that Montreal was even out-doing Quebec in public demonstrations. She adds, 'He had looked upon it quite as a sort of crisis and could not have hoped for a more favourable result.'[2]

During these days in Montreal Lord Durham laid before a group of seven men, selected by Peter McGill, a plan for a federation of the British North American provinces. The Montreal leaders were, of course, all for legislative union and were opposed to federation because it would place them in a minority in the Lower Canada provincial government, where the French would undoubtedly secure an ascendancy. This feeling was strongly expressed in a letter of Moffatt to Colborne, in which he also objected to the abolition of legislative councils proposed by Durham.[3]

The party left Montreal on July 10, stopped at Cornwall and Kingston, where Lord Durham received and responded to addresses, and sailing from the latter point directly to Niagara arrived there early on the morning of the 13th. The Falls excelled all their expectations – 'the most sublime and beautiful spectacle in creation'. Lady Durham wrote to Lady Grey: 'How I long to have you enjoying this unequalled spectacle. . . . I shall almost consider this one sight has repaid us for the sacrifice of coming.'[4]

In the same letter Lady Durham stated that 'Lambton was up early, inspecting forts, docks, &c. But he is very well and seems quite equal to the work he has undertaken, but which, I assure you, is no slight one, even in respect to bodily fatigue'. Durham was impressed not only by the Falls but by the city of Buffalo and the possibilities of the Welland Canal. He wrote to Glenelg:

If this canal was completed and the St. Lawrence Canal, the water communication by the Lakes, the Rideau Canal, and the St. Lawrence to the sea by Montreal and Quebec would be complete, and all that immense trade which now flows from the West by Buffalo and the Lockport and Grand Canals to New York would pass through our provinces, and enrich all the towns and districts through which it was carried. . . . I feel it my duty to press it on the immediate attention of Her Majesty's Government. I would ask of them a grant of money to be issued on the same principles and securities as those which regulate the assistance given to harbours, railroads, canals, and other public works in England.[5]

This dispatch resulted in the appointment of Colonel Phillpotts, whose report led the British Government to give substantial aid to the Welland Canal.

Lieutenant Governor Arthur and Sir John Colborne joined Lord Durham at Niagara. There were reviews of troops. A number of Americans crossed over to the Canadian side. For these and for the Canadians of the district Lord Durham provided the most sumptuous entertainment. He went out of his way to show his friendship for the Americans. On the 15th he took the unprecedented step, for a Governor, of crossing to the American side. Lady Durham wrote in her journal:

It was reckoned something of a bold measure to cross in this way, he and his staff in full uniform among the Americans, and I believe if much had been said about it, or he had regularly consulted Sir John Colborne and others, that he would have been advised against it. We had heard a great deal on arriving of the bad spirit which prevailed across the frontier, but we met with nothing but civility, people even taking off their hats as we passed, an unusual mark of respect among the Americans. We heard afterwards that as soon as it was known we were gone across, our return had been watched for with some anxiety at Niagara.

Of Durham's hospitality and friendliness to American visitors to the review on the 17th, Lady Durham wrote:

It was the first occasion on which any attempt towards cordiality had been made on the part of a British Commander and the result completely exceeded his expectations. From that moment a marked change took place in the feeling of the people of the United States, and for the first time goodwill and friendly spirit seemed to prevail among them towards the English of the colonies. These dispositions were still further encouraged on his return to Quebec. He set apart a day for receiving all those who came with satisfactory references, and showed further civilities to such as prolonged their stay.[6]

Charles Buller said:

After the studied reserve that it had been usual for the leading persons in the British provinces to maintain towards their republican neighbours, it was most gratifying to the latter to be received with cordiality by the nobleman of the highest position with whom they had come in contact. I have often said to those who (after the fashion of petty carping, by which we are assailed) used to dilate on the seven or eight hundred pounds that were spent in the course of Lord Durham's visit to Niagara as a monstrous expense, that, considering the results attributable to it, a million of money would have been a cheap price for the single glass of wine which Lord Durham drank to the health of the American President. . . . Henceforth, instead of incivilities being offered to every British officer who chanced to cross the lines, the citizens of the United States vied with each other in hospitality and respect to them. Lord Durham continued this wise course after his return to Quebec, where he made a point of receiving the numerous travellers from the United States at his house during the summer. These were in themselves but slight acts and easy observances, but they were parts of a great view of international relations, and produced great and good

effects on the feelings and intercourse of two nations. It is only
the man of statesmanlike mind who can produce a great result
out of things so small as an invitation to dinner, or the drinking
of a glass of wine.[7]

While there is in these accounts a large measure of personal
devotion, they are amply confirmed by the American newspapers of the period. Buchanan, the British consul at New
York, writing to Colonel Couper of the remarkable change
wrought by Lord Durham in American sentiment, said: 'The
most violent democrats here are loudest in praise of Lord
Durham's courteous manner, and advocates of his "lordly
court", as they term the banquet they partook of at the Falls.'[8]

Previous Governors of Canada had maintained an attitude
of aloofness, and their antipathy to American ways and American institutions had been thinly veiled in their public utterances
and frankly expressed in their letters and confidential dispatches.
Durham's friendship for and admiration of the Americans were
spontaneous and sincere. His interest in popular government
was an element in this; he believed in the great American experiment just as he believed in the experiment which he himself
had launched in England. The Americans appealed to him also
as a progressive people, following keenly the trails blazed by
the Industrial Revolution. His habitual frankness and love of
liberty found for him ready affinities with the Americans.
Durham was a great Englishman, and in spite of many things
which he must have disliked he caught the conception that the
strongest traits of the American character were simply some of
the finer characteristics of old England transplanted to a new
soil. To what extent he was influenced by the fact that his father
and his father's friends had been ardent Foxites and the best
friends of the American colonists in the days of conflict, it is
difficult to say; it is probable that the influence of Fox is as
strong here as it was elsewhere. We boast to-day the longest
international frontier in the world, unarmed, unguarded, con-
secrated by over a hundred years of peace. But the new forces
began to play across that frontier in the short, fateful administration of Lord Durham. This significant fact of American
history is closely related to Durham's position in world-history
as the prophet and pioneer of British democracy and colonial
self-government.

On the 17th Durham wrote a long letter to Melbourne:

I shall privately and confidentially consult with all the Governors and the principal men in all the provinces, and, having collected their sentiments, shall be prepared, as I told you, with my plan, which you will receive by the end of November. Thus far all looks well. Everyone approves of the general principles of the scheme I suggest, and thinks it will work well in practice. . . . I mean to have all my consultations over in the month of October, having summoned all the colonial notabilities to meet me at Montreal in that month.

Everywhere I have said, and I hope I shall be sanctioned by you, that the object of my mission, and of my measures, is to perpetuate the connection between England and these colonies, indeed to render their separation impossible. You have no idea what general satisfaction this declaration has given. . . .

Adieu. You must excuse the hurried and indistinct manner in which this letter is written, but I have no time to spare. It is now five in the morning, and lately I am no longer master of my own time. . . .

If I had any right to insert anything of a private nature in this letter on public matters, I should say that I am now writing to you in sight of the grandest and most magnificent spectacle which ever presented itself to my eyes – The Falls of Niagara. They infinitely surpass the most extravagant notion I ever entertained of their sublimity. No man ever lived, but Milton, who could adequately have described them.[9]

At Niagara there came another break in Durham's health. His activity had been constant and he never allowed himself sufficient rest. He was sometimes up as early as four o'clock in the morning writing his letters and dispatches. The fatigue of the journey to Fort Erie on the 14th broke him down for the time being. Lady Durham complained that 'he never allowed himself sufficient time to recover but resumed his exertions before the attack was by any means dispelled'.[10]

After five days at Niagara he and his party left for Toronto, July 18, arriving there at four o'clock in the afternoon. Lady Durham wrote in her journal:

He was so ill when he approached Toronto that it was necessary to keep off the steamer and delay the landing for half an hour while he endeavoured by a hot bath for his feet, and such remedies as could be given for the moment to palliate the suf-

fering so as to enable him to get through the ceremonies of the public reception which awaited him. . . . He had such resolution and energy that he would never give in, where he thought the object required the exertion. On this occasion he seemed so entirely unwell that I was quite alarmed for the consequences.[11]

Toronto gave him a splendid reception. A public holiday was declared and every municipal organization, including the fire brigade, was turned out in his honour. He made a speech shortly after landing. After the other festivities came a dinner, at which he made two speeches.

So ended [wrote Lady Durham] a day of frightful fatigue, the effects of which he felt a long time. . . . Next day he was rather better but did not go out, altho' he was perhaps engaged in a more fatiguing manner, in holding a levee and giving interviews to numerous persons who were anxious to see him. . . . We saw Toronto to great advantage. It is in general spoken of as a dull place, but the number of people who had come in from the surrounding country, and the animation which prevailed in the town did not admit of such an impression upon us. We were rather struck with the appearance of the streets, which seemed to be better built and to consist of better houses than in any place we had seen. There also seemed to be some pleasant houses and gardens looking toward the lake.[12]

The Baldwins, father and son, called on him by appointment, but he could give them only twenty minutes. He was interested in their views of constitutional reform, and urged them to write to him fully in regard to them. One of the delegations represented the Roman Catholic citizens. The *Toronto Mirror* (Reform) gave the following account of the proceedings which followed the congratulatory address:

The deputation . . . called his attention to the late Orange procession in Toronto and to the probable consequence of further exhibitions of this nature. The deputation was received in the kindest manner and was assured by the noble earl that Orange processions were illegal – that the actors ought to be proceeded against as much as those who had taken up arms against the Government, and that he would use his utmost endeavours to put down the system of Orangeism in the province. He further pledged himself as the friend of civil and religious liberty, and the deputation returned highly gratified with their reception.[13]

Lord Durham may not have expressed himself as strongly as the *Mirror* indicated, but it seems probable that something of the sort was said.

Lord Durham left Toronto on the afternoon of the 19th, having been in the city twenty-four hours. On the return journey he stopped at Kingston and Prescott on the 20th, John Beverley Robinson accompanying him from Toronto to Prescott. He spent the 22nd and 23rd with Edward Ellice, Jr., at Beauharnois, his father's seigniory. The second day of this visit was one of enforced rest, as Durham was too ill to go on. On the 24th he arrived at Montreal, where he remained for two days. He had intended to tour the Eastern Townships, but abandoned the project on account of his health and returned to Quebec, arriving on the 27th.

In connexion with this Upper Canada tour a cycle of stories developed, centred about Lord Durham's haughty manner and quick temper. Kingsford incorporated a number of these in his *History of Canada*. He arrived at Kingston late at night,[14] there was no guard of honour to receive him, and he administered to Colonel Dundas of the 83rd a severe reprimand. The very smell of tobacco was distasteful to him, and no one was permitted to smoke in his presence. On a steamer one night he detected the disagreeable odour and ordered the captain to discover the offender. After some time the captain reported that Vice-Admiral Sir Charles Paget was ensconced in a remote and comfortable corner, smoking a cigar. The admiral was allowed to finish his cigar in peace. On the return journey a clergyman who, with the permission of the captain, had attempted to travel by the steamer reserved for the Governor and his party was stranded at Coteau Landing, sixteen miles from his destination.[15] Kingsford, writing in 1898, apparently believed these stories, but gave no authority for them. Most of Kingsford's stories and a number of others are to be found in Richardson's *Eight Years*. Richardson was a contemporary and in fairly close contact with Lord Durham, but his book was written nine years after 1838. He told the stories as one who did not believe them, and was confident that they were later inventions due largely to the antipathy to Durham of the Family Compact and the dethroned official clique of Lower Canada. He was a great admirer of

Durham and went out of his way to argue that his haughtiness and temper were very much exaggerated, yet he re-told with some gusto these stories that were going the rounds. While expressing disbelief in nearly all the stories he recounted, Richardson was in a position categorically to deny one of them. In presenting a cup at the Montreal races, Lord Durham was said to have angrily rebuked the Earl of Mulgrave, one of his aides-de-camp, for not placing it before him in the proper manner, and to have taken time to show him how it should have been done before proceeding with the presentation. Major Richardson stated that he was with Lord Durham in his box during the whole time, that he witnessed the presentation, and that he saw nothing of the sort. He added that he did not hear any of the stories until several years later.[16]

Buller, left behind ill at Niagara, wrote to Durham:

It seems to me here to be a mere question between a petty, corrupt, insolent Tory clique much of the kind we found in our old close boroughs and the mass of the people. You can hardly conceive how popular you are with the latter, and how furiously the others are said to rage against you. It is asserted that your proposing the President's health is an act of positive high treason: I have no doubt the judges & Orange juries here would so find it. Also you expressed yourself at Toronto in a manner hostile to Orangemen. Whereby you offended against religion as well as the constitution.

These fellows here will give you trouble: and I see how they will set to work by making objection to your powers and disputing the legality of your acts. . . . Your stopping the jobbing in the Canadas is death to the Family Compact; and they'll die hard, and make Arthur lend them a helping hand.

If a collision should take place between you and these gentry it is as well to know beforehand how the land lies, and I am for that reason anxious to know how it lies at Toronto especially. I want very much to spend a few hours there before I leave this part of the world.

I am told the Americans are quite captivated by your behaviour to them, and that at Buffalo they have had private meetings to contrive some mark of respect to you.[17]

Immediately after Lord Durham's return to Lower Canada Charles Grey wrote to his father:

Lambton has been very unwell, and consequently very irritable for the last three days. Having nothing to do with him he is always good natured to us, but I daily thank my stars that I have nothing to do with him. It is astonishing, taking everything of importance as coolly as he does, to observe how trifles upset him. With it all, however, he is very good-natured to those about him, and I think he is liked by them all.[18]

Before he had time to recover from this illness there arrived from England a series of communications on the Turton affair. Melbourne, of course, after having made his sweeping declaration, had been caught out when the news of Turton's appointment reached England. The Tories were quick to press their advantage against the Government, and Melbourne calmly made Durham the scapegoat. He informed the House of Lords that Lord Durham's dispatches had said nothing about such an appointment (which was quite true). The authority of the *Quebec Gazette* could not be questioned, however, and it was with surprise and regret that he had read the announcement.

This was July 2. Again Melbourne wrote Durham immediately:

You must be well aware, after the letters which you must by this time have received, . . . that this step must necessarily place us all, and me more particularly, in great difficulty and embarrassment. I have been questioned to-night in the House of Lords upon the subject by Lord Wharncliffe, and I could not, of course, say otherwise than that I had heard of the appointment with great concern and great surprise, and that when I had made my former statement – to which, of course, he called my attention – I thought that I had had reason to expect that no such appointment would be made. I could not say other nor less than this, because I must own it appears to me most wonderful that you should have done this so hastily, so precipitately, and so entirely without consultation. If the public feeling here was such as to render it advisable that no appointment should be made here before you went, you could not suppose that it could either be satisfied or evaded by making the appointment upon the other side of the water immediately upon your arrival. I write this upon my own account, and without having consulted with others. What steps it may be necessary to take in this matter it is impossible at this moment to say; but it must be considered and determined upon. With the exception of this unfortunate,

and from the beginning most ill-advised proceeding, your letters
seem to be satisfactory.[19]

Two days later Glenelg wrote a dispatch which covered the
same ground in a more formal manner.[20] Durham's reply to
Melbourne's letter is apparently lost. It would make interesting
reading, as it was probably no less spirited than his dispatch
to Glenelg[21]:

I beg most unequivocally again to remind your lordship, that
I stated to Lord Melbourne, before leaving England, that whilst
I waived any appointment by the Government at home for Mr.
Turton, I should feel myself at full liberty to employ him on
my arrival here in any way that I considered most advisable –
provided always that such appointment emanated from myself
alone, and did not require the sanction of Her Majesty's
Government.

Such is strictly the case at present: Mr. Turton is my own
secretary and not the Civil or Provincial Secretary, or one of the
secretaries named in the establishment submitted to Parliament.
His appointment as one of the Executive Council is not under
mandamus from the Crown, and is derived from myself alone.
I am not aware, therefore, that Her Majesty's Government are
called upon to take any cognizance whatever of Mr. Turton's
appointment, which, neither as to nomination or salary, can
ever come under their notice.

You will allow me, my lord, to say that I also on my part
have observed with 'great surprise and regret' the tone which
Her Majesty's Government adopted in the debates in the House
of Lords to which you refer me. Whilst the highest situations in
the Empire have been, and still are, held by those who have had
the misfortune to be convicted of adultery – it is most unjust to
denounce and devote to destruction the holder of a petty office,
merely because he is without political friends or family influ-
ence. I feel 'surprise and regret' that Her Majesty's Government
did not, at the outset, expose the hypocrisy of this proceeding,
and ascribe it to its true cause – the desire to embarrass political
opponents, and not a regard for that morality which had
repeatedly been violated without compunction or remonstrance.

Durham might have said more. He believed that the Government was betraying him, that it was wilfully placing him in a
false position in order to protect itself. But he was unwilling as

yet to make such statements in a public dispatch.

Durham's assumption that his appointment of Turton was none of Melbourne's business was a most remarkable one. Melbourne felt that his Government was in an extremely precarious position and was being weakened by this Turton affair. Avoiding trouble was always a first consideration with him, and the fact that this trouble was so unnecessary stirred his indignation against Durham, whom he had always disliked. To his mind, Durham was exasperatingly unconcerned about the bearing of his conduct on the fate of the Government, was acting as though his decisions as Governor of Canada were the questions of first importance, and was not even deigning to afford the British Government sufficient information on matters that were vital to its existence. Over the Turton matter both men were developing a state of mind that goes far to explain the fateful events precipitated later by the attack on the Ordinance.

The following quotations from Melbourne's letters to Durham of July 17 and 18 will illustrate some of Melbourne's substantial grievances against Durham and a tendency to reasonableness on his part, as well as his lack of tact in writing some of these things to a man like Durham. The effect of the words on Durham's mind in view of all the facts may be left to the imagination of the reader.

You never ought to have entered into any negotiation with him upon the suggestion of others without distinctly naming it to me. You must have known, as you did know, the objections that would arise.

When, in consequence of the state of public feeling here, you were persuaded that it was necessary to give up making the appointment, who could have expected that you would make that appointment the first act of your government upon your arrival? and, considering the ferment which prevailed upon the subject at the time of your sailing, you must have expected that the matter would be mentioned in Parliament; and was it ordinary discretion not to wait until you learned whether it had been so mentioned, and what had been said by the government upon the subject? . . . If these [Melbourne's last two letters] should make no alteration in your determination, I cannot, of course, take upon myself the responsibility of pushing matters to an extreme which would hazard the interruption of that course of policy in Canada which you have auspiciously commenced, but in that case you must be prepared for the result of any motion in Parliament upon the subject. I am prepared to resist such a motion; but if it should be carried, I hope that you will be prepared to acquiesce in it.

Upon all other matters, upon all parts of your conduct, except as far as relates to Mr. Turton, I have only to express, according to my present information, my full approbation and concurrence and my congratulations upon the good effects which your measures appear to have already produced. . . . It is incredible that a man of common sense should show such an ignorance or such a disregard of public feeling and opinion as you have done in the selection of these gentlemen. If their abilities and powers were superhuman they would not counterbalance the discredit of their characters. . . .

Only consider how you injure your own private character, by the association of such men with yourself and family. Only consider how you injure the Queen, whose age and character demand some respect and reverence.[22]

At the same time Durham received a letter from his friend Parkes:

In degree and publicity of offences, and public feeling for their nature, no two men in England could attract more prejudice or commentary in their public employment. . . . Under the circumstances of Lord Melbourne's last disclaimer and rebuke of you the question with all your friends is what course you can wisely take – your enemies and political opponents hoping that you will throw up and return. We, who know you, know you will disappoint them, and that you would never by resignation invite the responsibility of being visited with the onus of embarrassing the government. . . . We all think that after the position against you Lord Melbourne assumed (which I think was not necessary and might easily have been otherwise managed by him) Turton cannot remain. . . . It is a Pharisaical cant but there is no opposing force to stay it, especially when the female sex foment the outcry.[23]

On August 9 Durham wrote a long dispatch to Glenelg, embodying what was really a preliminary report.[24] The greater part of it is devoted to a description of the racial conflict in Lower Canada, which anticipates in outline a large part of the Lower Canada section of 'Lord Durham's Report'. As in the

Report, he has discovered 'the existence of a most bitter animosity between the Canadians [French-Canadians] and the British, not as two parties holding different opinions and seeking different objects in respect to government, but as different races engaged in a national contest'. As in the Report, the British are all on one side and the French all on the other; 'the mutual dislike extends into social life, where, with some trifling exceptions, all intercourse is confined to persons of the same origin; each side assumes false designations and fights under false colours', the French really being the more conservative, fighting for their old institutions, and the British the more liberal, desiring to break down the old ways in the interests of progress. Durham in this dispatch blames this situation on the early policy of the British Government, in precisely the same way as he did later in his Report. The lack of sympathy between the official group and the main body of the British population, the perversion of legislative powers on the part of the Legislature, the aggravating effects of the rebellion, the general disaffection of the French, and the attitude of the Americans are all viewed as in the Report. Almost a third of the long section on Lower Canada in Lord Durham's Report is clearly suggested here.

There is little attempt, however, in this dispatch at constructive suggestion. That is to be left until later. The commissions on education, municipal government, and crown lands were, it must be remembered, only getting well started in their work, and Durham would not care to attempt to anticipate their conclusions. Nothing is said about Responsible Government; it can be confidently asserted that this had not yet been adopted by Lord Durham as the great solution. In conclusion – still speaking, it must be remembered, of Lower Canada – he expresses the hope that the British Parliament 'will sanction such measures as will effectually provide for the abstraction of all legislation on British interests from the control of a French majority. I am of the opinion that this great object can be legitimately effected without violence to Canadian rights, and in strict accordance with the sound principles of constitutional government'. Everything points to the fact that his great reliance in this as in other respects was on federation.

This dispatch is also remarkable for its interpretation of the rebellion and its imputation to Canadians of a desire for war with the United States. As in the Report, Lord Durham associates the rebellion with a *general* disaffection on the part of the

French and expressed the belief that it would have succeeded had it not been for inadequate preparation and poor leadership. The weight of historical evidence – and there is a great deal of it – is directly against this. Lord Durham was anxious to know the whole truth, and desirous of being fair to all parties, but he hardly came at all into personal contact with the French-Canadians, while he had had many conversations with the British leaders. On the other hand, he states that the rebellion was 'precipitated by the British from an instinctive sense of the danger of allowing the Canadians full time for preparation'. The statement is a remarkably cool and confident one. There is some reason to believe that it was true, but in any case it could apply only to a small minority among the British.

The most surprising and sensational statement is the following:

Both parties are disposed to wish for a war between England and the United States. Though there are but few on either side who would make such an avowal, the truth appears from circumstantial evidence; such as the pains taken by the British organs of the press to affront and provoke the Americans, and the envious satisfaction and industry with which both Canadians and British of all conditions invent and propagate reports of a warlike tendency. No tale is too extravagant for the belief of either party, provided it encourages the hope of an American war, and every story of the sort is listened to and repeated with a degree of satisfaction proportioned to its absurdity.

The British wanted war, according to this dispatch, because it would place the French at their mercy. The French-Canadians wanted it because it would free them from British rule; an invading American army 'would operate in a friendly country'. We know of no historical evidence to support these astonishing assertions, and careful study of the newspapers of the period fails to confirm them. Lord Durham, subject from the first to the common English prejudice that the French were a rebellious race, was in this case reporting to the home government impressions that had been too quickly formed. Among other things, he had not yet learned that Canadian patriotism considered it necessary to nourish itself on loud, sometimes boastful, anti-American declamations which were usually mere pretence. That continued to be the case long after 1838. To assure itself of the support of good patriots and the applause of the *profanum vulgus,* a newspaper must, when the occasion offered, reach out and verbally tweak the noses of its American neighbours. Bearing this in mind, the statements made in the press in 1838 appear to be quite innocuous and leave one with the impression that on the whole the Canadian people of both races faced a delicate situation with remarkable coolness and that war was the thing farthest from their desires.[25]

There is no reason to believe that up to this time Lord Durham had any idea of advocating Responsible Government for Canada. Neither in his own utterances nor in the communications of others is there any indication of this. In Lower Canada it was neither desired nor understood. In his brief tour in Upper Canada he or Buller may have heard vague references to it, but, as we have seen, the idea was neither clearly understood nor generally advocated by Upper Canada Reformers. It was clearly formulated and urged as a matter of primary importance only by the Baldwins, Hincks, and perhaps a small group of their associates. It is a striking fact that in the letters addressed to Lord Durham by Upper Canada Reformers in response to his request for suggestions, there are only two passing references to Responsible Government, of which neither is at all definite and one is antagonistic. The only clear expositions of the doctrine were those given in the *Toronto Examiner,* a paper launched by Francis Hincks on July 4, the very day Lord Durham left for his Upper Canada tour. It is possible that Durham came across some of these statements and that it was by Hincks's pen that he was introduced to the idea which his own advocacy was to render a cardinal principle of British colonial policy. Considering how busy he was during the tour, it is doubtful whether his attention was attracted to the new newspaper. Copies of the paper were sent to him from the *Examiner* office, but at what time they started it is difficult to say. If his attention was not attracted to the *Examiner* during July, he would learn little from the references to it in the Lower Canada press immediately after his return. The *Montreal Transcript* of August 7 assumed that in advocating Responsible Government the *Examiner* meant an elective legislative council, which is exactly what the inhabitants of Lower Canada – and many of those in Upper Canada – understood by the expression. When the *Examiner* in its issue of the 15th took the *Transcript* to task for the misunderstanding, the latter printed a farrago of constitutional nonsense that betrayed a more profound misapprehension.[26] It was some weeks later that the *Transcript* grasped the simple but strange idea, only to attack it violently.

In the meantime, in the month of August, Durham received two very important letters from the Baldwins. That of the father, W. W. Baldwin,[27] gave a full account of the Upper Canada grievances and suggested Responsible Government, but did not give as clear an exposition of it, nor so forceful an argument, as did his son's communication of three weeks later.

Robert Baldwin's letter must have arrested Lord Durham's attention in a signal manner. There had been little time to discuss Responsible Government in the twenty-minute interview in Toronto, but in this letter Baldwin took full advantage of Durham's request for a written communication explaining his position. He enclosed a letter which he had written in England to Lord Glenelg, July 13, 1836, after the latter had refused him an interview. He relied on that as an exposition of his views. His letter to Durham was a personal appeal on the basis of that explanation.[28]

The letter to Glenelg had lain for two years in the Colonial Office, and on the few occasions on which the principle embodied in it was referred to, it was only to scout it as the wildest of impossibilities. When this letter was brought to the attention of Lord Durham, his adventurous and prophetic mind discerned its remarkable possibilities, and he advocated the principle it embodied as vigorously and as fearlessly as he had set the pace for his party in the championship of Parliamentary Reform. The conception was Baldwin's, and the view of Responsible Government for Canada presented in Lord Durham's Report as the most epoch-making feature of that remarkable document is, with a few differences of detail, some expansion of principle, and a more discerning application to imperial relations, the view expressed in this letter. It is a matter of pride that the principle on which the British Commonwealth of self-governing nations has been built, the principle which has held the British Empire together and afforded it permanence and vitality, was in its conception a Canadian idea. Without Lord Durham's advocacy, however, the voice of Baldwin would have been lost in the Canadian woods. It was necessary that some great British statesman be converted to this Canadian idea. Durham had the open mind, the gift of brilliant exposition, the forcefulness, the courage – nay, before the story was through, the heroism – that was needed. And fortune helped to set the stage and afford a dramatic opportunity for its promulgation.

After discussing several ineffectual remedies for the Canadian political situation, Baldwin put forward this suggestion: 'to put the Executive Council permanently upon the footing of a local Provincial Cabinet, holding the same relative position with reference to the representative of the King and the Provincial Parliament, as that on which the King's Imperial Cabinet stands with respect to the King and the Parliament of the Empire, and applying to such provincial Cabinet both with respect to their appointment to, and continuation in, office the same principles as those which are acted upon by His Majesty with respect to the Imperial Cabinet in this country.' This would require no legislative change in the constitution of Canada, the form of which it was desirable to preserve. It would amount 'merely to the application of an English principle to the constitution as it stands'. All that would be necessary would be to insert a clause in the instructions to governors.[29] 'From being an English principle, it would strengthen the attachment of the people to the connexion with the Mother Country; and would place the Provincial Government at the head of public opinion, instead of occupying its present invidious position of being always in direct opposition to it.'

Baldwin recognized that many of the popular grievances were exaggerated and some of them imaginary, but under the old system the discontent was bound to continue and the British Government would encounter more and more trouble and conflict. Under the system which he suggests government would work smoothly. If an Executive Council once in power neglected the wishes of the people, 'the people have only to return to the next parliament, men who would not give them parliamentary support and they would necessarily have to resign'. With this principle established, the remedying of all substantial grievances would follow as a matter of course.

The advice rendered by this Provincial Cabinet would be limited to the 'internal affairs of the provinces'. (Baldwin, however, made no attempt to draw the line between internal and imperial affairs as Lord Durham did in his Report.) There would be no conflict of responsibility. The Governor would still be responsible to the British Government. Collisions might occur between the Governor and his Council, and he might

*find it impossible to form an Executive Council which would
secure parliamentary support upon any other terms than concession. . . . The practical working of the principle would be sure
to postpone such collision to the latest possible period. The
intermediate steps of a change of the Executive Council, and of
appealing to the people by a dissolution, would at all events give
the Home Government the great advantage of not itself coming
in collision with the people till the last moment, and of ascer-
taining the exact point where the question of concession would
become one merely of expediency; in addition to which I would
remark that this objection is equally applicable to the practical
working of the principle in this country; with this great difference, that supposing the people of England to be wholly
unreasonable in their demands, the Crown has in point of fact
no means of resistance; whereas in the case of a Colony there is
as a last resort the application of that power, which, independent
of the influence which a knowledge of the possession of it would
necessarily give to the Representative of the Home Government,
in the course of the previous contest, will always rest in the
hands of the parent state to be exercised when all other means
fail.*

Lord Durham went far beyond that in his Report. He
recommended that in such a situation the British Government
should give no support whatever to a Canadian Governor.[30]
That meant that the Governor would have to bow to the will of
the Canadian people – as Durham had seen William IV forced
to give way to the British people. It meant that the Canadian
people would govern themselves in matters of purely Canadian
concern. ('I admit that the system which I propose would, in
fact, place the internal government of the colonies in the hands
of the colonists themselves.')[31] Lord Durham's Report blazed
the way to self-government much more clearly than did this
conception of Baldwin's.

Baldwin's letter conveys the impression that these views had
a much larger support in Upper Canada than it is possible for us
to believe that they did. This may account for the statements in
the Report to the effect that they were advocated by the Upper
Canada Reformers generally.[32]

In his letter to Durham in which this letter of 1836 to
Glenelg was enclosed, Baldwin set his panacea of Responsible

Government over against Durham's panacea (at this time) of Federation, with a strange blindness to the fact that the political future of Canada was to depend upon *both* of them.

I confess when I see the only man perhaps in the Empire who from his political reputation and peculiar position is in a situation to induce the Home Government to retrace its steps, concede to the Provincial Parliament its just influence in the direction of the local affairs of the Colony, and thus place the affairs of my native country upon a foundation from which permanent tranquillity may be looked for, about as I believe to waste the energies of his master mind in an experiment of the failure of which I entertain not the slightest doubt, I feel that I should be criminal if I did not in terms the most distinct and unequivocal express my entire and unqualified dissent to any such experiment being made. . . .

Your Lordship has been the first statesman to avow a belief in the possibility of a permanent connection between the colonies and the Mother Country.[33] . . . Your Lordship has gone farther, you have said that the connection must be preserved. I sincerely feel grateful to Your Lordship for this announcement. It will I trust put an end to the repeated references to the arrival of a time when these Colonies must cease to be a part of the British Empire which have not unfrequently proceeded from the very servants of the Crown. . . .

If Your Lordship then after the solemn announcement of the great principle that the connection must be maintained can but happily succeed in giving us a system which by its own working shall tend to establish and strengthen that connection you will have indeed done a great public service to your own Country but you will have conferred a far greater benefit upon these Provinces. . . . Your Lordship must adapt the Government to the genius of the people upon and among whom it is to act. It is the genius of the English race in both hemispheres to be concerned in the Government of themselves. I would ask Your Lordship, would the people of England endure any system of Executive Government over which they had less influence than that which at present exists? Your Lordship knows they would not. Can you then expect the people of these colonies with their English feelings and English sympathies to be satisfied with less? . . .

In this month of August Durham was confronted with serious difficulties. Sir John Harvey sent him from New Brunswick a confidential memorandum which indicated obstacles in the path of federation.

The 'British Party' in Lower Canada was becoming impatient with Durham's tenacity in regard to that policy. They had expected to convert him to their idea of a legislative union of Upper and Lower Canada long before this.

At the same time distrust was developing among the French. They were not averse to Durham's policy of federation, and they continued to approve of many of his public acts. But it was known that in visiting Montreal both on the way to the upper province and on the way back he had spent a large proportion of his time in political conversation with the British leaders and that he was still in communication with them. On the other hand, his contact with the French leaders had been limited to dinner invitations and casual social meetings. They were somewhat stand-offish and in some cases, perhaps, inclined to sulk, but Durham could have secured their attention had he sought to do so. The fear was developing that he would fall into the hands of the British party, and the more impatient among them began to express discontent. Buller and Wakefield mixed quite freely with the French-Canadians and frequently discussed the political situation with their leaders. But Durham was the only one they trusted. Of Buller they knew little; of Wakefield they knew too much. If Durham's idea was to deal with the British himself, while Buller and Wakefield dealt with the French, it proved a failure.

Lafontaine was the key-man among the French-Canadians. As a young liberal he had been attracted by Durham's career in English politics. He had looked forward to Durham's coming with hope that bordered on enthusiasm. He had a deep respect for his character. He had written of him from England and from Paris in the highest terms. One cannot but feel that if Durham had himself gone to Lafontaine in that straightforward way of his, mutual understandings would have been developed. Instead of that Lafontaine was left to Wakefield, with some assistance from Buller. Lafontaine's attitude towards Wakefield was one of disguised, but constant, suspicion. He thought that he was trying to trick him. If Wakefield was not attempting to deceive Lafontaine, he was grossly disloyal to Durham. The latter conclusion is a difficult one because of the many evidences of Wakefield's personal devotion to Durham, a devotion of a peculiarly generous and unselfish type.

The relations between Wakefield and Lafontaine need not be described in detail here, except in so far as Lord Durham is involved. Wakefield stated that Durham knew nothing of his unsuccessful attempt to see Papineau at Saratoga, and that he made no report to Durham on his conversations with the French leaders. 'I took several opportunities of solemnly assuring those whom I met that I had no mission from Lord Durham, or from any one connected with him; that I spoke for myself alone, as a well-wisher of theirs, who had a right to say and do what he pleased without reference to Lord Durham.' He added that Lord Durham never asked him 'a question about my intercourse with the French-Canadian leaders'.[34] Although Wakefield's statements are open to suspicion, these are probably true, in their literal sense at least. At the same time, Lord Durham undoubtedly was aware of the fact that Wakefield and Buller were meeting very frequently with the French, and he probably expected that they would in the course of time inform him of their impressions.

A few weeks later Lafontaine was to be further estranged by the harsh and haughty conduct of Buller and Leclerc in regard to the treason charges against himself and Viger in relation to the rebellion. Durham in a most unnecessary manner threw himself open to implications of at least a lack of generosity and conciliation. This matter also was left to subordinates and mishandled by them. Both the state of Durham's health and his absorption with the general situation made that necessary in most matters of administration, but that he should have permitted the Lafontaine and Viger cases to proceed the way they did shows that he was singularly blind in his failure to realize the importance of Lafontaine. In this he flew in the face of fortune, which had offered him a good start in Lafontaine's correspondence with Ellice. He was too ready to swallow what the 'British party' had to say about the dour and unconciliatory attitude of the French. He missed the hope for the future that lay in the French moderates. This mistake recurred in his famous Report; the fact that it did not seriously undermine that work of genius was due largely to the lofty statesmanship of Lafontaine himself.

The French-Canadians were further irritated by Durham's

selection of Adam Thom as his principal Canadian adviser. Thom had been a schoolmaster in the north of Scotland. An acute mind and a brilliant, vigorous, violent, and occasionally scurrilous pen had brought him to the front in the new colony. He had been for some years the editor of the *Montreal Herald* and had vigorously championed the British cause against the French, notably in the *Anti-Gallic Letters*. He had retired from the editorship a few months before Durham's arrival to take up the practice of law, but he still had influence with the *Herald* and wrote for it on occasion. The fact that he had been their ablest opponent in the literary field had much, no doubt, to do with the antipathy of the French, but certainly if there was one Britisher in Lower Canada whose head they would willingly have had on a charger, it was Adam Thom. And this was the man whom Durham on August 25 appointed to co-operate with Kennedy on his Commission for Municipal Government, the first appointment in which he deviated from his rule of having nothing to do with the old parties. This was the man who henceforth acted as though he were the Dictator's minister, whom Durham permitted to speak as one inspired, and who was certainly consulted on every important problem.

If French feeling might be disregarded, there was much to be said for the selection. It was Wakefield and Turton over again. Durham wanted the best man, and took him. Thom showed an intimate knowledge of the whole political situation, a discerning appreciation of the real difficulties, and also an unexpected streak of liberalism that must have appealed to Durham, fatigued by the die-hard attitude of men like Moffatt and many of the Montreal merchant-leaders. Thom saw the disadvantages of their favourite solution of a legislative union of the provinces, and was willing to afford appreciative consideration to Durham's plan of federation.

Much of the glory and tragedy alike of Lord Durham's life lies in the fact that counting the cost was not one of the things he did best. He paid too great a price for Adam Thom. French suspicions were now increased. Etienne Taché (later Prime Minister and Chairman of the Quebec Conference) was appointed to the Municipal Commission at the same time, but refused to act with the arch-enemy of his race. The French press attacked the Governor, although *Le Canadien* still urged the French-Canadians to be patient and not give up their high hopes in Lord Durham. However, the enthusiasm and eulogies of even *Le Canadien* were somewhat dampened from this time on. Not yet recovered from his illness, awaiting the next move in his quarrel with the British Government, Durham now saw that the French were clearly turning against him, and it was easy for a man of his temperament to think that it was through no fault of his, and to accept the interpretation that was being poured into his ears that the French were all intractable.

At the same time, in these closing weeks of August, friction was developing with Lieutenant-Governor Arthur and the Family Compact of Upper Canada. Arthur had shown a previous tendency to be jealous of Durham's powers, but his protests had been mild and his letters friendly.[35] In a dispatch of August 16 Durham informed Arthur that application for clemency had been made to him in the case of two political prisoners, Chandler and Wait, and asked for a report on these cases and all others in Arthur's hands. In reply Arthur stated that the pardoning power was vested in him during Durham's absence from the province of Upper Canada and characterized this action as 'depriving the officer administering the Government of Upper Canada of the powers expressly vested in him by the Royal Commission'. Durham in a dispatch of August 24 insisted on his authority and maintained that the Lieutenant-Governor's pardoning power was a power delegated by the Governor-General and to be exercised in subordination to the latter. He proceeded to question the wisdom of some of Arthur's actions, and several of his phrases had a sharp edge. The controversy was continued in a number of letters and dispatches, and Arthur referred it to his Executive Council, which supported him and drew up an imposing list of unfortunate consequences which would ensue if the Governor-General insisted on hearing appeals from the decisions of the Lieutenant-Governor. The matter is not of primary importance in the life of Lord Durham, but it added to the troubles that were piling up for him at the end of August and beginning of September, and dug deeper the chasm that separated him from the Tories of Upper Canada.

It was a sick man on whom these troubles in England and Canada were accumulating. He had felt sufficiently recovered to go to Montreal for the races from the 18th to the 22nd of August, but the trip prostrated him for several weeks. At Montreal he met 'Tommy' Duncombe, who had been a gentleman jockey at the Lambton Park races, a sensational bankrupt, a showy if not brilliant figure in the House of Commons which he was to startle at a later date by the presentation of the famous Chartist petition, at all times an enthusiastic member of 'Durham & Co.' Duncombe kept a diary. 'Aug. 21 – Reached Montreal. . . . Joined Durham on the race-track where I found him in all his glory.' Just why Duncombe should have come to Canada to add his bankruptcy scandal to those of Turton and Wakefield it is difficult to discover. Durham selected the other two because they were the best men for certain tasks, but there is no evidence that 'Tommy' Duncombe did anything in Canada but prove an entertaining companion – he was always that – to Durham, Buller, Wakefield, and Turton. His talk of going to Canada to post Durham on the English situation is not convincing. He had expressed a desire to visit him in Russia. The diary runs: 'Aug. 26. Durham ill. . . . 27. Durham still ill. . . . 28. Durham better and dined at table. . . . Sept 1. Went to sit with Durham; still very ill. . . . Sept. 2. Durham somewhat better. . . . Sept. 3. Durham too ill to appear. . . . Sept. 4. Durham attended the races.'[36] Lady Durham wrote to her mother on September 1: 'He has never recovered from the attack he had at Montreal and I have not seen him so unwell as he has been within the last few days since the winter at Petersburgh. Of course this disheartens him very much and I dread very much his prospects for the winter.' She refers to their return to England, which she hopes 'may take place early in the year'. In her journal she wrote that he was 'many days confined to his room' and that even after he went out 'he was still often ailing and a good bit worried by his anxiety for accounts from England. Several things had passed in Parliament which were far from satisfactory, and he became more and more doubtful . . . as to the manner in which the ordinances of June would be received and the support which he would obtain from the Government at home.'[37]

On August 25 Durham had written to Sir Willoughby Gordon: 'I am tired to death of my task and wish it were over.'[38] But the greatest light is thrown on his state of mind at this time by a long and remarkable letter written to him by Charles Buller, September 7. The handwriting of a draft of this letter, towards the end, bears the marks of Wakefield's co-operation, and it is a fair assumption that much of it was suggested by the latter. It is difficult to imagine the gentle Buller writing such a letter unless goaded on by the venturesome and aggressive Wakefield.

Day after day I have gone to you with the intention of making you acquainted with the view of affairs which all those, who have your interests most at heart, concur in taking and expressing among one another; and every time I have been turned away from my purpose either by that despair of the ultimate success of your mission, which now frequently crosses me and makes me refrain from what I consider fruitless labour, or by getting alarmed at the effect which what I said seemed to have produced on your health. I will not, however, without an effort deliberately abandon myself to the former of these feelings: and an attempt must be made even at the hazard of temporary injury to your health, to rouse you from a state which threatens the worst consequences not only to your health, but to your reputation and happiness. I am the less tender of your health because no one can have observed you without seeing that, be your bodily disorders what they may, the real cause of your sufferings is in your mind, and that you have no chance of recovery without raising yourself from your present morbid state of feeling. I should be wanting in the first duty of a friendship which, believe me, though of recent date, is very true and very strong, were I not to make an exertion to save you from a catastrophe, after which I believe in my conscience that you and your best friends will attach little value to the preservation of your health or even your life.

You will think this exaggerated language. . . . You seem to think that if not properly supported at home and here, you have nothing to do but resign, and vindicate yourself by proving the withdrawal of the confidence which you regard as essential to your success. . . . But I think you must have had proof enough by this time of the utter ignorance of the public at home as to the affairs of Canada. They know nothing of the real nature of your difficulties; nothing of the causes which render the want of support, of which you have reason to complain, peculiarly embarrassing. . . . You have undertaken in time of danger, the maintenance of one of the most exposed defences of the Empire. The post was entrusted to you simply from the general confidence in you as the only person capable of maintaining it. . . . Why then do you suddenly abandon the post of honour and of danger? You cannot do this without accounting for it to most severe judges. And in proportion to the high hopes which a nation has formed of you, and the high trust which it has reposed in you, will be the fearful recoil of its unexpected disappointment, and the terrible downfall which you will experience from the noblest position ever occupied by any public man in England since the first Pitt. You have followed no ordinary path to fame and power. You have courted those high and daring enterprises. which end in triumph or political death. . . .

You have been attacked by the Tories. Did you ever expect anything else? You, – who have been without any exception their deadliest enemy, who gave them the most fatal blow they ever experienced, and have ever held them up in the most unqualified language to public scorn and reprobation? . . . Depend upon it, the Tories hate you more than any man in England, because you have given them the most reason to hate and fear you. They will do everything to damage and ruin you in public estimation. It is natural that they should do so. Everybody anticipated it; almost everybody expected you to triumph over it. . . .

The Ministers have not given you the support you had a right to expect. They have betrayed you.[39] *But you will get little sympathy in England if you urge this as a mischief, which you did not foresee. Nobody ever imagined they had any love for you. Every one regards you as the most formidable rival or rather actual competitor that they have to dread. . . .*

Your line is to produce good measures in perfect assurance that they will produce good feelings and ensure you that amount of public confidence which may be necessary to give those measures a fair trial. This is the line you took when instead of throwing yourself into the hands of a party, you composed your Executive and Special Councils of persons representing no will but your own. By so doing you declared your intention of pursuing your own course careless of the opinion of parties here. This system has perfectly succeeded, as yet; all parties have acquiesced in it or rather approved of it. . . . But what is the dissatisfaction expressed towards you? Till within a month ago, you had every proof from every party, if not of confidence, at least of as confiding a disposition as the circumstances permitted. What public manifestations have you had of a contrary feeling? Nothing but the mere mercenary and insane blackguardism of a press which represents no one and guides no one. The people of England gave you despotic power because they thought you had courage, wisdom and justice enough to use it for this people's benefit, in spite of this people itself. And they will hardly believe that such a power has proved inadequate in consequence of the impertinences and slander of one penny and 2 half penny papers.

My opinion is that the reasons which you regard as justifying failure or withdrawal from your charge will not be considered sufficient. . . . Imagine, for your imagination is fruitful in that line, taunts from the public press to which those which have hitherto produced an effect on you that I cannot comprehend, will have been mere trifles. Picture to yourself the delight with which you will be regarded by Ld. Brougham and Sir James Graham, the torture of having to be thankful for an exculpation by Ld. Glenelg, and the ignominy of being spoken of in the same category with Ld. Gosford. . . .

Here you must conquer success in spite of the government and the opposition at home. You are Governor General, – you have your Special Council for Lower Canada. These are your means of saving yourself, and saving yourself by a success which will send you home incontestably the most powerful public man in England.

When I turn from those feelings in your own breast the knowledge of which fills me with alarm, and look to the past acts of your government I find no reason to doubt the correctness of the most sanguine views which I have ever expressed or formed. I see no reason to doubt that by conciliating the United States, you have removed all immediate danger, and achieved more than half your task. Nor do I see any doubt of the correctness of the great principle on which at the outset you professed to me your intention of acting, . . . the principle of making this a thoroughly British province as rapidly as was consistent with the necessary regard for the feelings and present state of the French Canadians. It is in fact that of purchasing from them a concession of their bad usages and laws, in short of their nationality by great lenity and consideration towards them now that they are down in consequence of their late insurrection. . . .

It is perfectly obvious that a very unfavourable change has been produced in public feeling in these provinces by the late debates in Parliament,[40] and the inference which is being naturally drawn from them, that you are not strong enough at home to carry your own policy into effect. . . . This effect you foresaw to be inevitable from the moment you read these debates. Your part was by all possible means to counteract this impression by showing yourself utterly unmoved, by allowing no abatement *of courage or cheerfulness to attract public attention, by rather displaying increased energy and devotion to your great task. You have done exactly the reverse. You have allowed yourself to be more influenced by these debates than any are in the Province; you have formed an apparent determination to fret yourself until the next despatches arrive: in the meantime you feed yourself on anything next most harassing that comes in your way and worry yourself by reading blackguard attacks in the newspapers, and imagining even worse as likely to assail you hereafter; so that at last anxiety and mortification combined have acted so on your body as to produce your present state of health, and just now when your presence in public was most wanted, keep you at home or allow you to appear only as an invalid. This unfortunately has produced the worst results. In this little town everybody speculates on your state and movements. Some exaggerate your bad health and represent you as in a very alarming state: others say that you are yourself making the most of your illness in order to have a pretext for going home. . . .*

The explanations which you have given of your plan for the constitution have been half understood and much misunderstood. The people here take it for Roebuck's plan, and neither party likes it. I think your own experience must show you that it requires reconsideration. Time begins to press: and no progress is made in this your most important work.

The reforms you promised at the time of the amnesty have not yet been produced. I do not think they could have been. You have shown that you were engaged on some of them. But the public generally knows of no progress made, of nothing actually achieved. . . . The one great remedy is rousing yourself to a better state of spirits. If you cannot cease to think of the despatches which you expect from England, do nothing at least, I beseech you, to favour the notion that you attach much importance to them. If you entertain the idea of resigning, you should not tender your resignation in the first place to Mr. McGill. While there is even a chance of your remaining you must not act so as to mar your future policy. While you retain the title, do not abandon the functions of Governor General. Above all I implore you as I value your comfort, your dignity and your freedom of action, to pay no attention to the press. It cannot serve you either by guiding or warning you: its only effect is that of irritating; and that you can obviate by simply not reading any papers, in which you expect to find anything offensive.

Your constitutional plan requires a good deal of reconsideration and amendment, and if you mean to do anything towards perfecting it, you must not delay it long. It is now quite in a state for discussion. Let us discuss it; and if any important alterations or additions are suggested, you will be able to set some one to embody them in it. . . .

I have explained my views and feelings at great length. I have expressed them in a language of plainness – even of roughness to which you have not been accustomed from your friends, and which your first impression will be that I have no right to use towards you. But I know that you have too much justice, too much generosity to mistake the feeling which has prompted me to use it. I report to you the substance of what all your friends, all who have made your interests their own, say in speaking of you; and which it is but just that one of them should say in speaking to you.

I have more right than any one else so to speak to you, because I have more community of interest with you than any one else. I have left prospects of no little attraction at home, in order that I might follow you in what I trusted to you to find the path of a higher ambition. My position in public life was such as least that I could not leave it without its being asked whither I went. Others, if you succeed, may catch some rays of glory. I alone shall share the responsibility of failure. So much do I feel this, that I sometimes think that rather than return home after the failure of your mission, it were better that I should take my passage from New York with poor Turton, and hide my head in India. . . .[41]

For I am convinced that on the course you pursue now depends your own honour and happiness – the welfare of this much injured people – and the preservation of the integrity of the British Empire. . . .[42]

❁ ❁ ❁

CHAPTER V

The Storm Breaks

While Lord Durham at Quebec, his pride wounded, and his health broken, was facing these difficulties, and contemplating resignation on account of what he felt to be constant betrayals by the Melbourne Government, Fate was preparing the stroke that was to break his administration and provide the setting for his crowning achievement. Lord Brougham had fallen from a great height and must regain it. For over a year now he had been intriguing with the Radicals on the one hand and the Tories on the other in the hope of humiliating the Government which had excluded him. He loved neither the Radicals nor the Tories, but he was willing to play a desperate game to win again a place in the king-row. Now, with the arrival in England of the Bermuda ordinance, he had his great opportunity. His legal eye seized on one clear flaw and a number of dubious points which could be magnified by his matchless oratory. Would the Government defend Durham? If it did, he had probably succeeded at last in finding an issue on which Radicals and Tories would unite to defeat it. If it abandoned its proconsul he would have brought it to its knees and greatly weakened its prestige. At the same time, he would get his revenge on Durham; he never allowed a grudge to escape him unpaid.

Brougham opened his attack on July 30. He called attention to the newspaper reports of an ordinance of Lord Durham's, 'which if the noble earl presumed to carry into effect, he would be guilty of no less a crime than murder'. His commission only permitted the Governor-General to make general laws. It did not empower him to sentence men to banishment without trial and declare them guilty of death if they returned to Canada, a procedure 'utterly at variance with the known and just and established law of this country'. Glenelg had little to say in reply except that it was premature, in view of the lack of information, to condemn the conduct of Lord Durham, who had gained the confidence of both parties in Canada. Lord Melbourne characterized such an attack on Lord Durham's authority as 'imprudent' and 'unpatriotic' in view of the extent to which Imperial interests were affected. They should have confidence in Lord Durham, who had the best means of judging what was expedient in a most difficult situation.

While Brougham was preparing his case, the Government

submitted the legality of the ordinance to the law officers of the Crown.[1] They reported, August 6, that 'so much of this ordinance as directs the class of persons therein first enumerated to be transported to Bermuda and be kept under restraint there is beyond the power of the Governor and Special Council and void; but all the rest of the Ordinance is within their power and valid'. After pointing out that by Act of Parliament of that year the Governor and Special Council enjoyed all the power of the Legislature of Lower Canada, and referring to the powers conferred on that Legislature by the Constitutional Act of 1791, the opinion continued:

We conceive therefore that the old Legislature might have lawfully passed an act for banishing from the Province the first class of persons described in this ordinance, and enacting that if any of this class or of the second class should return to the Province without the leave of the Governor they should be deemed guilty of treason and being convicted thereof should suffer death. This could not be done by the proclamation of the Governor, but it is an act of legislation for which there are precedents in the Parliaments of Great Britain and Ireland. There is no pretence for saying that if this part of the ordinance really were put in force that the parties who suffer would be put to death without trial. Before they could suffer they must be indicted for having returned to the Province without leave of the Governor, which by law is made treason, and they could only suffer on being duly convicted of the offence laid to their charge. . . . With respect to that part of the Ordinance which is to be executed beyond the limits of the Province of Lower Canada, we are of the opinion that it would acquire no force by being confirmed by Her Majesty.[2]

On August 7 the greatest parliamentary orator of that generation was ready with his main attack. It was a masterpiece of legal casuistry, but the part of it which dealt with expediency rather than law was weak. He stated that when Durham was appointed the Government had explained that his acts would be subjected to the careful scrutiny of Parliament. The substance of his legal argument, apart from the part of the ordinance relating to the detention of the prisoners in Bermuda, which the Government admitted to be null and void, consisted in the citation of English statutes of 7 William III and 25 Edward III in regard to treason, and the insistence that Durham had no power to convict men of treason without trial or to declare that to be treason which was not treason according to English law.

Lord Glenelg's reply was not a strong one, but he was never a powerful speaker. He attempted to show the difficulties of Lord Durham's position and argued that the ordinance had given general satisfaction in Canada. Lord Melbourne was embarrassed by Durham's failure to supply the materials for an adequate defence. (He did not even have the paper the prisoners had signed; Brougham could make what use he pleased of documents which the Government had never seen.) On the legal side he satisfied himself with citing the opinion of the law officers of the Crown. He treated Brougham's points as too trifling to justify an attack on a Governor who was deserving of more confidence than was being afforded him. Melbourne was always nettled where Brougham was concerned and could not refrain from a reflection on the patriotism of indulging party feeling and personal animosity in such a situation. To this Brougham replied with heroics about opposing arbitrary power, and a reminder that he had solemnly protested against the Act creating Durham's powers, and had promised that he would watch its exercise and guard against its abuse. 'And am I now, at the end of the session, to be told that personal feelings have a share in these observations?'

On the 8th Brougham introduced a Bill 'for declaring the true import' of the Act which had defined the power of Lord Durham and his Council, 'and for indemnifying those who have issued or acted under a certain ordinance made under colour of the said Act'. It declared that the Act in question did not confer the power 'to make any law or ordinance for altering or suspending the course of the criminal law within the said province, in any particular case or cases, or for attainting or subjecting to pains or penalties, or otherwise punishing any person or persons not convicted by due course of law, or for declaring any person or persons not so convicted to be guilty of any offence for refusing to leave the said province, or for coming within the same, or for not returning within the same'. It indemnified against any prosecution which might be instituted for illegal action those who had advised and acted under the Bermuda ordinance. This Bill could be presented as a plausible way out of an obvious difficulty, but it was for the Government and for Lord Durham the most humiliating that could be devised.

It came up for second reading on the 9th. Brougham said that the prisoners had not confessed guilt. He repeated his contention that Durham had no power to declare that to be treason which was not treason according to the law of England, and laid special emphasis on a clause which on the suggestion of Sir William Follett had been added to the Act which had defined the powers of Lord Durham and his Special Council. This clause declared that they should not repeal, suspend, or alter any provision of any Act of the Parliament of Great Britain or of the Legislature of Lower Canada.

Lord Glenelg made a much stronger defence of the ordinance than on the previous occasion. He taunted Brougham with the fact that after all his diatribes he had stated in his Indemnity Bill that Lord Durham's ordinance was 'so much for the service of the public that it ought to be justified by Act of Parliament'. Since the matter of expediency was admitted, there only remained the question of law. The Constitutional Act of 1791 had empowered the Legislature of Lower Canada to make changes in the criminal law, and when Lord Durham was appointed no restrictions were made on that power. The Follett clause referred to had no relation to criminal law. It had been introduced specifically to protect clergy reserves, land tenure, and the maintenance of the Protestant religion.[3]

Lord Lyndhurst felt sure that Lord Durham had acted from the best of motives. But they could not countenance anything in the way of illegality. The Government should disallow the whole ordinance. He discoursed at great length on the imaginary suits which the Bermuda prisoners would bring against Lord Durham and others. If this learned ex-Chancellor had spoken of polar bears which he had seen in the heart of Africa, it would have been no less fantastic, but it was no doubt pleasant exercise to the legal mind, and the fact that he was injuring the Government was as incense to his soul; the integrity of empire might well be overlooked as a trifling consideration. He renewed the old attacks on the composition of Lord Durham's Special Council, and before sitting down solemnly assured the House that Sir William Follett had told him that he had intended, in proposing his amendment, to prevent Lord Durham making any changes in the criminal law. That statement is of interest to us only because of its inconsistency with what Sir William had said at the time and Sir William's denial a few days after this debate that he had so much as thought of the criminal law. But the disclaimer was made after Lord Lyndhurst's statement had done the harm that it was designed to do.

Lord Melbourne urged that on account of the extraordinary powers which they had conferred upon Lord Durham he should be supported by an unusual degree of confidence. His powers were admittedly so great and his appointment had been so universally approved that to condemn him now on the basis of a legal quibble would make it appear as though they had laid a trap for him in a manner unworthy of the British aristocracy. He defended Lord Durham's action in appointing his Special Council from his own official staff as being in harmony with the statesmanlike policy of keeping clear, so far as possible, of the rival parties in Lower Canada. He boldly stated that to pass this Bill would mean undermining the authority of the Governor and the possible loss of the colony. All in all, and in view of his lack of information, for which Durham was solely to blame, Melbourne made a fairly strong defence. There were no lofty eulogies of Durham, but Melbourne, who was a sincere man, did not have them in his heart.

The Duke of Wellington, who had not yet taken part in the more severe attacks on Durham, made a spirited reply to Lord Melbourne's insinuation about a trap. If Lord Durham had got into trouble it was the fault of the Government and not the House of Lords. The House had given those large powers to a Governor who was to exercise them on the advice and with the consent of a Special Council. The Government had failed to issue any instructions as to the constitution of the latter. The Governor, taking advantage of that, had set up a shadow Council consisting of his secretary, his aides-de-camp, and a few other subordinates. And as a consequence they had this ordinance. It was clearly illegal and the indemnity was necessary. Men could not be banished without trial, nor could they be put to death for returning to the country.

The Indemnity Bill passed its second reading by a substantial majority, with the ministerial peers voting against it. Next day Melbourne announced that the Ministers were prepared to advise the Queen to disallow the ordinance. They cannot fairly be blamed for not sanctioning illegality. Since the ordinance was illegal in part, they must disallow it or attempt to pass supplementary legislation. They did not attempt the latter because they feared a defeat in the Commons. A small number of Radical votes added to those of the Conservatives would effect that. The Ministers had probably known for some days that Brougham had planned his attack in conference with Roebuck, Leader, and other prominent Radicals, and that they were confident of the support of enough Radicals in the Commons to defeat the Government. But the attitude of the Conservatives as a party was not clearly indicated until the last stages of the debate. After the Government had surrendered, the declaratory part of the Bill was dropped and the indemnity stood alone. Brougham agreed to this reluctantly. He probably realized that he had won too much to imperil his victory by pressing it too far. A year's effort had yielded its harvest, and for the moment he tasted something of the power that has been his when he had held the fate of the Grey ministry in his hand and when he had sat in his 'hill-fort'. In moving the third reading of the Bill on the 13th he said that it should not be his part to provide an indemnity. 'However, as I have been *accidentally* mixed up with the business, I have no hesitation in moving the third reading of this bill, as it now stands, although quite sensible that I am making this motion on behalf of Her Majesty's Government.' Then when all were agreed to pass an indemnity, the reasons for which they could not agree on, the Lord Chief Justice rose to state that he doubted if the Bermuda part of the ordinance was illegal, and that he was convinced that the indemnity was constitutionally unsound.

It fell to Lord John Russell's lot to introduce the Bill in the Commons, a task for which his honest soul felt a repugnance which he could not conceal. He made a spirited *personal* defence of Durham. 'I ask you to pass this bill of indemnity, but telling you at the same time that looking at the conduct of Lord Durham as a whole . . . his zeal for the welfare of this country . . . I shall be ready to take my part with him in any responsibility.' Durham might have packed a jury but had been too honourable to do so; he might have transported the prisoners to a penal colony but had been too merciful to do so. In spite of any illegality or informality that might be discovered, Lord Durham in a most abnormal and difficult situation had pursued a 'wise and statesmanlike policy' and had 'reconciled the ways of mercy with the safety of the province'.

If Lord Durham be able to impose tranquillity and good order without the infliction of the punishment of death and to re-establish a free constitution, not only unimpaired but

*improved, – he need care for no violence or invective, for no
refinement of sophistry, for no bitterness of sarcasm, accompanied by professions of friendship, attempting to disguise but
not succeeding in disguising the petty and personal feelings at
the bottom of all these attacks, for he will have deserved well
of his country, well of his sovereign and well of posterity.*

Leader revealed the temper of the extreme Radicals in
championing Brougham and attacking Lord Durham. Sir John
Campbell, on the other hand, deprecated the whole idea of
indemnity, which was officious, insidious, and unnecessary since
no one would think of prosecuting. Sir William Follett made a
lengthy speech which betrayed an amazing ignorance of what
Lord Durham had really done, in the course of which he made
the interesting admission: 'I can assure the House that I had
no intention of fettering the Governor with reference to the
criminal law. I had not the subject in my mind at all.' Lush-
ington, himself one of the best lawyers of the day, cited the
divergent legal opinions stated in the debate by the Lord
Chancellor, two ex-Chancellors, and the Lord Chief Justice. If
any one of these was right, the others must all be wrong, from
which it followed that if Lord Durham had been assisted in the
preparation of his ordinance by the most distinguished legal
talent in England, he would probably have produced something
to which much more exception would have been taken.

The Government had been placed in a difficult position from
the time that the law officers of the Crown declared that the part
of the ordinance relating to Bermuda was illegal and that no
ratification of theirs could remedy that. Some action had to be
taken. Lord Durham's authority could have been fully sustained
by the passing of an Act of Parliament supplementary to the
ordinance. But the Government had no more chance of passing
such an Act than it had of defeating Brougham's Bill. A considerable number of the Radicals were sure to vote against such
a measure in the Commons, and if the Conservative party took
a stand against it, it would be defeated in either House. In any
case the Commons must be faced – sooner or later – and a defeat
in the Commons would finish the Government. If they had been
willing to put justice to Durham and the Canadas first they
would have invited defeat on that issue and appealed to the
electorate. But Melbourne refused to sacrifice his government
for the sake of a far-off colony or of a man whom he had always

disliked, who had treated him cavalierly and who in this instance had withheld the information essential to a strong defence. And politicians in power have a way of convincing themselves that a change of government is the greatest of national calamities. So he refused to introduce such legislation or to fight Brougham's Bill in the Commons. He played for a compromise. If the Government sacrificed Durham and the interests of Canada, it did so to save its own life. It did not, as it has been accused of doing, weakly surrender to the criticism of the Lords. At the same time, we may agree with Lord Grey's statement in a private letter that neither he nor Althorp would have acted as Melbourne did. Either of them would have fought to the last and found honour in defeat.

Through all of this the sympathies of the public went strongly with Lord Durham. Realizing this, the Conservative press taunted the Government with a heartless betrayal of him, and the ministerial press, for the most part, attempted to throw the blame on Brougham and the Tory lords. *The Times* said:

> *True to their base and selfish instincts, the time-serving Whigs, in deference to whom the noble Earl had at great personal sacrifice placed himself in the van of their Canadian conflict, have at the first shot deserted, dishonoured, and dismissed him, . . . finding their cabinet to be in dangerous waters, they have flung him and his ordinance overboard in order to save themselves.*[4]

The treatment of an individual was not the most serious feature of the situation. The Canadian newspapers were to describe that clearly enough a few weeks later when the news reached Canada. The integrity of the Empire and the very life or death of Canada was dependent on the shifting alignment of political parties at Westminster which represented phases of opinion on British questions but which did not reflect any comparable body of opinion on Canadian questions. Nothing could make that clearer than what had just occurred. Some way must be discovered of terminating that situation for all time to come. Canadian politics must determine Canadian issues. Lord Durham, although he felt the personal wrong with all the sensitiveness of his temperament, saw that and acted accordingly.

We have left Lord Durham reading Charles Buller's long frank letter of September 7. On the 10th he heard of Brougham's initial attack on the ordinance and by the 13th he knew something of the early stages of the debate in both Lords and Commons.[5] But he knew nothing of the disallowance – nor had he the least suspicion that the Government would think of such a thing until he read of it in an American newspaper on the afternoon of the 19th. The circumstances are described with dramatic simplicity in Lady Durham's journal.

Wednesday, 19th. – A day I can never forget! We went a longer drive than usual, crossing a ferry over a small stream beyond Cap-Rouge, continuing along the banks of the St. Law-rence to Lake Calvaire and returning across the country by the St. Fois road. We were a merry party – the children, Charles and Caroline (I think) and Mr. Buller, enjoying the little adven-tures and difficulties of crossing the ferry, laughing at Mr. Cavendish and his drag following us – and delighted with the beauty of the scenery. As we returned we saw from the heights the steamer from Montreal, arriving with the post and bringing with it, tho' little did we guess it, the intelligence of those events whose fatal consequences, we were, alas! so far from anticipat-ing. We had returned late from our drive and it was time to dress for dinner when we got in. Before I was ready, he called me into his room and I could see that something unusual had occurred. He had received a bag with letters and dispatches from England – containing the account of the reception of the Ordinances, with private letters from Lord Melbourne, Lord Glenelg, and others, rejoicing over the manner in which the difficult affair of the prisoners had been settled, and bidding him 'go on and prosper' with other expressions of unqualified appro-bation – there was also a letter from the Queen to me, in answer to those we had written on her Coronation day expressing her thanks and her satisfaction at all that was going on.

If the steamer had only brought this bag from England what could have been more gratifying than these communications! but a New York paper with later intelligence from home reversed all these visions of success and happiness – it contained the account of the proceedings in Parliament! – the disallow-ance of the Ordinances! and as it proved, the doom of his fate. I can well remember now the feeling of consternation which came over me on first hearing the news, and then of grief for him, and indignation and bitter resentment towards those who had so cruelly betrayed him. He said but little, but I was only the more unhappy, and when he finished his dressing and went with little delay to dinner, behaving as usual, my heart ached as I looked upon him as he sat opposite to me, and I thought of the feelings which preyed upon his mind.[6]

Buller too had vivid memories of the event and its immediate consequence:

I well remember what we saw, and how we talked, and how we laughed under the bright Canadian sky on that fine autumn day. As I was walking back from the carriage to my lodgings some one told me the news in general terms, but I supposed it to originate either in joke or in mistake. . . . When I got into the carriole to go with Mr. Turton to dinner, he told me that the report was quite true, and when I arrived at the house Lord Durham sent for me, told me the news, and almost more by manner than words, let me know that his mind was made up to resign his government.[7]

Durham probably turned from the news of his betrayal by the Government to read – or read again – the letters of the Prime Minister and the Colonial Secretary.

Lord Melbourne had written, July 28:

I am most obliged to you for what you have written to me [about the ordinance] which is most distinct, clear and satisfactory. I have not time to do more than to acknowledge it – I have nothing to express but the most entire approval and concurrence. I am very happy to hear that you have settled the very difficult affair of the prisoners and settled it so well. We must deal with them as well as we can at Bermuda. I understand some difficulties may be apprehended. Your ordinance will have no validity nor confer any power there. . . .

You are quite right in making use of your present power to introduce as many good laws as you can. . . . There can be no doubt of the feeling of satisfaction that prevails in the province —It must be like a sudden transition from the discord of Hell to the peace of Heaven. . . . A strength which at once puts down all parties is naturally agreeable to all.

Make a constitution, but for God's sake make one that has a chance of working. All colonial assemblies, it appears to me, are always resisting to the extreme of their power, and if they do this, they necessarily further their own destruction. . . .

Affairs must go on, and if they cannot go on with the assembly they necessarily proceed without them.[8]

Adieu! My Dear Durham. Remember me to Lady Durham and believe me

Yours faithfully,
Melbourne.[9]

Lord Glenelg's letter was written July 31, the day after the attack on the ordinance was launched:

You will see by the papers that our old enemies attacked your ordinance and proclamation last night. These attacks are after all impotent in this country. I trust they may be equally harmless in the colony. All reasonable people here approve your conduct. My colleagues and I entirely approve – our opinion is that, although there may be some legal inaccuracies of form, the substance is entirely right and the result satisfactory. You have solved a very difficult question most judiciously and ably, in a way at once merciful and just, and equally grateful to rival parties and impartial judges. I congratulate you on this – and on the confidence which, I hear on all sides, all classes in Canada repose in you. Go on and prosper. . . .[10]

After writing thus, Melbourne and Glenelg had remained silent for fourteen days (Durham as yet knew not how long), and allowed him to read the story of their disallowance of this great healing measure in an American newspaper!

While the Dictator – who by virtue of this action was dictator no longer – held his wrath in check and fretted his sick body at the Chateau, the news spread through the narrow streets of the ancient capital. Men recently wakened from despair lost hope again. 'The most violent language was openly held in the streets. Separation from England was talked of, and it was said that it would be better to be connected with the United States than with a country that was so reckless of the interests of its colonies.'[11]

Lord Durham had told Buller that night that he would resign. Next day he wrote to Sir John Colborne that immediately on receiving official intimation of the disallowance of the ordinance he would tender his resignation, returning to England as soon as possible. Since the administration would devolve on Colborne as senior military officer he was giving him timely notice.[12]

That day, the 20th, the Governor and his party went for an

excursion on the *Medea*, but the Chateau was besieged by crowds who put down their names as a token of esteem and an indication that they shared Lord Durham's indignation at the action of the British Parliament. It was said that during this and the following day this action was taken by every respectable British inhabitant of Quebec. On the night of the 21st Durham went to the theatre. The house, usually poorly attended, was packed, and they gave Durham a remarkable ovation.[13] This was the Reform struggle again! once more he was the leader of revolt – steady, constitutional, but nevertheless revolt against an outworn system of government that permitted British politics to paralyse Canadian progress. The new system of Canadian self-government was already forming itself in his mind, but his own experience was lending force and feeling to his vision.

On the 22nd the delegates from the Maritime Provinces presented an address to him, expressing gratitude for his personal kindness, confidence in his administration, and a desire that he should not resign. In the course of a formal reply, he said: 'I have been arrested by the interference of a branch of the English Legislature, in which the responsible advisers of the Crown have deemed it their duty to acquiesce. Under these circumstances, I have but one step to take: to resign that authority the exercise of which has thus been so weakened as to render it totally inadequate to the grave emergency which alone called for its existence.' He assured them that his interest in and efforts for their welfare would remain unabated.

That much certainly occurred. But the story goes that in a more informal speech he expatiated on his personal wrongs; he had expected such treatment from Lord Brougham but 'he was compelled to say that *he had been put down – sacrificed by his friends!* – those whose duty it was to stand fast in his defence, at a period when his personal enemies were using their utmost efforts to destroy him' – here he was so moved that he had to retire from the room; after a few moments he returned, apologizing for the display of feeling and proceeded. This story has always been adverted to in accounts of Durham's resignation. It is undoubtedly a good story, but it is pure fiction. It was invented – or too hastily accepted – by a travelling correspondent of the *New York Commercial Advertizer*, [14] was printed in New York, and went the rounds of the Canadian papers. But the *Quebec Mercury*, which was recognized as being in a special manner the organ of the administration, denied it in the following terms:

We are authorized to state that it is incorrect in many particulars. His Excellency used no such expressions as are imputed to him with regard to his friends in England; nor was he under the influence of any such emotions as are described. His Excellency felt very grateful to the deputation for their warm and friendly address, and, we doubt not, evinced that feeling by his manner previous to delivering his reply. His short speech subsequently delivered neither called for nor produced any particular expression of feeling beyond the earnestness which naturally pervaded the tone of what he said.[15]

As happens so frequently, the denial was lost and the story lived.

The Lower Canada newspapers, without an exception, supported Durham and bitterly attacked the British Government. The *Quebec Gazette* stated that a prospect dark enough before was rendered gloomier than ever. 'We see in the conduct of those noble lords who supported Lord Brougham's bill, either an utter ignorance of the state of the Canadas, or worse, a disregard for the preservation of this important portion of the Empire.' The *Montreal Herald,* the organ of the extremists of the British party, described the situation bluntly. 'The Canadas appear to be a trump card in the hands of the political gamblers in the Imperial Parliament.' The *Montreal Gazette,* representing the moderates, said: 'We cannot conceive how any man of high spirit could submit to the utter degradation of serving a government who have neither the power to support him in the exercise of his public functions, nor the courage to defend him and themselves from the factious insults of party politicians or the more infamous inroads of personal and jealous enemies. . . . It is therefore no wonder if the Earl of Durham has resolved upon abandoning the future administration of the affairs of these provinces.' The *Populaire* reminded its French-Canadian readers that while nothing that had been done under Colborne had been declared tyrannical or illegal, 'the only act that was practicable, the only act which could have sheltered the greater number by inflicting a light punishment on the few, is declared null and void'. It urged Lord Durham to 'breast the storm'. If he throws up the game his political career will be destroyed, and that, no doubt, is the aim of his enemies. *Le Canadien,* leader of the French-Canadian press, said: 'The proceedings of the House of Lords have thrown all classes of society into a turmoil of anxiety, of which our history, fertile in events palpitating with interest, can offer few parallels. Every one can feel, touch, see, the disastrous consequences which have been prepared in Canada by noble Lords sitting tranquilly in their comfortable senatorial chairs, who have transformed the Canadian question into a plaything or weapon of party. . . . A political adversary, powerful and dangerous to them, placed in an exceptional position, finds himself, on account of acts of a similarly exceptional character, taken on the flank by men who pretend to judge him as if he were in an ordinary position. To profit by the disadvantage at which this man is placed by attacking him may compromise the peace and integrity of the Empire. That is a matter of no consequence; here is an adversary, a redoubtable competitor in the struggle for power, and cost what it may, one must attempt to defeat him, to destroy him.' *Le Canadien* concluded by urging that every possible public demonstration be made to persuade Lord Durham to remain.

The Upper Canada press were as outspoken and as unanimous. This was the only occasion in the troubled history of these years in which all groups and parties (except the friends of Mackenzie and the Nelsons, the few who were planning a second rebellion) were united in a common feeling. The news of the disallowance of the ordinance reached Toronto, through American channels of communication, almost as soon as it reached Quebec, and the leaders of the Family Compact did not lose a moment in sending their heartiest expressions of sympathy and support to the statesman whom they had always feared and were already beginning to hate. Among these Archdeacon Strachan was particularly cordial and appreciative.

On the 21st Colonel Fitzgibbon, hero of 1813 and 1837, issued an appeal to the loyal inhabitants of Upper Canada to be ready in case the action of Brougham and his allies encouraged the rebels to another effort. This he sent on to Lord Durham with the following message written on the back: 'My Lord, Do not abandon us. It will be, I humbly think, more noble to stand by us until you shall have accomplished your labours, than to return and punish the unworthy men who assail you. An old Soldier.'[16]

On the 22nd, Lieutenant-Governor Arthur, dropping his controversy, and putting behind him all sharp words on both sides, wrote as follows:

My dear Lord Durham,

Your Lordship has, I am aware, such a pressure of business upon you that I most reluctantly trouble you with a private note; but, conscious as I am, of the depth of anxiety which you have manifested in the great objects which have induced you to undertake the Government of Her Majesty's North American Possessions, and of the solicitude which Your Lordship has felt to restore stability and security to these tottering provinces, I cannot see you so unjustly assailed as you have been by Lord Brougham without expressing the deep concern I feel, in common, I believe, with all classes of persons on this occasion. . . .

There was not, I will be bound to say, one individual in these provinces who ever thought for one moment that it was Your Lordship's intention to visit Papineau or any of his gang with death – every one saw distinctly the end Your Lordship had in view, and the difficulty you had in accomplishing it, and were disposed to look at Your Lordship's ordinance accordingly. The silence of the whole press is a remarkable proof of this.

The first impulse of Your Lordship's high spirit will be to resign; but I do trust you will not yield to it. The people in both provinces ought immediately from every district, to send in addresses to Your Lordship and I hope that the citizens of Toronto will, at once, lead the way upon which subject I have just been speaking to Mr. Ellice.[17] A measure of this kind is very necessary to remove the injurious impression that may be made upon the disaffected portion of the community by the disallowance of the Ordinance. It is not to be disguised that we are in a very critical position. [18]

Four days later Arthur sent on to Durham a copy of the resolutions to be moved at the public meeting in Toronto and the resolutions and address to be proposed at Cobourg.[19] Similar meetings and addresses were by this time being organized throughout both provinces.

On the evening of the 25th, Lord Brougham was burned in effigy in the Place d'Armes. A large crowd gathered for the event and, although there were angry mutterings against Melbourne and Glenelg, Brougham was the only victim. A week later, in Montreal, the tragedy was more elaborately staged:

Two transparencies, each six feet by nine, were mounted on a carriage and drawn by some jackasses, and followed by a transparent coffin, borne by pall-bearers, who carried lighted torches. On the coffin the word 'Brougham' was painted. One of the transparencies represented Lord Brougham seated on a jackass, with his face to the animal's tail, an imp of darkness leading the ass and exclaiming, 'Come along, old boy!' while his Lordship says, 'I protest against the legality of this ordinance;' and a second devil, who has a hold of the ass by his tail answers, 'Protest, and be d——d.' A fingerpost, stuck up at a short distance, having on it the words 'Road to Hell'. The other transparency represents his Satanic Majesty as having fastened a cord around the necks of the three Lords [Brougham, Melbourne, and Glenelg], and hauling them to their appointed place, very much against their will. His Majesty says, 'No mistake; you must come'. These two transparencies form the sides of a box, on the ends of which is painted, 'Thus may the enemies of British interests perish.' . . . Lord Brougham and his noble fellow traitors were publicly hanged and burned in effigy, amid the cheers of thousands. . . . We had almost forgot to mention, that Lord Glenelg was represented as asleep.[20]

One wonders what were the thoughts of Durham while Brougham was being burned on the Place d'Armes. Did his mind travel back to the friendship of early years when Henry Brougham had comforted him and drawn him back to politics after the death of his young wife, their battles side by side in the Commons, their electioneering in Westmoreland, the gay days that followed at Lambton, their standing one by the other in the face of an impending duel, that day in the Lords when he had introduced Brougham as his friend and the Chancellor of the realm, that other day when they had sat side by side as Commissioners declaring the Reform Bill the law of the land, their two names the most beloved among statesmen in the homes of the people; and then the drifting apart, the clash at Edinburgh, the stormy days that followed? – and now thousands of miles away in this new country, out there in the public square thousands who knew scarcely more of Brougham than his name were hissing and cursing it as the epitome of all that was vile, because of what they deemed a treacherous attack upon himself and upon them. Whatever he thought, his lips were sealed. In these weeks when his friends on both sides of the sea were raging against Brougham, he, the man of pride and temper, spoke no word against him. Personal feeling was already buried in a passionate cause. From this night to the night of his death twenty-two months later, he discussed publicly no aspect of this conflict but that which had been forgotten by the mother of parliaments – the future welfare of Canada.

When men had cursed the borough-mongers and reached out their hands towards fire and sword, he had framed the law that had set Britain on the road to popular government. What appealed to him now was not the wrathful indictment of individuals, whoever they might be, but what lay back of it in the desire and right of the Canadian people to govern itself. The plan was already shaping itself in his mind, and thanks to Brougham, whose effigy the crowd was burning, a dramatic situation was being created in which the whole British world was looking on in fever-pitch of sensation. Durham possessed not only the genius of far-flung vision but that ability to play up to a dramatic situation – partly consciously, partly unconsciously and spontaneously as out of the very essence of his being – which at every turning-point of history some outstanding individual has exerted.

Durham knew what all this meant – these glowing epistles and public meetings, resolutions, addresses, burning of Brougham and carting of Melbourne, all Canadians except last year's rebels united for once in a common feeling. It was not universal love for him, although there was a heartfelt sympathy and a deep respect; he could have no illusions regarding Strachan or even Arthur, good-natured as they might be for the time being; nor had hundreds of others grown affectionate over-night. It was because the Parliament and Government of Great Britain, playing their party game, without thought of Canadian interests, had reached their hands across the seas and overturned the policy of the government of Canada in such a manner as to threaten its peace and its future. It was an expression of *Canadianism*, in which all these discontented groups could unite. And not Canadianism only, but that deeper understanding of British interests which was ultimately to enable the Canadian people to give to the world the finest and most effective blending of nationalism and imperialism.

To many it seemed, and to many students of the situation it may still seem, as though the remarkable unity supporting Durham at this time should have decided him to yield to their petitions, refuse to resign and build on this situation that permanent unity which he had come to desire as ardently as the most intelligent Canadian patriot. But the fact that Durham could not get away from was that the source of power was at Westminster. With these tricks already won and all the trumps still in their hands, Brougham and his allies would never throw up the game. What had happened in August would happen again in October and November, and there was no limit to the number of his acts which might be disallowed. The Melbourne Government possessed no courage adequate to the situation, even if such courage could avail. There can be no questioning the sincerity of the refrain that ran through all Durham's dispatches, letters, and speeches of this period – his 'authority' was 'undermined'. What the Canadian people needed most was a generous measure of self-government. Given that, national unity and other developments would follow. That was the larger issue of which this incident was but a part. And that issue must be settled at Westminster.

It was on the day that Brougham was burned in effigy that Durham committed himself irretrievably by writing to the Colonial Secretary that he had decided to resign. His first impulse, communicated to Buller on the night he heard the news of the disallowance, was perhaps one of pique and anger, and a similar fit may have been on him next day when he wrote to Colborne. But he waited six days before he wrote a word to the British Government, and when he did so he expressed the result of a process of cold reasoning applied to the Canadian situation. He wrote in a spirited style which always characterized his utterances, but the words are not those flashes of wrath which he had been wont to release on his colleagues in the Cabinet. In view of our description of the situation, his statement of his case need not be recounted here. The ability displayed in this dispatch of the 25th and those of the 26th and 28th was recognized by the very men whose actions he criticized. In their private correspondence they conceded that high praise that Durham's writings always elicited.

Durham did not send off these dispatches until he had received Glenelg's official notification of the disallowance of the ordinance. He accompanied them by a private letter to Glenelg.

I am bound to tell you privately that I never could have anticipated the possibility of such treatment as I have received. Having succeeded, far beyond my most sanguine hopes, in restoring tranquillity and inspiring confidence, all over the

Continent of North America, I little expected the reward I have received from home, — disavowal and condemnation. . . . In these circumstances I have no business here — My authority is gone — all that rests is military power, that can be better wielded by a soldier, and Sir John Colborne will, no doubt, do it efficiently.

I shall appear in Parliament not to defend my conduct, for it needs no excuse, but to expose the cruelty, injustice, and impolicy of those who have trifled with the best interests of these Colonies for purposes of personal enmity or party hostility.

As soon as I can make the necessary arrangements, I shall deliver over the government here to the Administrator and return by the United States, where I hope my influence (which permit me to say, is apparently greater than in the House of Lords or the Cabinet) may be beneficially exerted for the purpose of confirming and extending those friendly feelings towards England, with which I had, at some labour, succeeded in inspiring them.[21]

His health did not improve, and two days later he was again confined to his bed.[22]

There is little historical value in discussing whether the circumstances justified Lord Durham's resignation. What is really important historically is that if he had not resigned and returned to England, his Report would not have been as effective and would probably never have been published except in a very mutilated form. In all probability it would have been further buried under a decided administrative failure. Durham's relations with the Whig leaders, his temperament, and the doubtful character of his administrative ability would all have militated against his succeeding for any length of time as Governor of Canada.[23]

But the readers of a biography may be interested in knowing the attitude of his friends and advisers towards his resignation. It was very much divided. Many who had signed the innumerable monster petitions from all over the country asking him to remain may have questioned the wisdom of his doing so and regarded the petitions rather as a demonstration. There can be no doubting the fact that the three Lieutenant-Governors who wrote to him all felt that the resignation was a mistake, much as they sympathized with his feelings. Governor Arthur's letter has been quoted already. Sir John Harvey, who had developed a real affection as well as a respect for Durham, wrote from Fredericton a most friendly letter, lamenting the whole incident and expressing his fear that it might be fatal to British connexion, but also clearly regretting Durham's decision. Sir Colin Campbell wrote frankly from Halifax to Lord Durham and to Colonel Couper condemning the intervention of English party politics and wishing that something could be done to persuade Durham to remain until the spring. The press, with a few exceptions, urged him to remain. One of the Catholic clergy made a similar appeal in a personal letter marked by patriotic fervour.[24]

Joseph Parkes added a characteristic contribution, from a Radical viewpoint, which Durham could not adopt.

Every real and well judging friend you have here, holds but one conversation – 'We hope Lord Durham will not be driven by false friends or Tory enemies into the pit fall dug for him – resignation.' . . .

I am still decidedly of opinion that you should if possible complete your plans by Christmas and appear in Parliament to advocate them. Whether they pass the Legislature of the Mother Country or not, whether they are rejected or modified by the Ministry or be thrown out by the Tories in the Lords, matters not, provided the Liberal Public approve them; . . . Faustus concocted all this abominable attack on the Ordinances at Leader's house wtih a Cabinet of Roebuck, Falkner & Co. Molesworth I hear would be no party to it. . . . Lay down the keel of a good representative system and elective municipalities, and then let the Colony go to the devil its own way. It will inevitably and beneficially ultimately outgrow the authority of the Mother Country – notwithstanding you, your Ordinances and schemes of Government. All you have to do is to prepare the launch.[25]

On the other hand, Lady Durham stated that all of those who were closest to Lord Durham at the time were convinced that resignation was the wiser course.[26] This, we know, included Colonel Couper, the military secretary, who had a considerable knowledge of Canada through previous residence, and it included Sir John Colborne and Adam Thom. The latter told McGill that 'His Excellency could, under existing circumstances, do more for the country by going home than by remaining here'.[27] Sir James Macdonnell, Commander of the Guards, thought that resignation was the only possible course.[28]

In a letter to Lady Durham, which showed that his father the 'Bear' had not exhausted the shrewdness of the family, Edward Ellice, Jr., who had come out to Canada as Lord Durham's secretary, and was now living on his father's seigneury at Beauharnois, took the same position. He stated that many agreed with him that it was a good thing Lord Durham was going home.

I am convinced that the moment the other measures of local and immediate interest were disposed of, the whole community here, French and English, would immediately commence a system of attempted bullying and intimidation (which, though without effect, would be most annoying) to carry into effect their secondary objects, all self-interested ones, and no three people agreeing cordially on any one point, except that of opposing a just and impartial settlement of their several differences. Lord Durham will now leave this country the most popular Governor that ever ruled it, and the situation in which he has been placed by his attempts to bring about a peaceable state of things, and do justice to all parties, will be most fully appreciated by every inhabitant of it, without distinction of race or origin. . . . All this cannot fail to give his opinion in Canadian affairs both here and at home far greater influence than it would otherwise have had, especially as it will now come from a disinterested Peer of England and not from the Governor of Canada.[29]

The Melbourne Government more than half expected Durham to resign. On the very day they notified Durham of the disallowance, they wrote to Colborne urging him not to abandon his post as he had intended doing.[30] On August 9, in replying to Brougham's attack, before he had surrendered to him, Lord Melbourne himself had said in the House of Lords: 'The disallowance of the Ordinance would be destructive of the moral effect of the noble Earl's government and almost the same as pronouncing the termination of his connexion with the colony.'

The two men who were closest to Lord Durham in Canada, Charles Buller and Charles Grey, his brother-in-law, both felt that, with much to be said on both sides, their advice to him to persist in this decision to resign was rendered inevitable by the state of his health. Buller wrote, in his sketch of the mission two years later:

Without surmising the real nature or extent of the mischief, I saw that Lord Durham's health was fearfully affected by all that had passed. Such a degree of nervous agitation did his disease produce, and such a reaction of that agitation on his bodily health was constantly going on, that it was evidently impossible for him to bear up against the anxieties and labour of his government under existing circumstances, and display that energy and promptitude of decision which had so eminently distinguished him when his health was better. I felt convinced – and unhappily it is now too clear that I was likely to be right – that Lord Durham's life would very soon have been the sacrifice for his continuance in Canada, even for two or three months, and that at any rate he was liable to have his energies impaired by illness at moments in which any relaxation of them would have been fatal to success. I lamented his resignation then: I deplore it yet more deeply now; but I approved of it then, and approve of it now, as an act done in compliance with a stern and sad necessity. I must not be understood as admitting that his return home was calculated to injure the interests of the Province; *on the contrary, I still think that in the difficulties then impending the preservation of the Province was more* safe *in the hands of Sir John Colborne than in those of Lord Durham, weakened as they were by the repeated proofs of his being unsupported at home.* It is for his own sake – *for the sake of the influence which his continuance in his government under such circumstances would have ensured him – and for the sake of all the strength that would thence have accrued to the popular cause at home,* that I regret that the state of his health compelled him to abandon this chance of fame and power, *and that even this sacrifice came too late to avert the blow which disease had already struck.*

Charles Grey wrote to his father, September 30:

For himself I could not advise him to stay. I really think it would kill him. I never knew a man so affected by the attacks upon him both in Parliament and the newspapers, and his mind works upon his body to a degree that is quite fearful. . . . The feeling in this country, as far as he is concerned, is certainly most satisfactory and flattering to him. . . . He obtained their confidence, to an extent, I believe, never before reached by any governor. . . . He certainly had been very diligent in endeav-

ouring to obtain every possible information respecting the country.[31]

That, however, was not Lord Durham's own reason for his action. He probably never gave a thought to it. He seldom, if ever, considered his health when there was a pressing call for public service.

In the meantime the mass meetings, protesting against Lord Durham's treatment at home, lauding his administration and urging him to remain, were being held in all parts of the country, and every day brought to Quebec another sheaf of the monster petitions embodying these sentiments. The petition from the City of Quebec bore over four thousand signatures on twenty-four sheets of parchment, and its presentation was made the occasion of a great procession and a meeting which was described as the largest ever held in Canada. Lady Durham and her family were present and shared the honours. In her letters home she spoke of it with the utmost gratitude and satisfaction. In his speech of reply Lord Durham said:

I do not return to England from my feelings of disgust at the treatment I have personally experienced in the House of Lords. If I could have been influenced by any such motives, I must have re-embarked in the very ship which brought me out; for that system of parliamentary persecution pursued me from the moment I left the shores of England. . . . My post is where your interests are really decided upon. . . . I assure you that to the last hour of my existence you will find me your faithful and devoted friend, bound to you by the strongest ties, both public and private, of respect and gratitude.[32]

It was this day, October 9, on account, no doubt, of the preparation for a demonstration, that Lord Durham, with his *flair* for the dramatic, selected for the performance of the task imposed upon him by the Home Government, in fact written by Brougham into his Bill, the proclamation in Canada of the Act of Indemnity and the disallowance of the ordinance. He made of this proclamation a defence of his action to the people of Canada, an explanation of his persisting in his resignation in spite of their appeals to him to remain, and a promise that as surely as he could exert influence on the political situation in England their interests would not be neglected in the immediate future as they had been in the immediate past.

There had been too much mystery in the public statements of Governors. With a people from whom he had received such gratifying proofs of attachment he could have no reserve. He had proclaimed at the beginning the principles by which he would govern. He must now explain why he could not continue. To effect the objects of his mission it had been necessary that he should have the means of acting for himself 'without a perpetual control by distant authorities'. This had implied not only extraordinary legal powers, but also 'the moral force that could be derived from the assurance' that his 'acts would be final' and his 'engagements religiously observed'. He had believed that he would enjoy these powers and 'that even party feeling would refrain from molesting' him, 'whilst occupied in maintaining the integrity of the British Empire'. He had been disappointed.

From the very commencement of my task the minutest details of my administration have been exposed to incessant criticism, in a spirit which has evinced an entire ignorance of the state of this country. . . . Those who have in the British Legislature systematically depreciated my powers, and the Ministers of the Crown by their tacit acquiescence therein, have produced the effect of making it too clear that my authority is inadequate for the emergency which called it into existence.

After a lengthy vindication of his Bermuda ordinance, he continued:

The good effects which must necessarily have resulted from any settlement of this difficult question had already begun to show themselves. Of these the principal were, the general approval of my policy by the people of the United States, and the consequent cessation of American sympathy with any attempt to disturb the Canadas. This result has been most gratifying to me, inasmuch as it has gone far towards a complete restoration of that good-will between you and a great kindred nation, which I have taken every means in my power to cultivate, and which I earnestly entreat you to cherish as essential to your peace and prosperity.

It had been absolutely necessary to insert in the ordinance the statements regarding the disposal of the prisoners in Bermuda; he had expected the British Parliament 'to supply their insufficiency in case of need'. But the co-operation which he had a right to expect had been refused him and 'the usefulness of my delegated power expires with the loss of that support from the supreme authority which alone could sustain it'.

With what confidence can I invite co-operation, or impose forbearance, whilst I touch ancient laws and habits, as well as deep-rooted abuses, with the weakened hands that have ineffectually essayed but a little more than the ordinary vigour of the police of troubled times? . . .

The proclamation contained an entire amnesty, qualified only by the exceptions specified in the ordinance. The ordinance has been disallowed, and the proclamation is confirmed. Her Majesty having been advised to refuse her assent to the exceptions, the amnesty exists without qualification. No impediment, therefore, exists to the return of the persons who had made the most distinct admission of guilt, or who had been excluded by me from the province on account of the danger to which its tranquillity would be exposed by their presence; and none can now be enacted without the adoption of measures alike repugnant to my sense of justice and policy. I cannot recall the irrevocable pledge of her Majesty's mercy. . . . If the peace of Lower Canada is to be again menaced, it is necessary that its Government should be able to reckon on a more cordial and vigorous support at home than has been accorded to me. No good that may not be expected from any other Government in Lower Canada can be obtained by my continuing to wield extraordinary legal powers of which the moral force and consideration are gone. . . . It is with feelings of deep disappointment that I find myself thus suddenly deprived of the power of reforming the administrative system there, and eradicating the manifold abuses which had been engendered by the negligence and corruption of former times, and so lamentably fostered by civil dissensions. I cannot but regret being obliged to renounce the still more glorious hope of employing unusual legislative powers in the endowment of that province with those free municipal institutions which are the only sure basis of local improvement and representative liberty, of establishing a system of general education, of revising the defective laws which regulate real property and commerce, and of introducing a pure and competent administration of justice. Above all, I grieve to be thus forced to abandon the realization of such large and solid schemes of colonization and internal improvement as would connect the distant portions of these extensive colonies, and lay open the unwrought treasures of the wilderness to the wants of British industry, and the energy of British enterprise.

He hoped that his Report would be productive of great results. He concluded:

I fervently hope, that my usefulness to you will not cease with my official connexion. . . . It must be, I humbly trust, for the advantages of these provinces if I can carry into the Imperial Parliament a knowledge derived from personal inspection and experience of their interests, upon which some persons there are too apt to legislate in ignorance or indifference, and can aid in laying the foundation of a system of general government which, while it strengthens your permanent connexion with Great Britain, shall save you from the evils to which you are now subjected by every change in the fluctuating policy of distant and successive administrations.[33]

This proclamation was received with almost universal favour by English-speaking Canadians and with nearly unanimous disapprobation in Great Britain. French-Canadians were disturbed by parts of it which seemed to confirm their fears that Lord Durham had been captured by the policy of the Anglification of Lower Canada.

The strongest condemnations of the proclamation in Great Britain are to be found in private letters rather than in the public press. Many of these letters were written by Lord Durham's intimate friends. Lord Grey, who had rallied to him loyally and indignantly in the matter of the ordinance and severely condemned the 'shabby' conduct of the Government, now felt that he had lost his head completely. 'All the faults of his character from which I always feared that it would turn out unfortunately for himself, his family and the country, seem to have broken out at last with a violence proportionate to the control under which he seems previously to have held them.[34] Edward Ellice, who for all his private criticism of the Government believed that it should be publicly supported and who was perhaps offended at the fact that Durham still favoured federation, wrote an angry letter to Melbourne which began: 'Well, has not this meteor finished his career in the blaze I always predicted? What a proclamation, – and if I am not mistaken in one important, the only important, point in it, – in defiance of his instructions.'[35] To Durham himself, in a letter full of friendship and advice, he described it as 'a document, with all its merits of composition and ingenuity, without precedent in the annals of our colonial government, and which I hope may never be taken as an example. . . . You will find that this is not only the opinion of one, but of all parties in this country'.[36] Leslie Grove Jones wrote to Durham: 'It is but what I owe to you to tell you candidly and in confidence that your proclamation is disapproved of by several who are warmly attached to you and whose favourable opinion you value.'[37]

In his proclamation Lord Durham had attacked both the Tory and Whig parties, and in ordinary circumstances he might have expected severe reprisals from both. Some newspapers attacked him bitterly, but others criticized him in terms tempered to a delicate political situation. The *Morning Chronicle* practically satisfied itself by quoting and commenting favourably – for once – on a statement from the *Standard* which summed up the most reasonable ground of offence: 'We cannot think that it [Lord Durham's criticism] has been made in the proper place. The whole paper looks too like an appeal from the decision of the Queen and Parliament of Great Britain to the sense, if not the feeling, of the people of Canada, – surely an unbecoming character for a proclamation issued by the Queen's representative.'[38] *The Times*, however, displayed its characteristic vigour, roundly attacked the proclamation as inflammatory and seditious, and dubbed Lord Durham 'the Lord High Seditioner'.

The Government, moved no doubt by Melbourne who talked a great deal at this time about 'not truckling to Durham', felt that it must vindicate its authority, and Glenelg sent Durham a dispatch which contained the following:

> They [*her Majesty's confidential advisers*] *consider, as open to most serious objection, an appeal by such an officer to the public at large, from measures adopted by the Sovereign, with the advice and consent of Parliament. The terms in which that appeal has been made, in this instance, appear to her Majesty's ministers calculated to impair the reverence due to the royal authority, to derogate from the character of the Imperial legislature, to excite amongst the disaffected hopes of impunity, and to enhance the difficulties with which your Lordship's successor*

will have to contend. The ministers of the crown having humbly submitted this opinion to the Queen, it is my duty to inform you, that I have received her Majesty's commands to signify to your Lordship her Majesty's disapprobation of your proclamation of the 9th of October. Under these circumstances, her Majesty's Government are prepared to admit, that your continuance in the Government of British North America could be attended with no beneficial results.

This cannot be regarded as a dismissal from office. Lord Durham had not formally resigned, but he had indicated clearly his determination to do so; he could not have changed his decision after writing his dispatches and the proclamation; and Lord Glenelg had, at his request, arranged for a ship to take him home.

Some of the Radical papers defended the proclamation, but by far the most influential statement in its favour was that of John Stuart Mill in the December number of the *Westminster Review*. He pointed out that the proclamation was not inflammatory; public opinion in Canada was already so inflamed that it was calculated to temper it. It was not an appeal from the decision of the British Government to the feelings of the Canadians; their verdict had already been rendered.

All the addresses, all the resolutions were solicitations to him to retain the government; the proclamation was his answer. . . . Though no longer their Governor, his connexion with them was not to cease; upon him it was to devolve to watch over their interests in England. He was the only man in the kingdom of first-rate political influence, the only man ever thought of as minister, or as a party leader, who did not at that moment stand convicted, in the minds of those whom he was addressing, of the grossest ignorance of all the circumstances of the colony, and the most presumptuous incapacity in legislating for it. When this last specimen of presumption and incapacity was making the whole British population of both the Canadas join with the French Canadians in denouncing the principle of distant colonial government, and the very officials talk familiarly of a separation, was it nothing to show to Canada that there was one British statesman who could understand her wants and feel for her grievances – that from any councils in the mother country in which he had influence she might expect justice – and that the man, on whose constancy and magnanimity so much depended, was not throwing up his mission from personal disgust, but returning to England because the manœuvres of his enemies had changed the place where he could serve them from Quebec to the House of Lords? . . . So far from being inflammatory, it was probably the only kind of address to the people which in the then state of men's minds could have any healing effect.

Of similar tenor is the statement made by Charles Buller two years later in his account of the mission. But Buller was able to speak of results as well as intentions. 'No disorder, no increase of disaffection ensued; on the contrary, all parties in the province expressed a revival of confidence; and we had it very clearly shown to us that one effect of the proclamation had been that of inducing a much more general readiness to enlist in the volunteer corps, and take other measures for the defence of the provinces.'

It does not appear, at first sight, why it was necessary to create a bad impression in all quarters by publicly inviting back to the province the very men whom the ordinance had sought to exclude from it. Charles Buller wrote a defence of that part of the proclamation in an appendix to his sketch of the mission, where he stated that Lord Durham had very reluctantly inserted it at his – Buller's – suggestion. Buller's defence is sound so far as it goes.[39] But it is remarkable that he made no mention of the fact that Glenelg had suggested to Durham that he should issue a new ordinance excluding these men from the province. Lord Durham gave as his reason for refusing to do so the feeling that this would be withdrawing the Queen's forgiveness after it had been granted, since the proclamation of amnesty covered them now that the ordinance which excepted them had been disallowed. But even if the amnesty did include them now – which is open to question – they might be amnestied for the treason committed in the rebellion and at the same time be legally excluded from the province because they were persons dangerous to the public order. The Government had defended the legality of that part of the ordinance and would be bound to defend another covering the same ground. And Durham and Buller must both have known that such an ordinance could not be successfully attacked in Parliament, once Lord Durham had turned over the government of the province to Sir John Colborne. The Duke of Wellington was the Conservative leader in the Lords, and the Duke, who was the soul of loyalty, would never interfere with the government of Colborne, who was both a personal friend and one of the Duke's best officers in the glorious days when they had beaten Napoleon.

So the matter appeared from the legal and political points of view, but when it came to individual cases there were greater difficulties. A few days after the news of the disallowance of the ordinance had reached America, Louis Perrault and Georges Etienne Cartier, two of the exiles affected by it, applied to Lord Durham for permission to return to Canada. They believed that the amnesty now applied to them. This was the more embarrassing because Louis Perrault had not been in the province at the time of the rebellion. He had been one of those whose arrest had been ordered on the eve of the rebellion, but he had gone to the States on a business trip some time before. These facts were now well known in the United States as well as in Canada, and to refuse his application would play into the hands of those whom Durham and Buller knew to be plotting another insurrection. Buller wrote to Simpson, September 22, that Lord Durham would deal with this application after he had received the dispatches which he expected in a few days.[40] Then came Glenelg's dispatch suggesting a new ordinance. To issue such an ordinance would mean in Perrault's case that he would have been unjustly exiled in the first place, then amnestied, then after respectfully applying on the basis of the amnesty for leave to return to his home, made the subject of an ordinance continuing his exile. That would have been the crudest injustice, but to issue a new ordinance and omit his name might very well do more harm. Buller's suggestion would seem the simplest way out. Nothing was said of this application in Buller's defence; he left it to be disinterred now from his official correspondence. But he said: 'When the subsequent insurrection actually did break out, the rebels could allege no harsh act on the part of the Government as a provocation.' None of the exiles who returned after the proclamation took any part in the second insurrection, and in view of the part which he played in the making of the Dominion, there can be no regrets that Georges Etienne Cartier was permitted to return to his home rather than excluded by a second ordinance. Buller generously assumed responsibility for this part of the ordinance. He concluded his defence with the statement:

I am bound to take on myself whatever blame is due to me, for well I know he never would have cast it on me. Every man who has to act on a great variety of matters of importance must rely on those whom he employs and trusts; and Lord Durham was necessarily compelled in much that he did to rely on me and act on my advice. Some steps that he took at my suggestion were among those that were most fiercely assailed either at home or in Canada. Yet never have I any reason to believe that he threw on me even the blame that I deserved. Never certainly, though often he might justly have done so, did he reproach me with the consequences of my counsels, never at least but once, in a moment of very natural excitement, and then he repaired the reproach in half an hour.

The most unfortunate result of the proclamation was one which received no attention in England and was not mentioned by Buller in his apologetic statement. We have noticed the sensitiveness of the French-Canadian moderates, their misgivings in regard to Durham's relations with the British leaders, and their indignation at his appointment of Adam Thom. But until the proclamation of October 9 the more optimistic of them had continued to hope for the best, an attitude reflected in *Le Canadien*. After that a marked change is to be seen. The breach was widened to the point where no one believed that it could be bridged. Lord Durham is still respected as an upright and conscientious statesman, but he has fallen into the nets laid for him by the British party. In the words of his proclamation his aim is to 'elevate the province of Lower Canada to a thoroughly British character', 'to raise the defective institutions of Lower Canada to the level of British civilisation and freedom, to remove all impediments to the course of British enterprise in this province', to 'touch ancient laws and habits as well as ancient abuses'. That might be a more graceful way of putting it, but it was what Adam Thom and his friends had been talking for years – the Anglifying of the French-Canadian race through the destruction of their cherished institutions. *Le Canadien* had been the most favourable to Durham of the Lower Canada papers until the appointment of Adam Thom; after that it was more subdued in its eulogies and somewhat suspicious; its attitude after the proclamation may be judged from the following quotations:

Of what black ingratitude, what odious oppression would not England render herself guilty, if after having favored for half a century . . . the existence and extension of certain 'social arrangements' under which this people has grown up and with which it has been identified, she were to decree arbitrarily the overthrow of this social existence or of any of its essential parts. It would have been a thousand times less hard, less cruel never to have established these rights. . . . It is not in this manner that a statesman will ever add a jewel to his crown.

Nobody could consider it strange that he [Lord Durham] an Englishman, and a patriotic Englishman, should believe that the laws, customs, and social institutions of his country were superior to all others and that he should desire their introduction in this country, but nobody could reconcile himself to the idea that, consistently with his political doctrines, he could and would impose laws, customs, and institutions, against their will on a people to whom other laws, other customs, other institutions are guaranteed. This noble peer of the United Kingdom, as a Protestant would no doubt have liked to see Ireland adopt Protestantism, yet as a liberal statesman he fought for the religious emancipation of Ireland against any measure which attempted to force the Protestant religion on a Catholic people. . . . By what strange perversion of principles can he act toward Lower Canada in a way that he could not toward Ireland? . . . What hope can remain to us to-day, ask Canadians most favourable to our present political existence, when we see one of the most liberal and distinguished statesmen of Great Britain, with a reputation for political talent, subscribe to those views of factious ascendancy which have been the curse of this country?

When Lord Durham sailed from Quebec on November 1 the leader of the French-Canadian press, who had welcomed him with the utmost enthusiasm, spoke these words of farewell: 'He was an envoy to pacify a country torn by political dissensions, envenomed by national distinctions, and into the midst of elements so inflammable, he throws a burning brand, he declares himself for the national destruction of a whole people.'[41]

We now turn back to trace the fortunes of 'the plan of government'. We have already noted that the first plan prepared by Lord Durham, probably in England, was modelled closely after the scheme of federal union of all the British North American provinces submitted to him by Roebuck.[42] The only important additions were the inclusion of all provincial officials among those who were to be subject to impeachment before the general assembly and the elaboration of the powers of the federal government, which were now to include militia, customs, administration of crown lands 'as far as the crown would consent', and all boundary questions as well as currency, bankruptcy, interprovincial communications, post-office, and general trade. This plan had been submitted to the Montreal leaders early in July. Its reception, though unfavourable, was not discouraging. A few days before, Durham had given a document embodying his plan to Sir John Harvey, Governor of New Brunswick, who had come to visit him at Quebec and who took it home for further study.[43] He submitted a very similar paper for consideration and criticism to John Beverley Robinson – Chief Justice of Upper Canada and the giant of the 'Family Compact' for nearly the whole period of their power – possibly when Robinson accompanied him from Toronto to Prescott on his return from Upper Canada.[44]

John Beverley Robinson's criticisms of this plan indicated by pencilled marginal comments are of interest not only on account of their influence on Lord Durham, but also because of their remarkable similarity to the provisions of Confederation as it went into effect twenty-nine years later. Not least significant is the revelation of the limited geographical vision of Canadians of that day conveyed by Robinson's writing opposite to 'all such future provinces as may arise' the remark: 'There will scarcely be any additional provinces unless by subdivisions of those now existing.'

Ultimately Lord Durham adopted nearly all of these amendments suggested by Robinson. Legislative Councils were to be retained, Roebuck's idea of giving revisionary powers to Executive Councils dropped, and the provincial constitutions to remain as they were. Members of the federal parliament were to be elected by the people, not the provincial Assemblies, and the number for each province raised from five to ten. The provision for shortening the duration of Parliament and for summoning and proroguing Parliament at fixed dates were struck out of the plan. Judges were to be appointed by the Crown only, and boundary questions left to the Privy Council. On the other hand, Durham apparently continued to favour the original provisions for the constitution of Executive Councils and impeachment, Canadian control of the post office, and the idea of a Canadian Supreme Court.[45]

Durham's remarkably open mind welcomed suggestions from all sources, Family Compact or Reform, Roebuck or Adam Thom. But these contributions of Robinson's came from a man who was not only one of the best political thinkers in the country, but who could probably win the Upper Canada Tories to any plan that satisfied him. Since the French-Canadians and the Upper Canada Reformers could be counted on to support any reasonable project of confederation, that would mean three out of four parties in the two Canadas, even if Adam Thom could not win the 'British party' in the Lower Province. The two most important of these changes, the retention of Legislative Councils and the election of federal members by popular vote rather than by the Assemblies, were also advised by Thom,[46] and it is easy to see why they were calculated to make federation more acceptable to his party. Another change which crept into Durham's plan was probably also designed to conciliate the 'British party' of Lower Canada, whose leadership and main strength was centred in Montreal. The district of Montreal, the Eastern Townships (the English-speaking part of rural Lower Canada), and the eastern part of Upper Canada were to constitute a separate province, making out of what had been Upper and Lower Canada three provinces, each of which would have, as nearly as possible, racial homogeneity.[47]

In the meantime there were the Maritime Provinces to contend with. The documents in which Lord Durham's plan was embodied had retained Roebuck's suggestion that Upper and Lower Canada might be federated first and provision made for the other provinces to come in later at their option. But the federation of all British North America had appealed to Durham's imagination and everything that he wrote during these months shows that he was driving for the immediate creation of the nation of which he dreamed. He had invited Sir Colin Campbell and Sir Charles Fitzroy, the Lieutenant-Governors of Nova Scotia and Prince Edward Island, to come to Quebec to confer with him after his return from Upper Canada. They arrived August 16 and remained until the 25th, during which time they accompanied him to the Montreal races. We know little of the results of this visit beyond Lady Durham's general statement that 'they both entered cordially into his views and he was perfectly satisfied in his communications with them'.[48]

While the other governors were at Quebec he received Sir John Harvey's comment on his plan of confederation. There was little discussion of detail beyond an adverse criticism of the abolition of the Legislative Council. Public sentiment in New Brunswick was at that time opposed to the whole idea of federation. The people were indisposed 'to connect themselves in any way with the French population of Lower Canada', nor would their representatives in the Assembly surrender a share of their recently acquired control over revenues to any federal body. He hoped, however, that if the plan were applied first to Upper and Lower Canada, the maritime provinces would realize its benefits and join at some time in the not distant future.[49]

Durham replied that he did not desire to force New Brunswick into federation, but that that province might regret its exclusion from the benefits which the other maritime provinces would realize from the union, especially the construction of lines of communication which they so badly needed.

Lord Durham had already planned a conference to be held at Quebec in September, to which each of the Maritime provinces was invited to send delegates representing all parties and classes. Before the Nova Scotia delegates left Halifax, Sir Colin Campbell wrote to him that while they believed that the confederation was desirable, they felt that the people of the province would not approve of it, and that the formation of two unions, one of the Canadas, the other of the Maritimes, was preferable. Sir Colin himself thought that the larger project was 'the only means of securing the tranquillity and strengthening the connexion of these flourishing provinces with Great Britain.'[50]

Into the midst of this conference came the news of the disallowance of the ordinance. Of the discussion of the plan of confederation very little knowledge is available. In view of the feeling reported by Sir John Harvey and the later statements in the Report to the effect that it might take some time before their consent to a general Union could be secured, it seems probable that at least the New Brunswick delegates suggested obstacles to the immediate adoption of any plan of confederation.[51]

Certainly Lord Durham still intended to recommend a British North American federation and not a legislative union of Upper and Lower Canada. Five days after the Maritime delegates left Quebec, Adam Thom wrote Buller that he would advocate the larger federal union in the *Herald*,[52] and at a meeting in Montreal, October 1, Thom stated that His Excellency was strongly persuaded that a union of the two Canadas 'would cruelly disappoint the anticipation of its advocates'. The French Canadians and a small group of revolutionists in Upper Canada, Thom argued, would unite to form a majority in the union legislature. The interests of the British party in Lower Canada would be better served by a federation of all the provinces. 'If Upper Canada alone cannot give you a truly British majority, infuse an additional quantity of British blood and British feeling to be found in the unbroken masses in Nova Scotia and New Brunswick.' C. D. Day said in reply that in a federal union 'we should be cursed with the same *local* legislature, the selfsame French majority, and we should be represented by the same materials in the general legislature'. The meeting was enthusiastically eulogistic of Lord Durham, but it passed by a large majority a resolution in favour of a legislative union of Upper and Lower Canada.[53] Next day Lord Durham wrote to Richardson: 'I thank you kindly for your account of the meeting. . . . I fully expected the "outbreak" about the union of the two provinces. It is a pet Montreal project, beginning and ending in Montreal selfishness.'[54]

The proclamation of October 9 indicated a federation of all the provinces. On the same day a letter to Arthur drafted by Buller but authorized by Durham developed new arguments for a general federation.[55] On October 22, ten days before Lord Durham sailed, Buller wrote Strachan that he was 'delighted' to find in him 'an advocate of the federal union of the British North American provinces' which seemed to be the only way to secure good government.[56] Buller, in an article written nine years later, gives us the reason why his chief came to give his blessing to that policy which he had previously damned – the legislative union of Upper and Lower Canada. The discussion with the Maritime delegates had suggested difficulties in the way of federation, but

Lord Durham, when he left Canada, was still so much inclined to this original plan that he was disposed rather to wait for the period at which it might be accomplished than to propose in the first instance any less extensive union. The second insurrection, which broke out during his voyage home, convinced him that the disorders of Lower Canada would admit of no delay; and compelled him, much against his inclination, to admit that the present peril must be guarded against by an immediate union of the Canadas.[57]

The insurrection however was on them, in all but actual outbreak, before Durham sailed, and there are reasons for believing that he was wavering before he left Canada.[58] In a situation that called for immediate action, the vision faded but it did not vanish. Probably Durham never saw very clearly the permanent advantages of a *federal* form of union. In his mind federation was always a stepping stone to an ultimate legislative union of all the provinces. But everything noble in his imagination clung to the dream of one united nation, glorying in its nationhood and playing an ever widening role in the larger British world. Not the least of the values of Lord Durham's Report is the fact that it developed, with that lucidity and force which characterized everything he wrote, nearly all the arguments for the larger union which were employed at the time of the formation of the Dominion.

During his last days in Canada he completed a number of matters that were in process of settlement. Among these was the preparation of a Registry Bill which received the approbation of the principal advocates of that reform and of the best lawyers of both races; the conclusion of an agreement with the Seminary of St. Sulpice which laid the basis of the emancipation of the city of Montreal from feudal ties; the granting to squatters on crown lands of the right of pre-emption at upset price; and the conversion of the Home Government to the necessity of a good law of escheat in Prince Edward Island, thus removing a deep-rooted obstacle to the prosperity of that province. The Commissioners of Education and Municipal Institutions were left behind to complete their tasks; Charles Buller remained to gather up loose ends in connexion with the commissions for which he was responsible. Wakefield on the other hand was sent on to England in advance, probably to spy out the land and report to his chief on his arrival. Durham's last appointment, that of James Stuart (later Sir James Stuart) as Chief Justice of Quebec, repaired an injustice of an earlier administration and placed the man who was recognized everywhere as being the best lawyer in the province in its most important legal position, from the vantage-point of which he was later to play the leading role, so far as Lower Canada was concerned, in establishing the Union and guiding the administration of Lord Sydenham. Stuart was one of the leaders of the British party, and his appointment was interpreted as a gesture in their direction. But at no time in his life did Lord Durham allow any consideration to stand in the way of his appointing the best man to every office. Such a policy may occasionally imperil an administration, but it builds the future of a nation on its surest foundation.

The second rebellion broke out two days after he sailed. But he and Colborne, to whom he had surrendered all real authority for several weeks before it came, had seen it gathering for some time. Measures were taken to meet it effectively, but its prevention was particularly difficult because it was being prepared in the States with the hope that thousands of *habitants* would flock to its banners when it had once crossed the line. Durham sent dispatches to Glenelg giving details of the coming danger. With characteristic exaggeration and a tendency to centre the councils of the gods on his own wrongs, he blamed it all on the Government's disallowance of the ordinance. 'The whole of this has been occasioned (you will excuse the frankness with which I tell it you) by your late proceedings in the Cabinet and the House of Lords.'[59] Sir George Arthur, who faced a similar situation in the upper province, while recognizing that the rising had been planned since the early summer, agreed with this to the extent that he believed it might not actually have broken out had not the Government's action encouraged the insurgents by disarming Durham's strong Government, and taking under its own protecting wing the leaders of the first rebellion.[60] It is difficult to accept that conclusion, but the political game in England had certainly helped to keep trouble boiling in Canada and made it easy to convince many a *habitant* that the Government of Canada was so weak that it could not even punish its rebels, and that it had no substantial support from Great Britain.

Although arrangements for his return had been made for some time, Durham came to feel in the middle of October that he should stay and face the impending rising. He had no misgivings about the decision, made a month before, that it was his duty to return to England, but here was a new factor in the situation. Could he honourably leave his post on the eve of battle? Buller and Colonel Couper, his military secretary, both told him he must go. Failing to persuade him they appealed to Colborne, and he, in his blunt fashion, said that at such a time all authority, military and civil, should be in the hands of the Commander-in-Chief, that a civilian governor would only be in the way and that the people of the British Isles were in dire need of enlightenment in regard to Canada, which Durham could best afford them. Couper wrote to the latter: 'I cannot help thinking that, at this crisis, your Lordship laments you are not a soldier.'[61] But it was a soldier's business and there could not have been a better man for it than Colborne.

That meant also the abandonment of the trip through the United States on which Lord Durham had set his heart. The Americans were in a most enthusiastic frame of mind in regard to Britain's most liberal statesman, who had been breaking down toryism and outworn systems in more than one British country and from his seat of power in the colony to the north had shown them a generous cordiality and affection. Great demonstrations had been prepared. The British consul at New York sent to Quebec a list of leading citizens who had been anxious to entertain him.[62] He was to have lived with the President at the White House as a national guest, which, according to Buller, was 'an honour never conferred on any one but Lafayette'. A few days before the change was made, Lady Durham had written to her father out of a heart that was aching for England and the old home scenes: 'If we missed this opportunity we should regret it all our lives.' But Durham regretted it more keenly than any. It would show his fellow-countrymen how the prophet on whom indignities were heaped at home was honoured in the new world.[63] And there was no doubt an impulse – hardly defined to himself because it was so spontaneous – to such a fine opportunity for display. But there was a greater cause. With him, along with that worship of the vanities, there went always a vision of permanent values. No Englishman of his generation appreciated as he did – none even approached him in this respect – the importance to the world's future of being an apostle of Anglo-American friendship. The good work begun at Niagara and Quebec might be completed at New York and Washington. Durham was bitterly disappointed at losing this opportunity to pursue what he had made an essential object of his mission.

On the 29th Sir James Macdonnell and his fellow officers of the two regiments of Guards stationed at Quebec tendered him a congratulatory dinner. The speeches were enthusiastic in their praise of Durham. It was made very clear, though not in so many words, that their admiration covered proclamation and all, and there was not a little implied criticism of the House of

Lords and the Home Government from which they held their commissions. An attempt was made next spring – after the fighting was over – to make this Guards dinner the subject of a sensational debate in the House of Lords. No doubt the proprieties were violated, not to mention the fact that it was galling to the Lords to have flung at them the fact that everybody in Canada, even to the British troops on whose valour the defence of the colony rested, supported Durham against them – everybody except the rebels, who had actually voted them congratulatory addresses. But the call to active service was only a few days off and these professional military men were plain-spoken fellows whose particular form of conceit was a belief that it was their business to clean up the blunders of politicians. Lord Durham improved the occasion with a graciousness and tact that never failed him when he chose to employ them. He proposed toasts to Sir John Colborne and the Duke of Wellington. The one was almost as much of a Tory as the other, but their names had been linked, as they were linked that night, in the annals of England's most vital military struggle. There were no two statesmen whose politics had been as diametrically and dramatically opposed as had those of Wellington and Durham. In the Reform Bill struggle each had been the hero of one side and the ogre of the other. But this was war, not politics. Durham's eloquent tribute to the Duke found its inspiration in the facts that the memory of his military genius and brilliant victories was an immortal possession of the British race, and that these men were called upon to fight for the glory of that race as it was to be expressed in a Canadian future which Durham alone of Englishmen had the eyes to see.

On the following day, the 30th, he was again seriously ill. More news arrived of the impending insurrection, he again spoke of remaining, and Colborne had to persuade him once more that his duty lay in England. With a renewal of his illness came a fit of depression, and he told Charles Buller that he did not believe that he would reach England alive.[64]

The members of his entourage had caught the spirit of their leader, and as they prepared to depart they felt deeply for the people of Canada. 'Tommy' Duncombe wrote in his diary:

It was impossible to leave them without feeling that we were going from a kind, loyal, and enterprising body of men, who would perhaps in a few weeks have to struggle for their lives and property, all owing to the imbecility of a Government, stationed four thousand miles off, enjoying every luxury and comfort that home could afford them, but totally ignorant of the high qualities and energies of those they presumed to govern and whose destinies were in their hands.[65]

This was too strong to be just, but it was the language of emotion, and the sentiment was a sound one.

It snowed on the night of the 31st, and the morning of November 1st broke clear and cold. Shortly before two o'clock in the afternoon, Lord and Lady Durham, with their suite, left the Chateau accompanied by a military escort, preceded by the friendly societies of the city, and followed by a procession of three thousand citizens. 'The streets were crowded; the spectators filled every window and every house-top; and though every hat was raised as we passed, a deep silence marked the general grief for Lord Durham's departure.'[66] But the scene is best described in the words of Lady Durham's Journal:

The gloom which prevailed seemed indeed as if the people were parting with what was most near and dear to them. I never beheld any public ceremony so deeply affecting, and all the feelings which pressed upon me on leaving England were slight in comparison with those I now experienced on departing from Quebec. Little did I imagine, on the first occasion, that I could ever feel regret on returning home; but there was now something so sad and solemn in the scene, so heart-breaking in the unmerited disappointment which had fallen upon him and upon a great people, that a long life of happiness afterwards could never have effaced the impression made upon me at that moment. . . . I seem to have been speaking principally of myself, – of my own sensations, – but it was the sight of him, of his countenance which contributed to render them so intense. He said but little at the moment.[67]

We may well believe that that day was a vivid memory through the few years of life that remained to them both. Deep as the bonds had been that bound them to the Canadian people, they were rendered indissoluble by the emotions that it evoked. And in that personal consideration there broke the one ray of hope that grew until it had conquered all the gloom. Lord Durham was the most potent envoy that Canada ever sent to England. About to die, he was to render her the service that stands peerless in Imperial history. His Report was more than a work of genius; his whole conduct in the coming months more than that of a man of state. He wrought his miracles for the ages to come, not only through his superior intellectual gifts, but because he set behind him all personal ambitions and all personal feelings, conquered temper and pride, – dogging him through life, but subdued in that last great task. It was more than a vision of Empire. There was no solemn service, no sacred vows, but it was none the less a dedication. He was more a Britisher than ever; through storm and pain he had served Britain all his life, but he served her best by becoming now – a Canadian.[68]

✿ ✿ ✿

CHAPTER VI Return to England

After leaving Quebec the good ship *Inconstant* ran aground, was on fire twice, sailed through twenty-five days of continual gale and storm, and reached Plymouth harbour, November 26, in weather too rough to permit a landing for four days. Lord Durham could not find peace on either land or sea. A sick man when he went on board, he appeared at dinner the first evening, then ran a high temperature, was in bed for a day, got up too soon, and was tormented with the pains in his head and face for the whole of the three weeks and a half.

In the meantime his home-coming was causing much more of a sensation in England than even he realized. The country had been all agog over Canada and Lord Durham in August, not only because they formed the centre of a ministerial crisis, but because the majority of the people – who always like to have their politics dramatized by personalities – saw in the whole affair of the ordinance a renewal of the old duel between Brougham and Durham, its interest heightened now by the fact that both were at daggers drawn with the Prime Minister. This interest might have been thrust aside by the Chartist and Corn Law agitations, but Durham had prevented that, first by his sensational proclamation and now by coming home, as the popular imagination fondly believed, blazing with passion against the Government. The Ministry was in a more dangerous position than ever. A dozen Radicals voting against them in the House of Commons could effect its downfall, and the Radicals were nettled by Lord John Russell's repeated declarations about the finality of the Reform Bill. Disliked by the bulk of the Ministerialists and distrusted on account of his advanced liberalism, Durham was strong with the more liberal of the Whigs, among whom he had warm friends and disciples. The Radicals, though they would follow Brougham on a Canadian issue because of their sympathy with supposedly downtrodden colonists, had by no means lost their old fondness and admiration for Durham. All candid observers of the situation agreed that Durham held the fate of the Government in the hollow of his hand.

The ministers were more worried than at any time in their precarious career. As the *Inconstant* approached the shores of England they were fairly shivering in their official togas. A month before Melbourne had written to Russell: 'It is very odd to see the terror that Durham inspires. Everybody has always been afraid of him. They seem to me to fear him much more than they do Brougham.'[1] Melbourne himself did not fear either Brougham or Durham, yet by the end of November a strain of anxiety had broken through his insouciance.

And the duel between Durham and Brougham! Public interest looked forward eagerly to their meeting in the Lords. What a day it would be! Spoil-sports had prevented it four years ago, but it was sure to come off this time. The ends of the earth were watching for it. While Durham was still at sea, Macaulay wrote from India:

> Lord Brougham, I have a notion, will often wish that he had left Lord Durham alone. Lord Durham will be in the House of Lords, with his pugnacious spirit, and with his high reputation among the Radicals. In oratorical abilities there is, of course, no comparison between the men; but Lord Durham has quite talents enough to expose Lord Brougham and has quite as much acrimony and a great deal more nerve than Lord Brougham himself.[2]

Brougham was meting out justice at the Judicial Committee of the Privy Council, 'in high spirits and looking forward with exceeding zest and eagerness to the fun he is to have in the House of Lords'. Brougham would have enjoyed fighting Durham, no doubt, if the latter felt he must fight. But, now that he had evened accounts with him, the greatest fun of all would be to join hands with him to break Melbourne. Yet there was a cloud now and then across those high spirits, for as Durham's storm-swept ship was lumbering homeward, a new move rendered the situation more complicated than ever. Some of the Radical leaders revived the idea of forming a really Liberal party by bringing together Liberal Whigs and Radicals under Durham's leadership. The Whigs who dissented might then join the Tories, if they pleased; the progressive elements in the electorate would at last have something to wax enthusiastic over and, whatever happened in Parliament, the country would return the party to power with Lord Durham as Prime Minister. In behalf of that conception John Stuart Mill wrote a powerful article for the *Westminster Review*. Since the *Westminster* was a quarterly, this did not appear in its pages until December, after Durham landed, but advance-sheets were circulated and lengthy extracts appeared in the *Spectator* of November 24.[3] The article linked the advocacy of Lord Durham's leadership of a Liberal party with a review of his administration in Canada, from which the defence of the proclamation has already been quoted.[4] Only a few passages can be given here.

There were consequences dependent upon Lord Durham's mission to Canada calculated to make it the turning point of English politics for years to come and to raise every incident connected with it, however secondary in appearance, to an event in history.[5] *. . . In addition to so large a portion of territory, there was delivered into his keeping the character also of England; her reputation in the eyes of all nations for wisdom and foresight . . . at one of those critical instants when Europe, Asia, and America were looking on to watch how England would act under trial, – whether like an irritated tyrant, or a serious and thoughtful ruler, intent upon profiting by experience and gathering from her failures that most valuable kind of knowledge, that of her own mistakes. . . . There was one man to whom his party might look, to whom it had for years looked, . . . as the leader of a future administration, . . . Lord Durham. . . . And he alone was so marked out for the position by every consideration of character, situation, and past services, that if he chose to assume it he could do so without rivalry or dispute; and the whole of its effective strength would come forth at his voice and give him that decisive majority in the House of Commons with which he might again break the power of aristocratic faction.*[6] *. . . The battle for the good government of*

Canada, as well as for reform in Great Britain will have to be fought here. . . .

Mill had no political ambitions. This was a work of pure patriotism. 'Our noble friend Mill,' Wakefield wrote to Molesworth, 'is ordered to Malta. His lungs are not organically diseased, but will be if he remains here. He thought the other day the disease was mortal, but yet fagged away at this Durham case as if he had expected to live for ever.'[7] Few review articles have exerted such an influence. The public support of Durham's administration in Canada, imperilled by the proclamation of October 9, was recaptured by Mill's marshalling of fact and argument; and due largely to his eloquent advocacy, there was a widespread Durham movement by the time the Proconsul landed at Plymouth.

During the four days in Plymouth Sound before he landed, Lord Durham received three letters from Wakefield in London.[8] The first was written, December 24:

The beginning of a change of feeling has been produced partly by your near approach, and partly by a notion, now beginning to prevail, that the state of the case is generally misunderstood here, or not at all known. Your coming straight home to face your foes has had the effect that pluck *always has with Englishmen. People say now —* 'Well, he must have something to say for himself, or he would not return in this way — perhaps he will put everybody in the wrong after all'. *The Govt. people especially are puzzled and alarmed by this evidence of your resolution and self-reliance.* They will submit to your terms — *they feel that they are at your mercy. . . . I would not deceive you or mislead you for the world. You took me by the hand when I was proscribed; and I would die in your service. . . . The leading Tory paper of Liverpool has turned smack around in your favour since I was there — so will the* London Standard *next week, I think. . . . The grand point of Whigs & shufflers will be to spare you (for now, they no longer dare attack you) and to abuse your 'advisers'. I know, and will prove to you that the word of command has been given. 'Praise Durham; but fall hard on his* advisers.' *If this trick should succeed with you, they would then say that your acts in Canada were but nominally yours and really those of Turton, Buller, and myself. They go about now, saying that all the 'indiscretions' you have committed (such as the Proclamation) were our*

*doing. . . . I said that you would, and you do now, fill a larger
space in the politics of the world than any other man. . . . The
fright at your return is increasing every hour. . . .*

In his letter of the 27th Wakefield reported that Durham's
position was improved and that a description of the effects of
the proclamation had removed all objections with 'candid
people'. 'Scarcely anybody knows anything of Canadian affairs
– still less of the motives, tendencies, or results of your acts. If
I had remained here, I should have gone along with the class of
objectors.' While this letter of Wakefield's informed him that
he would be ruined politically if he supported the Government,
one from Ellice conveyed a solemn warning that he would be
damned both in this world and in the next if he did not support
it. Ellice warned him especially against the 'recommendations
of the writer in the *Westminster Review*'.[9] There were other
letters and plenty of advice, which Durham welcomed because
he had to make his running through a broken field. In his third
letter Wakefield stated that he was hastening to Plymouth and
that Durham should make no move until he arrived with news
that could not be trusted to a letter; he had heard from
Molesworth who would follow Durham 'through thick and
thin'.[10]

There is enough in Wakefield's letters to awaken a suspicion
that there may have been some truth in a statement by the
Devonport Gazette that there were intervals in the storm during
which Lord Durham might have landed, but he took advantage
of a good excuse to secure time 'to read papers, collect opinions,
and see how the public pulse beat'.[11] He made his landing at last
on the 30th. There was no official reception, and some of his
friends represented this as the ultimate 'shabbiness' of the Government, but it is not very clear that it was the Government's
duty to tender such a reception. Durham had shown before that
he had a way of imagining that certain honours were 'customary'
when they were not customary at all. But the popular reception
was most enthusiastic. Sir William Molesworth, who for a year
and a half had been attempting to line up the Radicals against
the Government and had come down from London to muster
all the local influence he possessed in behalf of the Durham
movement, occupied the chair at a public meeting at Devonport,
December 1. Addresses were presented to Lord Durham from
Devonport and Plymouth. After repeating his Glasgow creed

and speaking with frank boastfulness of his achievements in Canada, he said:

In this career of, I humbly but fearlessly venture to assert, complete success, I have been suddenly arrested. . . . To me personally such disappointment is great . . . but to the people of British North America the crisis is most alarming and dangerous and throws into the shade all personal considerations which can attach to the treatment which I have received. Every feeling, therefore, of my heart, every faculty of my mind is engaged in the task of providing here for the security and advancement of those important national interests.[12]

Wakefield, who was still spying out the land, as well as helping to stir up the Radicals, and writing for the papers 'an account of "Durham Manifestations in the West of England"' reported that all the Reformers who were not content to see the Reform Bill a finality were, after having been rendered apathetic by Melbourne, now roused to action.

'They say – "Now we have got a man who can, and will, go through with Reform.". . . Your return, in circumstances which lead them to hope that you will act independently of the Melbourne Whigs, gives them heart; and they will support you through thick and thin if you are true to yourself.'[13]

One wonders how far Wakefield was running ahead of Durham's wishes in all this. He was usually over-zealous in the causes that captured his heart. Durham himself gave no indication of taking a stand against the Government in his replies to addresses at meetings in his honour at Ashburton, Exeter, and Honiton. Before he reached Exeter, news arrived of the outbreak of the insurrection in Canada. His critics remarked that these events were hardly consistent with the boasted success of his administration. But for purposes of argument the insurrection was a two-edged sword, and in his Exeter speech he blamed the insurrection on the proceedings in Parliament and used it to show 'how the best interests of the Empire are affected by proceedings founded on party feeling and political animosity',[14] which was an ambiguous expression referable to either Melbourne or the Tories.

Brougham could use the news of the Canadian insurrection against both Melbourne and Durham. According to Greville:

Brougham, who is sitting every day at the Privy Council, is always growling at him [Durham] sarcastically, and was much pleased when news came of the fresh outbreak in Canada, and his disappointment was equally evident when he heard it was so rapidly quelled. He was reading the newspaper in my room when Denman came in and announced that young Ellice was released, and the insurrection suppressed. Brougham did not take his eyes off the paper and merely muttered, 'It will soon break out again'.[15]

Brougham was chafing these days at the Radical play for Durham, which seemed to be the only thing that could spoil his game. He may have extracted comfort from Paley's *Natural Theology*, which he was editing – and improving – while at the same time he was translating Cicero's *De Corona*, editing a volume of his own speeches, and writing his *Statesmen and Philosophers of the Reign of George III*.

Melbourne was much more displeased. This Durham excitement was threatening him from both outside and inside his political household. Greville, who disliked Durham quite as much as Melbourne did, wrote: 'If notoriety upon any terms could satisfy anybody, Lord Durham would have ample reason for contentment, as his name is in everybody's mouth, and the chief topic of every newspaper and political periodical.'[16] Melbourne was still determined not to 'court and truckle'.[17] but he appeared to be willing to do anything short of that. He went down to London to be there when Durham arrived, but Durham was loitering along the way – receiving ovations. Durham and his Glasgow creed, democracy, the middle class, this ranting about Reform – how Melbourne despised it all! Durham had been in a great hurry to leave Canada in order to lay important information before the British Government, but here was the British Government preserving its soul in patience until His Excellency was through with his triumphal tour! (As a matter of fact, the Canadian cause was being served very well by keeping Melbourne on tenter-hooks.)

When Durham reached London on the 7th to begin – or resume – the writing of his Report, he found at his house a duplicate of Glenelg's dispatch conveying the Queen's displeasure at his proclamation.[18] The language was severe enough, but bringing the Queen into it was particularly galling. A fresh wave of anger swept over him. He must control it. What he could do for Canada was the great consideration, and that would not be helped now by an attack on these contemptible ministers. But he would not meet them personally. Political action was one thing; personal intercourse was another matter.

The Government selected as their emissary E. J. ('Ben') Stanley. He was not a minister, but was chief government whip and Secretary of the Treasury. He had been at one time private secretary to Lord Durham and, like every man who had served him in that capacity, was devoted to him and enthusiastic about his ability and personal kindness. He had been a disciple of Durham in the days of the Reform Bill, and when invited to serve under Melbourne he had written to Durham stating that he would not do so without the latter's express approbation. Stanley saw him on the 8th and apparently they talked things over in a general manner. Durham was 'calm and quiet enough', but did not conceal the fact that he had been deeply hurt. 'He expressed no animosity or resentment against any one, but said that he thought the Government had acted towards him with ill-will, and that he had been made an object of persecution.'[19] Melbourne probably found this strange calmness as disturbing as any feature of the situation. Durham calm! and under such circumstances! Surely they were becoming invested with mysteries. Whatever might come, Melbourne would stand up to him. He appreciated the advice of the Duke of Richmond who had stood up to Durham during the stormy scenes in the Grey Cabinet over the Reform Bill: 'Be steady, be very firm with your ex-Governor, or there will be the devil to pay.'[20]

On the 10th Lady Durham, feeling the situation keenly, wrote to the Queen, resigning her position as a lady-in-waiting. She took this action on her own initiative, Lord Durham attempting neither to encourage nor to dissuade her. 'They [the Ministers] behaved most shamefully about the Queen, which rendered Louisa's resignation quite necessary.'[21] Lady Durham wrote to her mother: 'We did not come down intending to take this step and Lambton was prepared to be of what use he could to the Ministers.' But after the dispatch which they sent him 'expressing the Queen's disapprobation', there was no other course to pursue. In subsequent letters she wrote:

I feel a most sincere interest for the Queen and regret that any coldness should exist with her personally, but she is entirely in Lord Melbourne's hands, of course sees with his eyes, and I don't see how I could have kept my place about her without putting her in an awkward situation. . . . It grieves me very much

that the breach should be so decided with some of the Cabinet,
but I must own with regard to Lord Melbourne that I do feel
great resentment, and I don't think I shall ever be able to forgive
him. I think his conduct from the moment Lambton quitted
England was base and ungenerous to a degree. . . . Ld. John
Russell is the only one among the Ministers who has written a
kind letter in the whole proceeding. It does seem hard that the
result of an undertaking entered upon with most generous mo-
tives, at great sacrifice and risk, should be complete desertion
and proscription. . . . I cannot tell you how I long to have every-
thing known that has taken place with respect to Lambton. The
private letters from Ld. Melbourne and Ld. Glenelg approving
of the ordinance[22] can never appear, but I think enough must
come out to make his course very triumphant.[23]

Demonstrations in support of Lord Durham were being
rapidly organized throughout the country, and wherever Reformers met his name was cheered. This popular movement,
which had gained ground so quickly, offered him revenge on
the ministers who had betrayed and insulted him, a splendid
opportunity for personal vindication, and the chance of becoming Prime Minister. People were already speculating as to who
should hold certain offices when Lord Durham came into
power.[24] From the standpoint of English politics, such a course
was fraught with serious questions; from the standpoint of
Canada there was no question at all. It would take time; but
the Canadian situation, since the outbreak of the second insurrection, demanded that radical changes should be effected
immediately. His mind was all aglow with the conceptions
which he was writing into his Report and which alone could
save Canada for a prosperous future and create an Empire more
glorious, because more free, than any that had been conceived
before. But what chance had such a Report in the immediate
future if he allied himself with those who were seeking the
overthrow of Melbourne? A permanent bond of Empire on the
basis of Responsible Government! The Melbournites – Russell,
Lansdowne, Poulett Thomson, Howick, Duncannon – might be
converted to it, but these Radicals never.[25] If the ultimate success of such a movement should carry Durham to the Premier-
ship, most of his followers would be men who had no use for
the idea of a permanent imperial connexion, and since they were
doctrinaires of the most obstinate type, they would not be

brought into line. No, the fate of his Report, of Canada, of the Empire that was to be, was bound up with that of the Melbourne Government. He despised, and in his present mood probably hated, them all personally, and ambition and the honours of the day were as dear to him as to any man. But whatever might happen to himself, he had set his hand to the plough and he would not turn back, he would fulfil his promise to the people of Canada, he would follow his vision. In doing so he was accounted a fool by his best friends. Among others, Buller and Wakefield, thinking mainly of his political future, urged him to accept the Radical leadership and even to join with Brougham to overthrow Melbourne.[26]

That was the situation irrespective of his recommendation of the union of Upper and Lower Canada, which had not been finally determined upon; and may have been to some extent the result of the fact that he was as much dependent upon Melbourne for the other recommendations of the Report, as Melbourne was upon him for the life of his Government. Melbourne was averse to placing a provincial legislature (even in a federal scheme) in the hands of the French, the legislative union of the two Canadas had been advocated in the leading government newspaper, and the Montreal merchants, who regarded it as a matter of life and death, were in close touch with the Ministers through the English firms interested in the Canada trade.

Although Durham was in no hurry to declare his unwillingness to oppose the Government, an address from the Westminster Reform Association forced his hand. The address itself was innocent enough. It was of the usual complimentary order and the principles professed could be readily accepted. But the newspapers carried accounts of the meeting itself in the issues containing the address. The freedom with which these ultra-Radicals discussed their champion – one referred to him as a 'trump card' and another said that 'he considered all public men great humbugs but Lord Durham was as little a humbug as could be found among them' – might be overlooked. But the principles advocated went far beyond those of the address and were capable of being interpreted as favourable to Chartism, then in its physical force stage and regarded as a menace to the foundations of social order. Practically every speaker made a declaration against the Government. One said that 'there was little doubt but that the noble earl would stand in opposition to the Ministers', and another hoped that Durham and Brougham would form a political alliance. After reading the reports of the meeting Durham refused to receive the deputation that was to present him with the address. 'I will not pretend ignorance of ulterior designs on the part of those who agreed to the address, which are completely at variance with the objects and principles to which I have adverted.'[27] He ultimately accepted the address after receiving a letter in which the officials of the society explained that they did not accept responsibility for the sentiments expressed at the meeting.

This was sufficiently discouraging to the anti-Melbourne Radicals. Lord Durham worked hard at his Report and declined all invitations to speak at public meetings. Charles Buller wrote in the concluding section of his sketch of the Canadian mission:

Many of those who enthusiastically rallied around him on his return, have since reproached him that he threw away the opportunity of complete justification and satisfaction, and refused to take that position in the political world that seemed to invite him. But this course he took after full and anxious consideration, and took I think as wisely as I am sure he did it honestly. Abstaining from all public part in general politics, he reserved himself for Canada alone.[28]

In the meantime, Lord Duncannon had written asking to see him. Duncannon, a member of the Cabinet, had been Durham's colleague on the Reform Bill committee, was a brother of Lady Grey, had reconciled Grey and Durham after their quarrel in 1833, and frequently acted for the Government in delicate situations involving personal relationships. Durham replied to him that he could have no communication with any member of the Cabinet who had treated him so scandalously. A little later an attempt was made, at the suggestion of Henry Stephenson, to bring Lord Durham and Lord John Russell together. These two, never intimate, had always respected and admired each other, and Durham had recently written to Russell a warm letter of appreciation of his speech on the Ordinance, in which he implied that Russell was the only member of the Cabinet who had treated him decently. This good feeling between the two men who had made the Reform Bill was to assume historical importance in the establishment of a new order in Canada. But nothing came of the attempt to bring them together at this time. Durham adhered to his position in regard to personal relationship with members of the Cabinet until the middle of January, when he consented to see his brother-in-law, Lord Howick, and Lord Duncannon. It is not likely that family influence effected this, because Lady Durham's letters show that she was more bitter against the ministers than her husband, but the relationship made it easier for Durham to relent. Following this meeting, which proved to be quite amicable, something of a political entente was established. Durham had desired that in any case for the sake of his Canadian policy, but it had been difficult to effect so long as he drew the line in regard to a personal meeting. Even the Turton difficulty was overcome by agreeing to a statement which saved the pride of both Durham and Melbourne.

From his arrival in London, December 7, Durham had been working hard on his Report. Some of its analytical sections were probably written in Canada, but it is clear from Buller's *Sketch* that the constructive part was written after his return to England. He declined a number of private as well as public invitations on account of this work, and even refused to allow himself any Christmas vacation. The Government, who probably thought it was farther along than it was and had no idea that it was so lengthy, were constantly pressing him. He assured them that it would be ready by the opening of Parliament, and he kept his promise. Lady Durham remarked in her journal that 'he worked incessantly until he had completed the Report'. Speaking later in the House of Lords he said that he had finished the Report before the meeting of Parliament 'at the cost of considerable labour and much anxiety of mind'. He wrote to his brother Hedworth: 'I am devoting myself to the winding up of my Canadian business', and to Charles Grey: 'I am, and all the staff, working very hard to get my Report as High Commissioner ready for the meeting of Parliament'.[29] Lady Durham wrote to her brother: 'We have not stirred from town since we came. Lambton has been very busy getting up his reports,[30] but he has been very quiet and I am happy to say very well.'[31]

After Lord Durham had been already working on his Report in London for several weeks, Charles Buller, who returned from Canada, accompanied by Adam Thom, on December 22, attempted to reopen the question of federation – if indeed it had ever been closed. This appears from Edward Ellice's letters to Durham.

Ellice wrote, Sunday, December 30:

I think of going up on Thursday to remain with you a couple of days before another visiting expedition to the north. I will then say all my say about Canada plans and should like, if there is no objection to it, to have a free conference with you, Buller, and Wakefield on this subject. If you see any objection to this, I will discuss them with you alone. In answer to a letter from Ld. J. Russell asking me to write my ideas on paper, either to Ld. Melbourne or Ld. Glenelg, I have told him that I wait to hear what you have to propose, with an anxious hope that I may be able to concur in your recommendations to the Government and to support them in Parliament. . . .[32]

Ellice's next letter is dated merely 'Tuesday evening', probably Tuesday, January 8, after a delayed or protracted visit to London:

My dear D., – One word before I set off to say that C. Buller rather disturbed me last night by insisting very much on the recommendation of a Federative Union of all those provinces. Now admitting this course to be ultimately the best policy, – no man in his sober senses would advise, and no secretary of state would act upon his advice, that a bill should be prepared for this purpose, without previously consulting the Legislatures of N. Scotia, N. Brunswick and U. Canada, – and if you will only give the loop-hole to the Colonial Office, they will of course avail themselves of it to defer a settlement until they have time to consult them, – or ad Graecas Calendas. . . .

Your way of viewing the subject leads to very different conclusions, – an immediate settlement of the Canada question, to come into operation at the earliest possible period, as not only politic but absolutely necessary in the temper of many minds [?][33] in Canada, – but so framed as to be the foundation of the wider scheme if the colonies should think an union of the whole advisable to promote their interests and to secure their connexion with this country. If you decide on the main features of the lesser plan, Wakefield and Thom would work up the details for you.[34]

In his next letter, written towards the end of January, Ellice says that he has not written, 'for I have nothing to add to what we talked about so fully in town'. He regrets Durham's inability to get off on a holiday to the country, but appreciates the fact that 'it is essential that you should get your work off your hands to enable you to have your mind and your time free for the House of Lords'. He is glad that Durham has seen Howick and Duncannon and hopes that they will support Durham's views in the Cabinet.[35]

As these are the only passages in Ellice's letters to Durham which refer to the latter's 'plan', and the two men did not meet except during the brief visit to London to which reference is made, Ellice's direct influence on the Report was limited to that occasion and the letter which followed. This was in the direction of confirming a decision which Durham had already made to recommend the legislative union of Upper and Lower Canada in the face of Buller's persistent advocacy of an immediate federation of all the provinces.

We have referred to Buller's later declaration that Lord Durham gave up his federation project because of the second insurrection and to the statement in the Report to the effect that it was abandoned because it was dangerous at the time to give the French-Canadians control of a provincial legislature under a federal plan. But it may have been quite as much the influence of the second insurrection on the attitude of the British Government and electorate. If Durham himself was hesitant, the knowledge of the Government's position on the matter was decisive. He realized that the fate of his Report and that of Canada was bound up with that of the Melbourne Government. He had conceived a great imperial dream, revolutionary in its character, epoch-making in its scope. To some features of that – even its greatest, Responsible Government – he might hope to convert the Ministry. But in regard to giving the French-Canadians control of a Lower Canada legislature under any plan of government, they were adamant. As Melbourne put it, 'We can never suffer the French to govern or to have much influence in Canada again, and they being the majority in Lower Canada, this will make it difficult to establish anything like a popular government', and again: 'It is laid down by all as a fundamental principle that the French must not be reinstated in power in Lower Canada.'[36] Melbourne had behind him in that position the great majority of the British electorate, lamentably prejudiced against the French-Canadians and shocked now by two rebellions. Furthermore, what would happen to Lord Durham's recommendation of Responsible Government if it were accompanied by that of a federal scheme? That would mean the setting up of a French Cabinet in Lower Canada and the control of every department of a provincial government by French-Canadians. It would have provided the crowning argument against Responsible Government. And Lord Durham's Report would have interest to-day only as one of those magnificent wrecks that lie strewn along the by-ways of history. The recommendation of the legislative union of the two Canadas cleared Melbourne's difficulties, and also left the way open for Responsible Government and for an ultimate union of all the provinces into that nation of which Durham dreamed. The Great Reform Bill and Lord Durham's Report opened the gates to developments whose possibilities astound each succeeding generation. They did so safely and effectively, they produced neither tumult nor reaction because the principal author of both was not only one of the greatest of political visionaries but was wise enough to so frame his recommendations for immediate action that he secured the largest realization of his visions that was possible in the existing political situation. The Melbourne Government sympathized with Lord Durham's ultimate aims as little as had the Reform Bill administration, but the one as surely as the other – and as unconsciously – took irrevocable steps towards their fulfilment. By playing his game adroitly in the existing political situation, Lord Durham succeeded in placing first the people of Britain and then the people of Canada in a position from which they could control their own political futures. They justified his faith and completed the fulfilment of his hopes – and much more besides which even he could not foresee.

Proof-sheets of the Report were submitted to the Ministers on the 31st of January 1839 and it was officially presented to the Colonial Office on February 4. On the 5th Parliament met. All the excitement of a ministerial crisis prevailed, and Durham and his affairs were still the centre of attention. It was not yet known that negotiations had taken place between him and the Government, and all sorts of rumours were in the air. A political public, bewildered and animated, was on the look-out for every straw that indicated how the wind blew. Hardly was Parliament opened – the speech from the throne was not yet read – when Lord Durham was on his feet to ask when his Report would be laid before the House. Lord Melbourne replied that the Ministers would need some time for its consideration, and that he would bring it down as soon as possible.

On the 8th *The Times* printed a large section of the Report and announced that other instalments would follow. It was splendid copy. Lord Durham's Report could hardly have appeared under more sensational circumstances. And the sensation was enhanced by rumours that he had sent it to *The Times* himself. That day in the Lords he asked again when the Government intended to bring down his Report. 'He had seen with the deepest regret the publication of a part and a part only of the Report.' Lord Melbourne replied that the whole of the Report would be laid before the House on the 11th. He said that the Government had now no choice in the matter and must present it all, since the newspaper in question undoubtedly possessed a complete copy.

There is a tradition to the effect that Wakefield sent the Report to *The Times*. One version has it that he feared that some parts of the section dealing with public lands, his particular field of investigation, were to be omitted and that he took the most effectual means to prevent that. Another story represents Lord Durham as giving his permission, then recalling it, and Wakefield replying, 'It has gone, my Lord'. But that is incredible in view of Lord Durham's statement in the House of Lords that he was not 'in any degree responsible or an accessory to the publication of the Report'. There were other places than the Durham camp from which a 'leak' may have occurred. Two thousand copies of the Report had been printed by the Government at Lord Durham's suggestion. They had permitted him to distribute some of these among his friends ('not more than half a dozen', Durham said). Durham had from the first intended that the Report should be published in full, and it is difficult, in view of their authorizing the printing of so many copies, to believe that the Government intended anything else. But parts of it were very frank, and Melbourne was probably well pleased when *The Times* forced his hand. It matters little who supplied *The Times* with a copy; the primary reason why the whole of Lord Durham's Report saw the light of day lay in a political situation, largely of Brougham's making, in which the Government was dependent on Lord Durham's support.

On the day *The Times* began the publication of the Report Lord Glenelg made an announcement. It is seldom that a minister rises in Parliament to state that he has been dismissed from office at the request of his colleagues, but that substantially was what Glenelg did. He had been offered another position in the Cabinet, but had refused it. The public, realizing by this time that the Government and Durham were working together, believed that Glenelg had been offered as a sacrifice to appease the wrath of the 'dragon'. Wakefield reflected another interpretation in a letter to Durham: 'Below the bar of the Lords yesterday, Ld. Glenelg's resignation was considered a great triumph for you. It was said "The Report has shot him; who'll be the next?" ' The inside story is that some of the ministers, and more especially Howick and Russell, who were presumably the most favourable to Durham, had been for some time disgusted with Glenelg's conduct of affairs in the Colonial Office. Just at the time when the Report was first presented to them, Glenelg and Howick clashed on Jamaican policy and Howick threatened to resign unless the colonial policy of the Government was placed on a sound basis, which was understood to include the dismissal of Glenelg. Russell stated that he would resign if Howick did. Then notice was served on Glenelg. Melbourne told the Queen that although he knew that Glenelg was incompetent, he would have retained him in office if it had not meant the break-up of the Ministry.[37]

Three days after this last sensation Melbourne laid the Report before the House of Lords. The Tories were still sniping at Durham. They rang the changes on the question – how did the Report get to *The Times*? – as though it were a great national issue, and their insinuations were as insulting as urbanity and mock-courtesy could make them. Then there was the eternal question of the expenses of Lord Durham's mission. A few days before, in the Commons, the old tale had been unfolded and a demand made that every champagne cork should be accounted for. Durham had stated that his personal expenses had all been paid out of his own purse, that he had refused a salary, and that he was £10,000 the poorer as a result of the mission. Now the Marquis of Westmeath stated that since Lord Durham made a claim of £10,000 against the Government perhaps the matter should be looked into. It would be too bad if the noble earl were not recompensed since (in a supreme flight of sarcasm) 'for aught he knew the Report was cheap at £10,000'.

Lord Durham replied that he wished 'to set the noble marquis right, if the noble marquis chose to be set right'. He had not said that he had a financial claim against the Government and would never think of presenting the matter in that light. He had simply made an explanation in regard to his personal expenses.

Was this the mode in which their discussion and their debates relating to Canada were to be carried on? If noble lords wished to indulge in personalities, he offered himself to them to pursue the course which seemed the best. Let them say of him what they pleased; let them set apart one day for personal attacks; but then let these things be finished, and then let them come to this great and important question and the mighty interests involved in it without any intrusion of low, petty and personal feelings.

On this day that saw the presentation of Lord Durham's Report to Parliament *The Times* published its third instalment. Other English papers were already printing it, and within a few months it was to appear – in part or in full – in serial form in the columns of Australian as well as Canadian newspapers. It was very different from the ordinary dry-as-dust state paper. It was free from the clap-trap of political speeches; it was lucid, spirited, forceful. Its facts and arguments were marshalled with a clarity and power which the common man could appreciate and admire. It maintained throughout a grandeur of style, thought, and spirit, and was as remarkable for an easy and natural eloquence as it was for an absence of forced sentiment and purple patches. Its faith and patriotism were as sane as they were inspiring. The common people received it the more enthusiastically because it was the work of one of their heroes. Britishers overseas adopted it as the corner-stone of Empire.

✿ ✿ ✿

CHAPTER VII Lord Durham's Report

Lord Durham's Report has never lacked high praise. In our own day competent historians, accustomed to write in a judicial spirit and chary in the use of superlatives, have referred to it as 'the Magna Charta of Canadian liberties', 'the Magna Charta of the colonies', 'the most valuable document in the English language on the subject of colonial policy', 'the most notable of British state papers', 'the most important document that has ever been presented relative to British America', 'that greatest of all documents ever published in regard to colonial affairs', 'the recognized source of the prosperity effected in Canada since the union'; and stated that it 'laid the foundations of a reasonable and practical colonial policy', 'has been the salvation of the Empire', 'broadened once for all the lines of constructive statesmanship in all that relates to the colonial policy of England', 'laid down the fundamentals of colonial liberty that have given to British imperialism whatever qualities of endurance it possesses', 'entitles him to the title of the greatest colonial statesman in British history', that all the self-governing dominions owe their freedom to it, and that 'the importance of the great Report can hardly be exaggerated'.[1]

All of these statements are literally true. Lord Durham's Report is more than the charter of Canadian democracy and self-government, the corner-stone of the first British nation beyond the seas. It is the great watershed of British imperial history. It is one of the few events of world-history of which one can say that this is the beginning of something absolutely new under the sun. When the unique type of empire which it created has completely worked out its destiny, it will be time to venture a final estimate of the significance of this Report.

But in its very greatness there lurks a peril for the student of history. Writers endeavouring to establish some particular interpretation of the facts of Canadian or imperial history frequently quote from Lord Durham's Report with a flourish as if to say 'That proves it'. Their readers need to be warned that although the principles of the Report belong to the immortalities, its record of historical facts is frequently misleading. It must be remembered that Lord Durham was not an historian, that he was only five months in Canada, and that although he had access to most important documentary sources, the whole period from his appointment as High Commissioner to the presentation of his Report was one year and sixteen days, crowded with practical problems, complicated politics, drama, worry, and illness. The result so far as historical accuracy is concerned is about what might be expected of a man of industry and analytical power, assisted by able lieutenants, but neither he nor they gifted in the arts of research and criticism. When the facts – real and supposed – passed from the stage of investigation to that of expression and description, they were further transformed by that habit of exaggeration which was the concomitant of Lord Durham's remarkable imagination and temperament. From this point of view, the worst part of the Report was the section on Upper Canada, in which province Lord Durham spent only ten days. Buller and some of his other assistants saw more of Upper Canada, and it may be assumed that they supplied the information in regard to that province. It is apparent that they picked it up from Reformers with the same facility with which they absorbed the Reform point of view. This section contains so many inaccuracies that the teacher of history, who is concerned only with facts, might do well to keep his students away from it altogether. But for those to whom the history of opinions is of equal value with that of facts, the section possesses an historical value, quite independent of those higher qualities which the Report reflects in almost every page; it is a remarkably clear presentation of the Reformers' interpretation of the political situation in 1838 with its historical background. It also contains a diagnosis that is more accurate than the history. And, even on this factual side, there is, when critically sifted, a mass of valuable information in the Report. For the British Government and people at the time, woefully ignorant in regard to Canada, its informative value far outweighed its misleading features.

But the greatest weakness of the Report – all the more striking because it marked Durham's only failure in the sphere of political prophecy – is its treatment of the French-Canadians. Lord Durham was a statesman of great breadth of view, but he was not that Utopian monster – a man without prejudice. The British merchants in Lower Canada took him at a disadvantage with their constant talk of the conflict being essentially a racial one and the only remedy a policy of anglifying the French-Canadians. Durham came to Canada with the prejudice of the British ruling class against the French-Canadians as a rebellious and contumacious race and an intense English feeling which sometimes closed the door to broader sympathies. This attitude was strengthened by the statements of the Radicals, the one group in England who sympathized with the French-Canadians. They had raised the cry 'emancipate your colonies'. Hume and Roebuck, who were known to be in constant touch with the French, had attributed to the latter their own desire that they should be freed from the fetters of British rule. In the weeks following the Lower Canada rebellion of 1837 these Radical leaders and their friends had repeatedly represented it as a rising of the *whole* French-Canadian people, who were desirous of establishing an independent republic on the banks of the St. Lawrence. It never occurred to Durham to doubt these statements – were not Hume and Roebuck the 'friends of Canada'? –

and he ultimately wrote these fallacies into his Report and marred what was in many respects a brilliant analysis of the situation in Lower Canada.

He over-estimated the racial factor in the conflict and under-estimated the economic, and even the constitutional. In relation to the economic situation, too, he was subject to a common failing of being unsympathetic on the reverse side of his enthusiasms. As the British statesman who saw most clearly and most gladly the vivifying effects of the Industrial Revolution on the British body politic, he saw many passing sights in Lower Canada that suggested nothing but elimination in the interests of progress. He saw in the aggressive British merchant-leaders of Montreal and Quebec the hope of the province, and he allowed them to give him an exaggerated conception of the backwardness and hopelessness of the French. He failed to realize that with their different outlook the French-Canadians had essential con-tributions to make to that nation of which he dreamed so nobly.

He paid the French-Canadians some sincere compliments. 'They are mild and kindly, frugal, industrious and honest, very sociable, cheerful and hospitable, and distinguished for a courtesy and real politeness, which pervades every class of society.' In religious matters 'a degree of practical toleration known in very few communities has existed in this colony [Lower Canada] from the period of the conquest down to the present time'. The Catholic priesthood 'have, to a very remark-able degree, conciliated the goodwill of persons of all creeds; and I know of no parochial clergy in the world whose practice of all the Christian virtues, and zealous discharge of their clerical duties, is more universally admitted, and has been productive of more beneficial consequences'. One paragraph is so sympathetic with the French that it might almost have been written by one of themselves, but it is followed almost immedi-ately by a description of their unprogressiveness that is so extreme that it would seem almost impossible that the French-Canadian people could ever forgive the man who wrote it into a Report which he was determined to publish as a standard British interpretation of French Canada. But the generous recognition by French-Canadians in recent years of the greatness of Lord Durham's contributions to Canadian history is one of the many evidences that they and we have been able to build a nation finer spiritually than even he dreamed that it might be.

He was entirely mistaken in regard to the ease with which

the French might be anglified. That attachment to their ancient institutions which, in his political realism and zeal for progress he so easily despised, has proved to be so tenacious that every assault upon them has only served to strengthen them. In this subject alone of those which Lord Durham dealt with during his whole life he failed to be the man of the future and was simply the man of his day. That day knew little of the toughness of nationalism as compared with our understanding of it. British Imperialism had had no previous experience with a people of European origin so deeply rooted in a country which, though conquered, was that of their nativity and their creation. The analogy which he pretended to find in Louisiana was pitifully inadequate to the situation. The French-Canadians may have suffered from some of the deficiencies which he ascribed to them, but they more than made up for those by a pride which he failed to understand and which we, their neighbours and compatriots, are only beginning to appreciate at its true worth. Short as was the period of his stay in Canada, he might have learned to know the French better, and what the historian finds it much harder to forgive than the prejudices to which he was subject is his failure to establish more vital personal contacts with them.

But if to Durham's love for democracy there had been added the most thorough-going sympathy for the French-Canadians, those feelings would not have led so sound a political thinker to apply his great recommendation of Responsible Government to Lower Canada so long as it stood alone as a separate province. He was no doctrinaire prating of 'self-determination' under all circumstances. He would still have seen that no one's happiness could have been served by granting self-government – even subject to the imperial reservations which he suggested – to a province on the Lower St. Lawrence, dominated by a people different in race and their whole point of view from the inhabitants of that larger territory whose entry and exit to the world were formed by that river. The primary recommendation of the Report was Responsible Government, but it was made conditional on the union of Upper and Lower Canada. Ultimately the Canadian people found in federation – with the interests dear to the French-Canadians conceded to the provincial government and 'trade and commerce', 'navigation and shipping', banking and all means of interprovincial communication assigned to the federal government – the better solution to this difficulty, satisfying alike the French agriculturists, the British merchants, and the larger national interests. Durham himself was one of the pioneers of the federal theory, but he had to find an immediate solution; federation was not practicable in his day, and so he turned to the union of the provinces. The policy of the Union was a sound one, in spite of the mistaken hope of anglifying the French. In itself the Union was a vast improvement over the previous situation; without it, neither Responsible Government in the 'forties nor Confederation in 1867 would have been possible.

With the exception of the anglifying of the French-Canadians, the recommendations of the Report were so well adapted to the situation that the passing of the years has only added to the appreciation of their wisdom. They undergird the life of Canada to-day at almost every point, and are reflected wherever British nations pursue their destinies under the inspiration of self-government and imperial partnership. They belong not only to our past, but to the larger future that beckons us. As we go back nearly a hundred years and follow the sweeping sentences in which they were advocated we find little that is offensive to our twentieth-century sentiments, and we seem to be reviewing political principles that bear the aspect of eternity.

The feature of the Report that is most commonplace now and was most revolutionary then is the recommendation of what has come to be known as Responsible Government. As no definition of what Lord Durham recommended in this respect can be adequate that does not follow the actual words of the Report, we quote here a few of its most significant passages:

'The wisdom of facilitating the management of public affairs, by entrusting it to the persons who have the confidence of the representative body, has never been recognized in the government of the North American colonies.'

Turning from this to the system of government prevailing in Great Britain he speaks of

'that wise principle of our Government, which has vested the direction of the national policy, and the distribution of patronage, in the leaders of the Parliamentary majority. . . .

It is not difficult to apply the case to our own country. Let it be imagined that at a general election the Opposition were to return 500 out of 658 members of the House of Commons, and that the whole policy of the ministry should be condemned, and every Bill introduced by it rejected by this immense majority. Let it be supposed that the Crown should consider it a point of honour and duty to retain a ministry so condemned and so thwarted; . . . and, I think, it will not be difficult to imagine the fate of such a system of government. Yet such was the system, such literally was the course of events in Lower Canada, and such in character, though not quite in degree, was the spectacle exhibited in Upper Canada, and, at one time or another, in every one of the North American colonies. To suppose that such a system would work well there implies belief that the French Canadians have enjoyed representative institutions for half a century without acquiring any of the characteristics of a free people; that Englishmen renounce every political opinion and feeling when they enter a colony, or that the spirit of Anglo-Saxon freedom is utterly changed and weakened among those who are transplanted across the Atlantic. . . . I know not how it is possible to secure that harmony in any other way than by administering the government on those principles which they have been found perfectly efficacious in Great Britain. . . . In England . . . when a ministry ceases to command a majority in Parliament on great questions of policy its doom is immediately sealed. . . .

'*Every purpose of popular control might be combined with every advantage of vesting the immediate choice of advisers in the Crown, were the Colonial Governor to be instructed to secure the co-operation of the Assembly in his policy, by entrusting its administration to such men as could command a majority; and if he were given to understand that he need count on no aid from home in any difference with the Assembly, that should not directly involve the relations between the Mother Country and the colony. This change might be effected by a single dispatch containing such instructions; or if any legal enactment were requisite, it would only be one that would render it necessary that the official acts of the Governor should be countersigned by some public functionary. . . . Nor can I conceive that it would be found impossible or difficult to conduct a Colonial Government with precisely that limitation of the respective powers which has been so long and so easily maintained in Great Britain. . . .*

I admit that the system which I propose would, in fact, place the internal government of the colony in the hands of the colonists themselves; and that we should thus leave to them the execution of the laws, of which we have long entrusted the making solely to them. Perfectly aware of the value of our colonial possessions, and strongly impressed with the necessity of maintaining our connection with them, I know not in what respect it can be desirable that we should interfere with their internal legislation in matters which do not affect their relations with the Mother Country. The matters which so concern us are very few. The constitution of the form of government – the regulation of foreign relation, and of trade with the Mother Country, the other British colonies, and foreign nations – and the disposal of the public lands, are the only points on which the Mother Country requires a control. . . . The colonists may not always know what laws are best for them, or which of their countrymen are the fittest for conducting their affairs; but, at least, they have a greater interest in coming to a right judgment on these points, and will take greater pains to do so than those whose welfare is very remotely and slightly affected by the good or bad legislation of these portions of the Empire. . . . The British people of the North American colonies are a people on whom we may safely rely, and to whom we must not grudge power.

The core of this recommendation is the adoption in British North America of the full system of British Cabinet Government – the establishment of a ministry controlled by Parliament, as Parliament was already controlled by the electorate, a ministry resigning or appealing to the people whenever it had clearly lost the support of a parliamentary majority. The Canadian people were to be permitted to govern themselves in matters of purely Canadian concern, in precisely the same way as the British people governed themselves. That central idea recurred time and time again in the Report. In the way of necessary machinery Lord Durham emphasized the issuing of instructions to Governors that they were to select as advisers only those who possessed the confidence of a parliamentary majority, the re-organization of the Executive Council so that it would consist, as did the British Ministry, of heads of governmental departments, and the adoption of the British rule that every official act of the Governor must be countersigned as a responsible minister. Recognizing that the new system must rest on practice and not on law, and that the maintenance of practice must depend on the Canadian people themselves, he recommended that the British Government should give no support to a Governor who found himself in conflict with a Canadian parliament on a Canadian question. Under these circumstances the Governor would be obliged to come to terms; and Lord Durham suggested that if the British Government, having once conceded the principle, were tempted to falter in its practice, they would be subject to the pressure of Canadian public opinion which could not under those circumstances be successfully defied and the operation of which, if a national union were ultimately formed, would be immediate and unquestioned.

But we must be on our guard against two fallacies, one that Lord Durham recommended in 1839 the Cabinet Government of 1927, and the other that he supposed that the usages of 1839 were to constitute for Canada a 'finality' that was to undergo no development with the passing of the years. While in 1839 the principle was fully established in Great Britain that the King acted on the advice of ministers who assumed responsibility for his actions, and who must be able to secure the support of a majority in the House of Commons, the sovereign exercised a personal control over the selection of such ministers which he does not exert to-day. Few Prime Ministers before that date had been able to secure from the King the appointment to ministerial office of all the men whom they desired to have. Some of the ablest statesmen of the time, including Charles Fox, had been excluded from cabinets because the King, for personal reasons, would not appoint them. When Lord Durham himself was selected for Cabinet office with the incoming of the Grey administration in 1830, he considered it to be a happy event worthy of comment that the King had given Lord Grey *carte blanche* in the matter of appointments. When Lord Melbourne formed his second administration in 1835, which was still in office in 1839, it was generally believed that the King would refuse to appoint either Lord Durham or Lord Brougham if Melbourne suggested them. The sovereign also exercised a wider choice in the appointment of the Prime Minister. To-day – except in very exceptional circumstances – usage always points to a particular individual whom the King shall invite to form a ministry. In Lord Durham's day he might select anyone, so long as the man selected could form a ministry which could secure a House of Commons majority. That difference may be largely due to the fact that the absence of the rigid party organization of the present day made it possible then for any one of a number of men to succeed in such a task, but certainly the King was afforded the opportunity of making a personal selection. According to constitutional usage at that time, the King might even dismiss a ministry that enjoyed the support of a majority in the Commons and ask the leader of the Opposition to form a government in the hope that he could secure such a majority; to-day the King does not dismiss ministries.[2] In 1835, Peel, leader of a party that was in a minority, formed a ministry, applied for a dissolution and, after the new Parliament met, was defeated both on the election of the Speaker and on the Address. No Prime Minister to-day would remain in office under those conditions, but Peel did so for several months, hoping to win over enough support to give him a majority. The historian of to-day may select 1835 as the date at which such practice terminated, and point out that both King and Prime Minister had learned their lesson through bitter experience. But that was not so apparent at the time. The correspondence of ministers and their friends shows that throughout the life of the second Melbourne Government the ministers feared that William IV would again dismiss them, turn the Government over to Peel or Wellington, and grant the latter a dissolution and thereby the opportunity of securing a majority from the electorate. In 1839, then, the rule prevailed that the sovereign must act with the advice of ministers who as a body assumed full responsibility for the King's government, who must secure the support of the majority in the House of Commons and must either resign or appeal to the electorate when it was clear that they had lost that majority, but so long as that rule was observed, the King exercised his own initiative in the selection of such ministers and in affording them very ample opportunities of securing the majority which they required; he might even dismiss a ministry who enjoyed the support of a Commons majority, if he could find another who could secure it.

We have called Lord Durham's recommendation for Canada of the British system of Cabinet Government under parliamentary control Responsible Government, because it was by that name that it came to be known historically, especially in Canada and those other Dominions which were to achieve self-government through its practice. But in the section of the Report in which that recommendation was made, it was not referred to as 'responsible government', and the use of the term 'responsible' in the Report is loose, general and varied, just as it was in popular parlance at that time, both in England and Canada. The refusal of a Civil List is referred to as a means of subjecting the officials to 'responsibility', popular leaders are said to be relieved of the 'responsibilities of opposition', and attention is directed to the prosperity of the United States 'under an eminently responsible government'. Lord Durham must have known that in the United States the Executives, as well as the Legislatures, were directly responsible to the people through popular election, and that there was an entire absence of that responsibility of the Executive to the people's representatives in the Legislature which he was attempting to establish in Canada, and which has come to be known in the British Commonwealth as Responsible Government; and there are clear indications in the Report that he was consciously diverting the government of Canada into British and away from American channels. He also knew that the Baldwins used the term in connexion with ideas very similar to his own, he was probably aware of the fact that since the previous July Francis Hincks had been doing the same thing in the pages of the *Toronto Examiner*, and he apparently believed, though mistakenly, that the Upper Canada Reformers generally employed the expression in that sense.[3] But he was so much concerned that his readers should understand the substance of this, his cardinal recommendation, that he refused to tie it up to a term that was liable to so many interpretations. The Reformers of British North America, however, seeing in the Report the great hope of the future, adopted it as a Magna Charta and accepted its principal recommendation as the classic expression of Responsible Government. Within a year after the publication of the Report, Joseph Howe's letters to Lord John Russell and Charles Buller's pamphlet on 'Responsible Government for Colonies', both based directly on Lord Durham's statements, had, along with Francis Hincks's *Examiner*, riveted upon the British world effectively and finally this meaning of the term 'Responsible Government'. Henceforward Responsible Government was government according to Lord Durham's Report.

By his successful recommendation of Responsible Government Lord Durham removed Canada's main political difficulty, the clash between an irresponsible Executive and an elected Assembly, placed the Canadian people in a position to remedy their other evils and solve their own problems, created an effective Canadian democracy for all time to come, established the full British constitutional system, and laid the foundation of Canadian self-government.

The question of *self*-government brings us to the consideration of the third aspect of the triple relationship involved in the setting up in Canada of Cabinet Government under parliamentary control. In addition to the relationship of ministers to Parliament and the King to the ministers which prevailed in England, there was in the case of Canada a third relationship, that of the Canadian Governor to the British Government. If the full British system was to be adopted in Canada, the Governor would bear the same relationship to his Canadian ministers as the King did to his British ministers. But while he was to be the analogue of the King in Canada, and act on the advice of ministers responsible to a Canadian Assembly, he was an official appointed by the British Government and responsible to that Government for his Canadian administration. Was the dual role practicable? That difficulty was one of the reasons why the British ministers had refused to give serious consideration to Robert Baldwin's proposals in 1836. They felt that the British system was possible only in a sovereign state, impossible in a colony. Baldwin himself pretended that no difficulty existed; the Canadian ministers would be responsible only for the advice they gave the Governor, and the British Government, while it would usually concede to Canadian opinion, would, if necessary, always have the means of asserting its supremacy and of securing through its Governor what it insisted on. But Baldwin was always better at conceiving theories – and there the British Empire owes him an imperishable debt – than he was in applying them to actual conditions. If, after the system of Responsible Government was once established, the British Government attempted to force action through its Governor, for which no Canadian ministry with a majority in Parliament would assume responsibility, the Governor would either have no ministry at all or an irresponsible one, Responsible Government in Canada would have reached a *reductio ad absurdum*, and a conflict would be created between the British Government and the Canadian Parliament which might be more dangerous to imperial unity than the old conflicts between the irresponsible oligarchic Canadian Executives and the representatives of the people.

Lord Durham recognized the difficulty and met it in his simple direct manner. He drew a line between Canadian and

Imperial questions. In matters of purely Canadian concern, Responsible Government was to operate fully and the British Government was to give no support to a Governor who found himself in conflict with a Canadian Parliament. In such matters the Canadian people were to govern themselves without any restriction. They would have the assistance of their Governor so long as he avoided such a conflict. But the ultimate seat of authority would be the Canadian Parliament, which to all intents and purposes would be, so far as Canadian questions were concerned, a sovereign legislature controlling executive action. In Canadian matters Canada would enjoy full executive self-government as well as legislative self-government. Downing Street and Westminster were to keep their hands off. He was too wise to put it that way, but that was what he meant. He took what was originally a Canadian idea and transformed it into a measure of self-government such as no Canadian had dreamed of. On the other hand, in matters of Imperial concern the British supremacy was to be maintained.

The distinction between Imperial and Canadian matters was not to be a vague one. He drew the line. 'The constitution of the form of government – the regulation of foreign relations, and of trade with the Mother Country, the other British colonies, and foreign nations – and the disposal of the public lands, are the only points on which the Mother Country requires a control.' In specifying these particular points Durham undoubtedly followed the suggestion of Buller, who had made the same reservations – with the exception of the constitution-making power which he took for granted – in drafting a constitution for New South Wales immediately before leaving for Canada.[4] Although Buller had not dreamed of Responsible Government when he made the New South Wales suggestion, which was merely a legislative restriction for a colony about to be granted representative government for the first time, the topics selected fitted in to Durham's scheme, and his suggestion to Durham that the latter's division should follow this line provided a most important feature of the Report. It afforded a practical answer to the strongest theoretical objection that could be urged against Responsible Government and completed the development by which this feature of the Report became a *modus vivendi* as well as a theory of government.

This line between matters of Imperial concern and matters of Canadian concern was broken down in the course of time –

by the changing conditions and the further developments of Canadian nationalism. (In fact the actual line, as the Report defined it, was never recognized, but the distinction in practice between Canadian and Imperial affairs was recognized.) But, like the limitations of the Reform Bill in Great Britain, this suggestion served its day and made possible the great essential step toward a new era. The statement of imperial powers indicated in the Report, with the single exception of the control of public lands by the British Government – and that was easily remedied – proved to be satisfactory at the time. The practical obstacles which Russell suggested seem to us now to have been trifling enough. They might, of course, have been more serious had it not been for a deep desire on the part of the Canadian people to maintain the British connexion if their essential needs could be satisfied. Lord Durham satisfied those needs and then trusted the future to the people of Canada, just as he had trusted it to the people of Great Britain in the Reform Bill. The confidence has been equally justified by history. Since the carrying out of his recommendations, the loyalty to British connexion and the ardent desire to harmonize nationalism and imperialism on the part of the people of Canada, and a rare blending of generosity, sweet reasonableness and practical good sense on the part of the people of Great Britain, have co-operated in perfect accord. Lord Durham provided the bridge on which they could meet, on which they could settle the problems of their future relationship as those problems developed, and over which, as the centuries pass, Britain and the British nations beyond the seas are destined to carry a larger and larger share of the responsibilities of modern civilization. He could not, of course, see that future in detail, but to suppose, as some writers have done, that he intended his definition of imperial and colonial powers to be a permanent one is to misunderstand his type of mind and to fail to recognize in him the pioneer of a new type of statesmanship. He had been the only one of the makers of the Reform Bill to argue against its 'finality'. He habitually thought in terms of a constantly changing world, and to him any true reform must be plastic and dynamic in character – conceptions which are commonplace to us but were still strange to his world of Whigs and Tories. For him two things only must be permanent, Canadian satisfaction and British connexion, and he succeeded in establishing both.

It would, of course, have been unwise for him to have

speculated in his Report on the manner in which Canadian self-government might in the future develop beyond the limits which he suggested for it. But there is enough to indicate that the Canada of which he dreamed was to be not simply a colony but a nation with a nationality, a patriotism, a pride of its own. He frequently employed the terms 'nation' and 'nationality', and spoke of 'a great and powerful people' who were to enjoy 'more of equality, of freedom, and of local independence', and who were to occupy a position in which there would be no feeling of inferiority to their neighbours. His vision was such that he was able to see what is obscure to a few Canadians as well as some Englishmen, even to this day, that a healthy nationalism within a healthy imperialism could alone keep Canada British, that a distinctively Canadian patriotism could alone preserve the boundary line between a *British* and a non-British North America.[5] He stands for all time between the little Englanders and the little Canadians on the one hand, and the little Imperialists on the other, as the prophet of the ideals on which our Empire's power and genius are built. For a moment, like all great innovators, he stood alone with this conception of nationality within an Empire, but within two generations there had sprung into being an Empire of nations, proud and self-conscious as well as self-governing, of which by virtue of his Report he was the creator as well as the prophet.

And so, having discovered the secret of Empire – that is, of Empire where men of European lineage are concerned – the keynote of his Report is that of a reasoned but passionate imperialism. That is the more striking historically because it emerged against a background where Britain sat aloof, conscious that the sun of her world-glory had been beclouded by the American Revolution, and without hope that it would ever fully emerge again; her most progressive political party preaching a gospel one of whose beatitudes was being well rid of colonies, and her other parties waiting with dignified patience until in the day of their maturity these colonies went their way of their own accord; her common people caring little about the matter at all except in some exciting period, when their pride was ruffled by some presumptuous colonials shooting at the British flag; and even her Colonial Office, while it tinkered at the old colonies as best it could, lukewarm about the acquisition of new ones and incapable of developing even a theory, let alone a vision, of Empire. Not only do the sweeping sentences of the Report never waver in their confidence that if its recommendations are carried out the bond between Great Britain and Canada will be a permanent one, but they everywhere insist that the basis of that imperial unity shall be *British*. It is British government, British institutions, British sentiments – wisely modified to suit an American environment, but retaining their essential British features – which are to prevail. To Lord Durham's mind, the greatest merit of those British institutions is that they 'link the utmost development of freedom and civilization with the stable authority of an hereditary monarchy'.[6]

His constant emphasis on the monarchy is not the least significant feature of his Report. In British politics 'Radical Jack' had never been quite willing to cross the line from the Whigs to the Radicals because he believed that many of the latter wished to destroy fundamental British institutions while he sought only to modify them, and that they were flirting with a republicanism which in British dress was as repulsive to him as it was unnatural. It would, of course, be a mistake to suppose that he foresaw with any clearness the day when the monarchy would be almost the only formal bond that would link the self-governing dominions to the Mother Country, and would at the same time symbolize and focus those British institutions and sentiments which he emphasized. And yet there is a peculiar fitness about the closing words of his Report. Canada can still take pride in that prediction that she would 'form one of the brightest ornaments in your Majesty's imperial crown'. Nowhere is the feeling towards the King and the royal family warmer or more devoted than in his Majesty's self-governing dominions beyond the seas. But if any Englishman of an antiquated and thoughtless type lets drop a phrase that suggests that Canada is in any sense a possession of the British Government or Parliament or people he is in for a bad half-hour and his hyper-sensitive Canadian friend for a worse one. It is a striking feature of Lord Durham's Report that though written nearly a hundred years ago there is hardly a phrase in it that could give offence to Canada's full-grown national pride. That is in keeping with the facility with which he grasped Canadian points of view, and it is not the least of the secrets of power in that self-governing Empire which was to be so different from the Empire of London-governed colonies.

While the recommendations in regard to Responsible Government, self-government, imperial relations, and the union of the provinces constitute the core of the Report, the other recommendations were of great significance for Canadian development. Lord Durham realized that an effective democracy needed the support of two foundations driven deep into the life of the community – education and municipal government. His own faith in the practicability of household suffrage at home had been associated with his observation of, and interest in, the progress of popular education, and no one appreciated better the part which local self-government had played in English history and the inevitable connexion between the Reform Bill of 1832 and the Municipal Act of 1835. Through his friend Joseph Parkes he had been in close touch with the proceedings which led up to the latter measure. On both of these subjects he had appointed sub-commissions, whose reports formed appendices to the main report. The report on education, written by Arthur Buller, brother of Charles, was incomplete when Lord Durham's Report was written. Its recommendations were not practicable in the form in which they were presented, but the Report contained valuable information, and much of the machinery it suggested was later incorporated into the educational system of the united province and passed on later to those of Ontario and Quebec. In his main Report Lord Durham's remarks on education were quite general, but his emphasis was strong. He observed that more attention had been given to secondary than to primary education where the great need lay. He especially scored the lamentable lack of primary education in Lower Canada. But, as usual, he painted too dark a background and was unfair in his criticisms of the British Government.[7] Such a strong emphasis on education in a document that was to become so famous in Canada proved a stimulus to Canadian effort, and the achievement of the main recommendation of the Report, Responsible Government, ultimately removed what had been the chief obstacle to educational progress in both the Canadas, by bringing educational policy under popular control, thus permitting the evolution of a system which corresponded to the genius of the Canadian people.

Lord Durham had taken with him to Canada William Kennedy, one of Parke's co-labourers in the English municipal reform, that he might study the Canadian situation and prepare a plan of municipal government. Adam Thom had been associated with Kennedy on account of his knowledge of Canadian conditions and his general ability. On the basis of the Report which they prepared – part of Appendix C to Lord Durham's Report – Durham's friend and successor, Poulett Thomson (afterwards Lord Sydenham), gave to Lower Canada municipal government and to Upper Canada a greatly improved system. In his own Report Lord Durham urged the importance of establishing a satisfactory system of municipal government[8] – to meet local needs, provide a training ground for democracy, free the Legislature from local jobbery and 'log-rolling', and establish in Canada another fundamentally British institution. It was his intention that this system of municipal government should form an essential part of the Union project and either be written into the Act of Union or be provided for by concurrent legislation.

The Report introduced other principles of stable government. Since Responsible Government with its corollary, the introduction of money votes by the ministers of the Crown, would put an end to the controversies over control of revenue, Lord Durham recommended that all revenues should be placed at the disposal of the Assembly on the concession of an adequate civil list. The judicial reforms which he suggested included the establishment of the independence of judges, improvement of the jury laws, the substitution of stipendiary magistrates for unpaid justices of the peace, and the formation of a Supreme Court of Appeal for British North America. His words appear to imply that the establishment of such a court would render unnecessary the continuation of the right of appeal to the Judicial Committee of the Privy Council. He recommended that all legislation of the British Parliament relating to the application of the Clergy Reserves and the resultant funds should be repealed and the disposal of these funds vested in the Canadian Legislature. He deprecated strongly any attempt to afford the Church of England any of the privileges of an established church. All religious denominations must be treated equally by the Government. His arguments for an ultimate union of all the British North American provinces were associated with the suggestion of a railway linking the Canadas and the Maritimes. This appreciation of the relation between public works and political development is evident throughout.

The Report reflects the defects of Lord Durham's temperament, particularly a tendency to exaggeration and to severe criticism of those who disagreed with him. It reflects also his courage, outspokenness, independence, analytical power, farsightedness, ability to see things in the large, his passion for reform, that combination of a liberalism which appeared rash to others with an instinct for safety which was adequate to the situation, and that gift which enabled him in more than one crisis to gather up a number of suggestions from various quarters into just that combination that brought order out of chaos, destroyed an old system, ushered in a new one, and provided a basis for a healthy and continuous development.

Sir Charles Lucas in his masterly introduction to the standard edition of the Report has recognized 'Lord Durham's constructiveness' as its outstanding characteristic.

To all times and to all sorts and conditions of men he has preached the doctrine, that for peoples, as for individuals, the one thing worth living for is to make, not to destroy; to build up, not to pull down; to unite small disjointed elements into a single whole; . . . to be strong and fear not; to speak unto the peoples of the earth that they go forward. In this constructiveness, which is embodied in all parts of the Report, he has beyond any other man illustrated in writing the genius of the English race, the element which in the British Empire is common alike to the sphere of settlement and to the sphere of rule. It is as a race of makers that the English will live to all time, and it is as a prophet of a race of makers that Lord Durham lives.

Lord Durham signed the Report, January 31, 1839. It was his last state paper. Disease had quickened its pace as he wrote. The time-glass of his life had but a few grains left. But genius had touched the fabric of Empire.

NOTE. *In this chapter no mention has been made of the section of Lord Durham's Report which deals with 'Public Laws and Emigration'. The ideas embodied in that section are entirely those of Gibbon Wakefield (no matter who may have actually written the section), and I have felt that they belonged to a life of Wakefield rather than to a biography of Durham. Nor has any reference been made to the appendices to the Report, which were prepared by Lord Durham's sub-commissioners. The contents of the appendices are listed in Vol. III of Sir Charles Lucas's edition of the Report.*

❂ ❂ ❂

CHAPTER VIII Immediate Reception
of the Report

That delicate balance of the political forces which made Lord Durham's return the chief topic of conversation and did so much to stimulate interest in the publication of his Report accounts for the caution with which it was at first received. Whigs and Tories alike were waiting to see what the Government would do. As soon as that was apparent their press would break out in the praise and abuse appropriate to the situation. In the meantime the Whig *Morning Chronicle* recognized that 'there is but one opinion in respect to the Report, that it is one of the most valuable papers laid before Parliament'. *The Times* finds that its theories 'are well stated and ably argued', and that 'this very remarkable writing of Lord Durham's is worthy of the closest attention'.[1] But as for the practicability or otherwise of any particular recommendation – not a word, until two weeks later *The Times* ventured to suggest that the Responsible Government suggestion was 'twaddle'.

Not so the Tory leaders of British North America! Whatever the British Government might do or not do, they felt instinctively that the Report would be fatal to their rule, if it were not discredited by every means in their power. Judge Haliburton of Nova Scotia, creator of 'Sam Slick', was in England. In mid-December he had been approached by 'a party in reference to the administration in Canada' who feared what was coming and wanted an account of the Canadian situation written by an eminent colonial to forestall and offset the Report. They believed that they had only two weeks in which to beat the Report, and when Haliburton replied that the time was too short, they promised to supply him with ammunition; 'the next morning eight hand carts of assorted documents were brought to his lodgings in Piccadilly'.[2] The result was the 'Bubbles of Canada', which made several bad guesses at what Durham was about to recommend, wasted much of its powder on an anticipated plan of federation, and headed up its personal attack in the sentence: 'When a nobleman advocates democratic institutions, we give him full credit for the benevolence of his intentions, but we doubt his sanity.'

The Report had proved to be worse than even Haliburton's suspicions, and the vinegar had been rubbed in by Lord Durham's ingenious citation, in support of one of his arguments, of 'a highly popular work, which is known to be from the pen of one of Your Majesty's chief functionaries in Nova Scotia'. The humourist was lost in the 'functionary' when Haliburton, fighting the battle of all the Tory officeholders of British North America, launched a wrathful series of attacks on the Report in the form of letters to *The Times*. Although the first of these appeared a week after the publication of the last instalment of the Report, Haliburton had not taken time to read that document very thoroughly, and the greater part of the second and third letters was devoted to bitter sarcasm at the expense of a supposed recommendation of a federal union, which, of course, was not in the Report at all. Those letters must have made good reading in Cleveland Row.

The proposed Intercolonial Railway, the recommendation in regard to Clergy Reserves, and, of course, Responsible Government were ridiculed in turn, along with a number of minor subjects. A few passages from these letters will indicate their spirit and substance.

I forgot that your Lordship . . . has provided us a railroad from Quebec to Halifax; and we make no doubt, when the great preliminary, but equally feasible work of a bridge across the Atlantic shall be completed, that the other will be commenced without delay. It was a magnificent idea, and will afford a suitable conveyance for the illustrious members of the great British American Congress. I will, my Lord, not ask you where the means for this gigantic undertaking are to come from, because that is a mere matter of detail, and beneath the notice of a statesman of your Lordship's exalted rank. . . . As a romance, my Lord, the production is not destitute of merit; the plot is well arranged, the language is above mediocrity, and it displays a fertile imagination; but as a state paper it is beneath contempt. . . . We have seen enough of rash innovations, of reckless change, and of dangerous experiments, of late years, not to tamely submit to follow the prescriptions of speculative men like your Lordship. . ... Your Lordship talks of a Government of the Colonies, responsible to the Colonies, and of a Governor ruling by heads of departments, amenable to the Legislature.

However this theory may apply to Great Britain, it is sheer nonsense as regards a dependent state. . . . If a Governor is to be controlled by his Council and that Council amenable to the Assembly, then the Assembly controls the Governor, the character of its political relation is changed, and it is no longer a dependent but an independent state. . . . The exhilarating gas which your Lordship has inhaled and caused others to imbibe has given rise to an extraordinary exhibition. Imagining their dimensions to be enlarged to their ideas, like the frogs in the fable they have wellnigh burst in unnatural inflation. . . . The most redeeming part of your Lordship's report is the zeal it displays in the cause of religion. The space devoted to this subject is so much larger than that allotted to your chaplain on your outward journey, that it has somewhat taken us by surprise. . . . [You only] pander to prejudice, and add fresh fuel to the war of Dissent against the Church. . . . You assailed your own church, represented it as having too much of public money, as comprising none but the opulent, and lauded the policy of stripping it of its lands to appease the craving appetite of others. . . . Should your Lordship unfortunately hear of a third insurrection, you will find 'the predisposing cause' in a certain report which has raised a 'hue and cry' against the Queen and the Church of God. . . . I am now about to take my leave of you, my Lord, for ever. If there are points in these letters calculated to give your Lordship pain, believe me, the infliction has been mutual. . . . The report of La Fayette on his return from the States subverted monarchy in France; the Report of your Lordship, equally laudatory of that republic and its institutions, is no less dangerous from its democratic tendencies.[3]

There was another prominent British-American Tory in England at the time. John Beverley Robinson, the Nestor of the Family Compact of Upper Canada,[4] was on the spot to watch developments. He was the ablest of early Canadian statesmen and there is nothing finer in our history than his long career of devoted public service. His gentlemanly attitude towards political opponents affords a noble contrast to the vindictiveness of many of the official leaders in both provinces (toward Durham for instance), and the abuse and unfairness with which he and his colleagues were attacked by many of the Reform leaders. He was always fair, always dignified, always statesmanlike (even when he was mistaken). Any one of his rapier thrusts was more

telling than all the blunderbusses of 'Sam Slick'. As soon as
Lord Durham's Report appeared, Robinson went down from
Cheltenham to London. He shut himself up with the Report for
days, studying its every aspect. He began to write a reply to it,
and after two days' steady work he 'had got to page 27 out of
119. How it worried me! – so much to say, such a wish to
shorten it'.[5] He did shorten it, but his letter to Lord Normanby,
the new Colonial Secretary, on February 23, was long enough
and we can only quote a few passages. The letter was begun at
half-past nine in the morning and finished at midnight with only
half an hour for lunch.

*No one will deny to this very important state paper the
merit of being ably written; but in respect to a document intended to affect such great interests, the style is but a secondary
consideration.*

*As it regards Lower Canada, there is much sound reasoning
clearly expressed; but my acquaintance with the history of that
province enables me to say that there are also in this part of
the Report some misstatements of material facts and some
erroneous inferences; and what I think is beyond measure to
be regretted is the unnecessary announcement in this public
document of certain opinions and convictions, the permanent
record it contains in highly wrought language of most painful
occurrences, and the recommendations of a rigorous policy,
which I fear it can serve no good purpose to throw before the
eyes of an exasperated and bewildered people. . . . [Lord
Durham spent only a few days in Upper Canada.] His Lordship
cannot be expected therefore to vouch for much, if for anything,
of what is stated, from his personal experience and observation.
But it is wonderful how he could have suffered himself to have
been so strangely imposed upon. . . . This Report [the Upper
Canada section] in regard to its most numerous, and most
important statements, either rests upon no evidence whatever,
or, if it has indeed been founded on any evidence, it has been
the ex parte evidence of an unknown number of unknown
witnesses, of whom unknown questions have been asked by
unknown parties, and possibly parties with unknown views, and
full of unknown prejudices.*

For the inaccuracy of at least half of the statements on Upper
Canada he can appeal to the authority of Sir John Colborne. He
is opposed to a legislative union of Upper and Lower Canada

because it is too vast for one government and because it will involve the Upper province in the troubles of the Lower. The English may outnumber the French, but they will be less coherent and so the French will get the upper hand. The recommendation in regard to the Clergy Reserves means that the thousands of Protestants who now inhabit the province and the millions who are to succeed them will be left destitute of all public provision for worship and religious instruction.

I do not believe that the Imperial Parliament will adopt and act upon the assumptions proclaimed in this Report of the hopeless inferiority of the French Canadian race, or of the eternal animosity between them and their fellow subjects of British origin. It is not in that spirit that the dominion over half a million of free subjects should be exercised; nor is it by measures that can be vindicated only by such reasons, that the tranquillity which long prevailed can be re-established, and security restored. . . . It will not appear, I think, to Parliament that any advantage to British interests or any support to tranquillity in the Colonies would be likely to ensue, from creating that new species of responsibility, which in reality, would be nothing more or less than a servile and corrupting dependence upon Party. It is but too obvious that a Colonial Government, such as would be constituted by a strict adherence to this suggestion in the Report, would be an anomaly without example in the British Empire, or in any other Country; and that in comparison with it the Republican Government of the United States would be strongly conservative.

What effect may be produced by the publication of such opinions, under such authority, cannot be foretold; but if the inhabitants of Upper Canada shall be led by them to desire, as a boon, what would be so destructive of their security and happiness, the taste will be a new one, and will have been created by the Report.

And whenever such a system shall be established, (if that be a possible contingency) from that moment may be confidently dated the decline of integrity and independence in public servants, of peace and contentment in society, of security for property, and attachment to British institutions.[6]

In a later letter he said:

It is not surprisng that his Lordship did not in this brief period attempt to transfer the scene of his personal observations to Upper Canada. He did, no doubt, intend to have applied the months or years that might be necessary for acquiring that knowledge from personal inquiry and observation, which His Majesty's Government was willing to rely upon for settling the most important public interests, but he did not in fact enjoy the opportunity. . . . It would be difficult to find any topic by which the dissatisfied members of the community, of which there are multitudes under every government, could be incited to distrust of their rulers and to a general impatience of their conditions which this Report has not dwelt upon, and in such a manner as to unsettle the public mind to the utmost. . . . The cause of popular agitation and of occasional collisions between the Assembly and other branches of government in the North American colonies is easily discerned. It lies on the surface. It is the tendency of democracy to swallow up everything, its impatience of any check. . . . Universal suffrage nearly exists in the colonies. [Let the British Government add universal suffrage to its system of responsible cabinet government and ask itself whether it would like to see established in Great Britain what Lord Durham is advocating for Canada.] . . . If it be thought desirable to remove every obstacle to the absolute sway of the multitude whether their inclinations be just or unjust and whether their views be sound or unsound, then undoubtedly the system recommended in these pages is admirably adapted to that object. But how it can be imagined that such a system will confer tranquillity on a country is rather inexplicable. . . .[7]

By the month of April it was apparent that Durham was standing with the Melbourne Government for better or for worse and he was once more fair game for the Tory reviews. The *Quarterly* had never felt much restraint in that respect. In its criticism of his Report it made him say a number of things that he had not said and in some cases the very opposite of what he had. Every unscrupulous trick of lifting quotations out of their context and giving fictitious meanings to isolated phrases was resorted to. The burden of the story was that the Report was 'a farrago of false statements and false principles, . . . the most fatal legacy that could have been bequeathed to our American colonies' and that its object had been 'to issue, under some colour of royal authority, the most democratic and anarchial principles'. It recognized as the 'key' of the Report the idea that 'the Houses of Assembly are to be in the provinces what the House of Commons is in England'. 'Yet it is the Queen's Ex-High Commissioner, . . . himself a Peer of Parliament, who promulgates these doctrines, this new and to us incomprehensible system of colonial *connexion*: the *Report* calls it connexion – to our understanding, it is absolute separation.' It would have been more honest to have boldly proposed to hand Canada over to the Americans, but this deceptive means of doing the same thing was calculated to be more effective.

In the meantime Lord Durham was receiving a number of letters expressing appreciation of the Report. E. L. Bulwer ('Bulwer Lytton'), always one of his admirers, wrote in regard to the section on recommendations, the first to appear in *The Times*, that it was 'absolutely colossal in the grandeur and scope of its views, in its singular frankness, boldness, and simplicity. And the lucid dignity of the style is worthy the splendour of the argument. . . . You have composed a masterpiece, that will lift your reputation as a statesman to a height that will command posterity'.[8] Charles Sumner, a recent acquaintance, thanked him for 'the friendly terms in which you have alluded to my country. Such language from so high a quarter will . . . give additional strength [in the United States] to the fraternal – perhaps I should say the filial – sentiment towards England. I avail myself of this occasion to express to your Lordship the great admiration with which I have read the whole of your masterly Report'.[9]

From his brother-in-law, Lord Howick, came a letter which is interesting because of his later work as Colonial Secretary, particularly in relation to his carrying out of part of Durham's policy. Howick expressed approval of the Report on the whole but revealed a tendency to work towards federation and to shelve the legislative union. The union of the two provinces should not, he thought, be put through without the consent of the people of Upper Canada, and any sort of constitutional government in Lower Canada would be dangerous in the immediate future. He suggested the holding of a Canadian convention which should make recomendations on the ultimate form of government. In the meantime, a Governor and Special Council in Lower Canada were to proceed to Anglicize that province. This letter quite justified Wakefield's comment that 'Lord Howick would substitute a whole plan of his own for the whole of your plan'. But Howick, while he was always independent, was always honest, and Durham, who respected his ability and tenacity, must have read with a glow of pleasure the concluding words of the letter. 'I entirely concur with you in your leading notions of allowing the colonists the most complete self government upon matters of mere internal regulation and local interest, and of binding the different provinces together by the closest and strongest ties which it may be practicable to establish.'[10]

Lord Durham's Report won its first public victory with the announcement to Parliament on May 3 that the Government would introduce legislation to effect a union of Upper and Lower Canada. But three days later, on the Jamaica Bill the ministry found their majority reduced to five, and they accepted that as the handwriting on the wall. They went out and Peel came in, but the ladies of the bedchamber and the clash between the reasonable demands of a political party and the equally reasonable affections of a lonely young Queen brought Melbourne back again. He rode valiantly to the assistance of a maiden in distress, but a 'working majority' was needed to carry on the Government; would the Radicals be reasonable again and supply him with it? It was more necessary than ever to conciliate them, and since their serious revolts had developed over colonial questions there must not be another colonial bill that session. Next session enough of the old team-work might be revived to put through the Canada Bill without danger of precipitating another crisis.

Russell, instead of presenting the Canada Bill which had received the ratification of the Cabinet two months before, presented to Parliament on June 3 two resolutions, one in favour of the union and the other that it was expedient to continue until 1842 the powers vested in the Governor and Special Council of Lower Canada 'with such alterations of those powers as may be deemed advisable'. He praised the Report of Lord Durham and expressed his approval of its recommendations not only in regard to the union of the two Canadas but also on municipal Government and the control of revenues by the assembly on the conditions suggested. But he disagreed with Lord Durham's contention that colonial ministers could be made to occupy a similar position to ministers at home. On this latter point Buller took issue with him, at the same time pressing for an immediate union of *all* the North American colonies. Replying to Buller, Russell denied that he approved of the practice of carrying on the executive government of a colony with a minority in the Assembly. He desired that 'the executive should be carried on in such a way that their measures should be agreeable and acceptable to the representatives of the people', but ultimate responsibility must always rest with the Home Government. Russell had been so far influenced by Lord Durham's Report that he was prepared to go some distance in the *practice* of Responsible Government if he could save himself from committal to its *theory*.

On the following Monday Russell withdrew even the resolution in favour of union. The reason which the Government offered for postponing the whole matter until the next session was the opposition of the Upper Canada Assembly. But they had been aware of that at the time they had prepared their bill. Melbourne and Russell agreed with Durham's statement in the Report that the Canadian situation was so urgent that not a single session should be allowed to pass before Parliament took action in regard to it.

The opposition of a Tory Assembly in Upper Canada would not have deterred them. But their estimate of the political situation at home was justified by the fact that while Peel, the Conservative leader, maintained a non-committal position, the only Radicals who took part in the Commons debate, with the exception of Buller, expressed antagonism to the union. (Buller, however, preferred the immediate establishment of a general union.)

In the debate in the House of Lords, Normanby dropped a remark which Brougham pounced on with great glee. The Colonial Secretary said that there were 'other reasons [than the news from Canada] which influenced the Government in withdrawing the Bill'. Brougham asked:

Did not every one know that during the whole winter Canada and Canadian affairs were the topics of conversation in all circles, and in fact that there was nothing else to be discussed? ... His noble friend, the late Governor-General of Canada, had laid before the country a Report of very great ability, showing very great industry, great resources, deep, if not successful, – for some persons differed on that point, – but at all events, assiduous, able, and skilful attention to the details, as well as the principles of the measures by which the country ought to be governed.

[Oh, that Macaulay had been in the Lords to recount the conversation in which Brougham had characterized the Report as 'a second-rate article for the *Edinburgh Review*'!]

Why, asked Brougham, was nothing being done? Why was the Report not being acted upon? They had heard the explanation of the Government.

But sometimes from the ruder and rougher individuals, who carry on the concerns of nations, – sometimes in a small parenthesis, and in an undertone, they drop out phrases which possibly, which peradventure, throw more light upon the whole conduct of the party than all the elaborate reasons, than all the prolix statements which have been formally put forth in explanation of the measures in question. 'There were other circumstances,' said the noble Marquis. . . . I believe there were. What think you of withdrawing the confidence of one House of Parliament from the Government that had never had the confidence of the other? What if it had been withdrawn on a particular question relating to colonial affairs? What if it had just so happened that the Jamaica Bill had been lost, and it was not expedient to risk the loss of the Canada Bill, which was very likely to follow? . . . And when the news from Upper Canada came, the light dawned, the clouds dispersed, the heavens opened, every heart was cheered. 'Now,' said they, 'we have a ground for doing what . . . we have so anxiously desired, now we have an excuse for putting off the Canada Bill.' . . . If they had gone on with it, another vote of the Commons would have led to another resignation. That is the plain English of the matter.

Durham came up from Cowes – where he had been trying to snatch a much needed rest – to support the Government and also to urge that a Canada Bill must be passed early in the next session. Ellice wrote to him: 'Your speech was excellent, and in the tone and temper, which always do equal credit to a man who may have serious wrongs to complain of and is disposed to sacrifice his personal feelings to the more pressing interests of his case.'[11]

The Government now decided to send a civil Governor to Canada to smooth the way for the Union and to carry out – with the exception of his full view of Responsible Government – the reform policies of Lord Durham's Report. They turned to an old friend and disciple of Lord Durham's – Poulett Thomson.

Durham had been estranged from him somewhat of late because he was a member of the Melbourne Government, but of those who sat in the seats of power and those who could bring to the task administrative experience, he was still the closest to Lord Durham's political views. He had been ill at ease in the Melbourne Cabinet; like Durham he had been too liberal for it, although he was as placid in temper as Durham was fiery.

Poulett Thomson sought out Lord Durham and conferred with him at length in regard to Canada. The latter coached him carefully, affording him 'all the information and assistance he was able to supply'. Durham and those who had accompanied him selected for Thomson the Canadians on whose advice he was to rely and wrote letters to influential persons in Canada with a view to securing support for him. Then at the last moment while the *Pique* was lying in Portsmouth harbour waiting for the new Governor, Durham, already under the shadow of his last illness, went over from Cowes to spend with him the few hours before sailing.[12] It was a 'bon voyage' for the next world as well as for this. Poulett Thomson sailed for Canada as Lord Durham's political executor and Lord Durham remained at home to die. In two years and six days Poulett Thomson (Lord Sydenham) was dead in Canada. But both men had done their work and the British Empire was born anew.

Before the *Pique* reached Quebec, an article from the *Colonial Gazette* which had appeared in England three days after it sailed, and had been carried across the ocean in one of the new steam vessels, was already reprinted in the Canadian newspapers as a forecast of his policy. The greater part of it is a repetition of the principles of Lord Durham's Report, announced now as the policies of the new Governor.

He has been convinced by Lord Durham's Report, dispatches, and conversation. . . . Notwithstanding Lord John Russell's declaration against responsible government, by that name, Mr. Thomson adopts the views of Lord Durham as put forth in the high commissioner's report. He conceives that representation is a mockery, and a very mischievous mockery too, if the executive is not made responsible to those in whom the people confide. By what special means he would secure this indispensable condition of peace and order under the representative system, we are not informed; but we have reason to conclude that he intends to be guided upon this point by the

*opinion of the leading men of the British race in both Canadas.
. . . [In the selection of some one to represent him in Lower
Canada, while he was in the upper province.] His choice, we
understand, has fallen upon the present chief-justice of Quebec,
Mr. James Stuart; of whom it may be said, without at all
disparaging others, that he is the ablest and most statesmanlike
person in British North America. He enjoys more than any
other, the confidence of the English race in Lower Canada and
more than any other Englishman the confidence of the French,
notwithstanding their hatred of him as the leader of the English.
. . . Mr. Stuart is the fittest man in the province to advise any
governor-general.*[13]

By this time Lord Durham's Report was known throughout
the British world. Most of the Canadian newspapers published
the whole of it – although it was a book in itself – and in
Australia several papers printed long extracts. The *Sydney
Monitor* advocated the distribution of five hundred copies of it
in New South Wales. Australian politicians studied it with care.
'The influence of that great pathfinder [Lord Durham],' writes
an Australian historian, 'upon the constitutional progress of
New South Wales and the other Australian colonies cannot be
over-estimated. Wentworth became saturated with it and made
reference to it over and over again.'[14] Lord Durham already
knew something of this before that first year was over.
Wakefield wrote to him, December 26:

*I send by this post two pieces of Van Diemen's Land news-
papers, by way of sample of the reception of your Report in
that part of the world. The principal paper of New South Wales
reprints the Report entire, and all the others that I have seen,
give large extracts with the most flattering comments. It seems
to have made almost as much impression in the Australian
colonies as in Canada. It has now gone the round, from Canada,
through the West Indies and South Africa, to the Australias,
and has every where been received with acclamations.*[15]

Returning to Nova Scotia a few weeks after his letters to *The
Times*, Judge Haliburton discovered that home was strangely
different from what it had ever been before. The (legendary)
'father of American humour' had failed to create the angry-
spouse-with-the-rolling-pin theme, but on this home-coming he
encountered every form of literary weapon that wrath and scorn

could lay their hands on. The Report had aroused Nova Scotia, and Haliburton's 'Reply' to it had aroused it still further. So beleaguered was the editor of the *Acadian Recorder* by anti-Haliburton contributions that within a fortnight he was obliged to warn them off on the grounds that he could not 'allow our columns to be wholly monopolized by one subject', and that they 'made use of personalities too gross and bitter for our acceptance'. One attack, after ridiculing his politics, his humour, and the weakness of his case, asserted: 'The Report of the Earl of Durham will stand a monument of imperishable honour to his memory when you and your bubbles shall have passed into long oblivion.' Haliburton's friends, to console him, organized a dinner in his honour, at which, speaking on behalf of his literary creation 'Sam Slick', he said: 'It gives him the greatest pleasure possible to hear all this abuse, for it is a sure sign that he is going ahead.' For once the principle did not apply. It was the Report that he had assailed that was going ahead. As for Haliburton his biographer writes: 'Even more disheartening than mere failure was his positive achievement. He had succeeded very largely in destroying his power to influence, one might almost say to interest his fellow colonials, – except as a target for their opprobrium.' His popularity never recovered from the set-back it received from the *Bubbles of Canada* and the *Reply to Lord Durham*. 'It was only after his death, when his reputation had become to a considerable extent mythical, that he was restored to the position of minor greatness he had once occupied in his native province.'[16]

At the same time the enthusiasm aroused by the Report in the Maritime colonies was being positively and constructively marshalled by a number of their public men, of whom Joseph Howe was the ablest and most aggressive. Already a reformer, he had heard of the 'responsible government' cry in Upper Canada, but while expressing some sympathy for it, he had given his preference to the demand for an elective council. Lord Durham's Report gave him the solution for which he had been seeking, and he hailed it as being 'perfectly *simple* and eminently *British*'. In September of this year he wrote his famous letters to Lord John Russell. Their arguments do not admit of brief analysis here. The letters themselves are readily accessible and are well known to students of history as brilliant exposition of Responsible Government, based directly on Lord Durham's Report and in some respects clearer and more convincing as they are also more detailed than those of the Report itself.[17] They probably exerted a considerable influence on Russell's colonial policy, which had already been shaped to some extent by the Report. Russell's mind could not leap quickly to great ideas as Durham's did, but he was open-minded and conscientious, and, when once convinced, courageous and aggressive.

In Lower Canada the British merchants were, of course, enthusiastic over the Report with its recommendation of provincial union. So long as that went through, they were content to say very little about Responsible Government, to which subject, in fact, they gave but slight attention. Their attitude was expressed in a letter from J. H. Kerr of Quebec to Wakefield:

Lord Durham has indeed redeemed his pledge to us, and this too he must have done at a great sacrifice of feeling against the Ministers who so basely betrayed him. . . . It is a fortunate event for us that Ld. Durham abandoned his government here; he was right in saying 'I can serve you better in England than I can here'.[18]

Charles Grey wrote to Durham from Quebec of the 'universal satisfaction' which 'your Report has given to every one who knows anything about the province'. In regard to the Upper Canada section 'there seems considerable difference of opinion'. The union of the provinces would be the greatest folly 'without they are further prepared to adopt your recommendation of a responsible excutive. People may talk till they are black in the face about its being incompatible with the principles which must regulate the relations between the Mother Country and a colony. The colony *will* have it before it is much older, in connection with you if you will allow it – but in spite of you if you force it to it.' To his sister, Lady Durham, Grey wrote: 'They can no longer have any excuse at home for misgoverning the country. And if his Report shall lead at last to right legislation for Canada, the whole merit of it will justly belong to him.'[19]

Some of the members of the old Executive Council which had been turned out of office by Lord Durham made the publication of the Report an occasion for renewed personal attacks, but they found themselves very lonely.

It was not to be expected that the French-Canadians should wax enthusiastic over the Report. Since the Union which it proposed had been the favourite policy of the British merchants, their political and economic opponents, and since it was frankly associated with an attempt to Anglicize them, they were bound to oppose it. Their antagonism was accentuated by the Union conditions suggested by Upper Canada. Lafontaine was as sincere as any in opposition to the Union, but as a practical statesman he knew that such opposition was hopeless. Conviction and political necessity alike induced him to oppose the Union until it was consummated, but long before that he must have realized how Union and Responsible Government combined could be turned to the advantage of the French-Canadians. For him and his followers Lord Durham's Report contained its own antidote. When the time for action came, he was to combine with the Durhamites of Upper Canada to render effective Lord Durham's primary recommendation, and then, as leader of a united and victorious Liberal party, utilize Responsible Government to nullify the policy of Anglicizing his compatriots and build a united Canada in which their institutions should be preserved. It has been supposed that the negotiations for a political alliance between the Upper Canada Reformers and the French-Canadians did not begin until the approach of the elections for the first legislature of the United Province. But the Lafontaine Papers show that Francis Hincks opened up the prospect to Lafontaine immediately Lord Durham's Report had reached Canada. Hincks had never met Lafontaine, and his letter, suggesting a liberal alliance on the basis of the Responsible Government proposed in Lord Durham's Report, was the first that had passed between them. In his reply Lafontaine stated that he liked the principles of Government laid down in the Report but they had no guarantee that they would be acted upon. In subsequent letters Hincks wrote:

We certainly must have such a guarantee and I have no doubt that we shall obtain it. . . . I can assure you that the Reformers of this province have never attributed to you any desire to promote national objects [i.e. an independent French-Canadian nationality]. . . . On the Union question you should not mind Lord Durham's motives but the effect of the scheme. Lord Durham, I think, wrote more against you than he would have done in order to carry the British party with him, and after the result of the insurrection it would have been difficult to go strongly against them. I am sure Lord Durham from his speaking of not subjecting you to the British minority of Lower Canada understood well that the Upper Canada British would be your friends. N'importe. I am sure they will be. . . . I can enter fully into your feelings toward that infamous (miscalled, believe me) *British party in Lower Canada, which I hate as cordially as you can do, and you may perceive that the love they bear me is about the same as if I were a French-Canadian. . . . I feel certain that we can send* [to the first parliament of the united province] *a majority of decided men who will resort to every constitutional means to obtain self-government as recommended by Lord Durham.*[20]

Within a few months of the arrival of the Report in Canada, *Le Canadien*, and all the French-Canadian papers but one, were supporting its policy of Responsible Government.

In Upper Canada, the Family Compact saw in the Report the handwriting on the wall, and resorted to every weapon in a desperate effort to discredit it and save themselves. The Reform cause, broken down by the Rebellion and still languishing, revived as though an elixir had dropped upon them from an unseen world; Francis Hincks, who had fought a single-handed battle for Responsible Government in his *Examiner*, was joined by a score of papers who adopted Responsible Government as defined in Lord Durham's Report as the sum and substance of their policy. A considerable number of the Tory party, including some of the most influential men in the province, were converted by the Report and joined the Reformers in an effort to secure its recommendations. With each of these groups Responsible Government was the main question and the Union a subsidiary issue.

The Family Compact replied to the Report in dignified and reasoned appeals to the British Government and – through its press – staged a campaign of abuse, innuendo, and flag-waving in an effort to prejudice the Canadian populace. Within a month of the arrival of the Report, select committees of the Assembly (controlled by the Tory majority secured by Head) and the Legislative Council had submitted Reports in reply to it. These were remarkably able documents. That of the Assembly confined itself in the main to the inaccurate statements of the Upper Canada section of the Report in an effort to show that Lord Durham's policies were enunciated in ignorance of the situation in that province. The section on Lower Canada was 'evidently drawn up with much greater care and, they believe, with much greater accuracy, than that portion of it which relates to this province'. The rather fantastic classification of the population of Upper Canada given in the Report was subjected to scathing criticism.

Your committee cannot suppose that Lord Durham has imagined such a state of society, – they are well convinced that some disappointed or discontented person has imposed upon his Lordship's credulity. . . . With respect to the exclusion of British and Irish emigrants from places of honour and emolument in the province, it is sufficient to state that the Vice-chancellor, the Master and Registrar of the Court of Chancery, the Receiver-General, the Secretary of the Province, the Solicitor-General, four out of five Executive Councillors, and twelve out of twenty-nine Legislative Councillors appointed since Sir John Colborne assumed the government of the country, two-thirds of the clergy of the Church of England, a like proportion of district schoolmasters, and the principal masters of Upper Canada College with one exception, have been taken from that class of gentlemen.

The Committee pointed out that Lord Durham constantly compared Canada with the United States, to the detriment of the former; he did not have eyes to see anything unfavourable in the Americans. It deprecated severely the insinuations made against commissioners in respect to the execution of public works without either the production or suggestion of evidence, and it indignantly denied that the local government had proscribed its political opponents and wilfully punished innocent men at the time of the rebellion. A bad mistake in respect to the number of petitioners in behalf of Lount and Matthews was also indicated. These points were well taken, they constituted a serious indictment of the Report, and the Committee was careful not to injure its case by attempting too much.

The greater part of the Report of the Committee of the Legislative Council was devoted to a frontal attack upon Lord Durham's recommendation of Responsible Government. It was not satisfied, as were many of the Compact's utterances in these days, with merely asserting that it was inconsistent with British connexion and 'must lead to the overthrow of the great colonial empire of England'. It sought to show that government possessed all the responsibility that was necessary – the local officials were individually responsible in that they were subject to impeachment and the Governor was responsible to the British Government – and that Durham's collective Cabinet responsibility would be subversive of the true ends of colonial government. The imperial Cabinet developed its policy 'with a view to the present prosperity and future greatness of a country in which England has a deep interest and above all things with the intention of preserving against all opposition the unity of the empire', and at the same time giving satisfaction in a general manner to the people of the colony. But, according to the system proposed by Lord Durham, these ends would all be defeated because those who would conduct it would simply be the servants of a Canadian political party – the one that happened to have a majority in the Assembly for the time being. In two well-reasoned paragraphs[21] Lord Durham's intentions are described with remarkable clearness, and then, having shown that the Governor must, under the new system, ultimately give way to the parliamentary majority, the Committee concludes that 'so far as the empire is concerned, he becomes the sovereign of an independent realm'. That would lead indirectly to separation, and then to annexation by the United States. It was true that Lord Durham proposed to confine the functions of the local legislature to affairs strictly colonial, but 'this limitation of powers is not practical under his Lordship's system'. Apart from a suggestion that, with the new order once established, the Canadian majority party would be in a position to get its way in imperial matters also, there was no attempt to substantiate that confident assertion. Whether or not the Committee felt that it was traversing a thin sheet of ice, it hastened on to another point, ignoring entirely Lord Durham's confidence in that desire of the Canadian people to continue the imperial connexion which was the safeguard of the Durham system, and has in point of historical fact made the British Empire of to-day possible. If the Durham system had not been established that desire would have been destroyed and no type of government could have held the Empire together.

The Committee attempted to show that the conditions of public opinion in the colony made Lord Durham's proposals dangerous to public safety. There was little party consistency in Canada on which the system could be built. It was necessary for the Government to possess a check upon the popular will, which was subject to gusts of sentiment. 'Most of the practical evils found in the colonies have arisen from measures popular at the time of their enactment. . . . A responsible cabinet must look to the party of the day and in its favour neglect the great future interests of the province.' (The argument was cleverly stated. In substance it amounted to this, that the people of Canada were not sufficiently grown-up politically to govern themselves, in matters of Canadian concern, under a democratic system. Lord Durham believed that they were. Again the issue was a clear-cut one.)

Having assailed the strongest part of Lord Durham's report, the Committee proceeded to riddle its weakest part – the inaccurate statements and unfair criticism of the Upper Canada section. The quotation of two illustrative passages must suffice here.

> *In what manner, we ask, did the dominant party make use of the occasion, to persecute or disable the whole body of their political opponents? Who were the numbers of perfectly innocent men thrown into prison? . . . And what severe laws were passed in* Upper Canada, *under colour of which individuals very generally esteemed, were punished without any form of trial? . . . Your Committee beg, ere they conclude, to observe that, as regards Upper Canada, Lord Durham could not possibly have any personal knowledge, the period of his sojourn in that province being of such very short duration. Your Committee regret that His Lordship should have confided the task of collecting information to a person, who, be he who he may, has evidently entered on his task with the desire to exalt the opponents of the Colonial Government in the estimation of the High Commissioner, and to throw discredit on the statements of the supporters of British influence and British connection.*[22]

While the leaders of the Compact were holding this high converse with the British Government, their newspaper supporters were applying to Lord Durham's Report all the adjectives in a fairly extensive vocabulary of vituperation. It was an 'evil-minded pamphlet', whose aim was 'to excite party virulence and religious animosity', 'to propagate discontent and democratic ferocity'. Lord Durham's 'chief scavenger, Mr. Charles Buller, was incessantly employed in searching the cess-pools of discontent, disloyalty and sedition'. Lord Durham's 'heart was rotten at the core and radically incorrigible'. He displayed 'the perfidy of all democrats'. 'Shun the curse of the new doctrine. . . . Shun the name of Durham as you would shun the war-cry of pirates and rebels.' When the writers were in milder moods the Report was 'that mischievous document'. Lord Durham was constantly represented as the dupe of traitors. But not content with making him out a fool, some of them had to make him a knave. The *Cobourg Star,* September 4, 1839, asserted that the cause of 'Lord Durham's perfidy to Canada' was to be found in the fact that he was the 'governor of a company whose trade consists in the purchase and sale of lands in New Zealand and whose profits must entirely depend on the number of people they can by any means induce to emigrate thither'. During the whole of a stormy career, his integrity had never been called in question; that remained for a newspaper, fighting ruthlessly to save the political life of the Upper Canada oligarchy.

The response of the Reformers to the Report was, if not so violent, even more demonstrative. One writer, in his haste to erect monuments before the victory was won, suggested that a statue of Lord Durham should be erected in every market-place in the province. The Reform cause everywhere took on new life. Despair gave way to hope. Instead of following vague and variant aims, the Reformers concentrated on a clear-cut policy – Responsible Government as in Lord Durham's Report. Francis Hincks literally woke up one morning to find himself sorrounded by journalistic allies in the preaching of the true faith of which hitherto he had been the sole exponent. A number of these papers not only printed the Report in their columns but also published it in pamphlet form. Hincks dedicated the *Examiner's* pamphlet edition to Robert Baldwin.

I have taken the liberty of dedicating this publication to you, who like your venerable father have been the zealous, eloquent, and able advocate of those constitutional principles which have been at last recognized by a Governor-General of Canada. . . . It is not now too much to assert that the people of Upper Canada have the means of good government in their power. If they rouse themselves from their lethargy and return a House of Assembly, pledged to demand firmly and constitutionally the system of Government advocated by Lord Durham, there can hardly be a doubt that it will be conceded.

A Whitby schoolmaster, about to leave the country in despair, but remaining now to see democracy triumph, wrote to a friend in the States, a month after the Report arrived:

I think I shall remain in the country some time as there is a prospect of the damned Family Compact being shivered and ripped to atoms. The Report of the democratical Lord Durham has just put new life and courage into the Reformers or rebels, as the damned (excuse the profane adjective) Tories call them; and they never could number so many in their ranks, or were so determinedly or triumphantly confident as they are at present. . . . [In another letter ten days later.] I live in a fine neighbourhood; there is scarcely a Tory in it. Reform is making rapid strides and must finally triumph. The people have great hopes of Lord Durham and the Tories hate and fear him as the devil does holy water. [23]

The most significant feature of the immediate influence of the Report was the number – and quality – of the supporters whom it won from the ranks of the Tory party. These varied from Egerton Ryerson, a temporary Tory, who had been a Reformer at heart, but who had distrusted the previous leadership and policies of the party and had put his church before all party considerations, to H. J. Boulton who had been a too-zealous member of the Family Compact. Ryerson at this time was editor of the Methodist paper, the *Christian Guardian*. In the first number after the arrival of the Report, he wrote:

Lord Durham's Report is no patch work affair. It bears throughout the impress of the same master hand, it is all alike fresh from the same fountain, permeated by the same energy, enlivened by the same interest, instinct with sound constitutional patriotism, luminous with most comprehensive views, and vivified with most loyal and benevolent feelings. . . . [It] secures to the inhabitants of these provinces the fullest advantages of British constitutional government. [24]

In a later number of the *Guardian* he said: 'We agree with Lord Durham; we maintain that the English, Irish, and Scotch inhabitants of Canada, as well as the natives of the province, are just as competent to appreciate the privileges and advantages of the British constitution, as are the inhabitants of Great Britain and Ireland on the Eastern side of the Atlantic.'[25]

William Hamilton Merritt, founder of the town of St. Catharines, promoter and director of the Welland Canal, had been a consistent Tory. The Report appealed to him as the great solution, he rallied to it as enthusiastically as Baldwin and Hincks, and within a few weeks was sharing with them the leadership of the movement for Responsible Government.[26] Governor Arthur in his dispatches to the Colonial Secretary frequently added to his general disapprobation of the Report expressions of regret that it was dividing the 'loyal party', by which, of course, he meant the Tories. From a Family Compact point of view it was deceiving the very elect. A. N. (later Bishop) Bethune wrote from Cobourg to Bishop Strachan that 'many respectable and loyal persons are abettors of that mischievous Report'.[27] Bethune was one of many who were sincere in their political and ecclesiastical flag-waving, and the limitations of his judgment in regard to 'respectability' and 'loyalty' were as severe as the pain which such a situation caused him.

For all the outcry against the Report as a hypocritical attempt to destroy the imperial connexion, welcomed and championed by rebels who were utilizing it to prepare another insurrection, reasonable men came to realize that a movement that was uniting the whole body of moderate Reformers with a number of Tories in the securing of popular government by legal and constitutional means, through a method that was as thoroughly British and eminently sane as that proposed by Lord Durham, was calculated to destroy all rebellious tendencies. Dr. O'Callaghan, one of the leaders of the Lower Canada Rebellion, had predicted that as soon as he read the Report. He wrote to Perrault: 'When this Report gets thoroughly before the Upper Canada people, I expect it will have the effect of tranquillizing the public mind in a great degree and thus militate against the "physical force men" at Rochester.'[28] The Rochester phrase alludes, of course, to Mackenzie. But it must be said for Mackenzie that his rebellion in despair of securing popular government in a legal manner had made Lord Durham's Report possible and that if any British statesman had offered such a solution in pre-rebellion days he would have welcomed it most heartily.

Within three months of the appearance of the Report in Canada, the *Toronto Examiner* wrote (June 24) : ' No document has ever been promulgated in British America that has given such general satisfaction as this report. . . . Thousands of copies have been distributed in pamphlet form, and the demand, instead of abating is greater than ever.' By this time a few 'Durham meetings' had been held. At Niagara a Durham Constitutional Club was formed. At these meetings 'Durham flags' appeared. On a number of these appeared the words 'Lord Durham and Reform'.[29] We have heard that before, and it had a familiar sound also to Canadians of that day. Canadian democracy was fighting its battle under a slogan adopted by the hosts of British democracy. Many of these Canadians had been in the old country in the days when it had rung through England and Scotland. The Canadian papers had reported with remarkable fullness many of Lord Durham's speeches between 1831 and 1835, and also the Glasgow dinner at which 'Lord Durham and Reform' had been emblazoned in the position of prominence and celebrated in song as well as in legend.

> The King, our homes, our wooden wa's
> Lord Durham and Reform.

The 'Durhamites' did not always have it their own way. They attempted to hold a meeting in Cobourg, a Tory stronghold, only to have it broken up by a hostile crowd 'some with shille-laghs and some without'. A shower of stones completed the rout, the Durham flags were 'torn into a thousand shreds and trampled on with contempt', and a bonfire was made of the hustings. The next number of the *Cobourg Star* jubilantly exclaimed: 'Should any more of these Durham flags be hoisted in any other quarter of the province, we trust there are British arms enough to level them to the ground and drive the rebels from the field.'[30]

These earlier meetings were small and sporadic. A great acceleration was given to the movement by a large meeting at Hamilton on July 29. While this was organized by the friends of Responsible Government, it was called by the sheriff as a meeting of the inhabitants of the Gore District. An attempt was made, headed by Sir Allan MacNab, to bring to the gathering enough opponents of that policy to secure a majority. On the eve of the meeting, the *Hamilton Journal* said:

Death to the Family Compact and up with the Durham Constitution! To sustain the latter, the masses are moving from Nelson and its back townships and the neighbourhood of Guelph, from Galt, Preston and Waterloo, from the Jersey settlement, Dumfries, Paris, Brantford and Ancaster, from Barton, Saltfleet and Glanford. . . . In numbers they will be overwhelming, in conduct they will be without reproach.[31]

The meeting mustered two thousand people. That was about equal to half the population of Hamilton at that time; to realize its relative size, one would have to imagine a meeting of 65,000 people in the Hamilton of to-day. Sir Allan MacNab had gathered his opposition hosts. He came down from Dundurn Castle in fighting fettle, spoke in opposition to each of the Durhamite resolutions as it was presented, and was outvoted by about three to one. He praised Lord Durham's Report in other respects but argued that the Responsible Government recommendations would sever the British connexion. The resolutions approved of 'Responsible Government as recommended in Lord Durham's Report' as 'the only means of restoring confidence, allaying discontent, or perpetuating the connexion between Great Britain and this colony'; called for a dissolution of Parliament and an appeal to the people 'upon the present state of public affairs, and especially upon the Report of the Earl of Durham'; and recorded a pledge 'to support at the next election such candidates and such only, as can declare themselves favourable to the leading principles of Lord Durham's Report'.[32]

The *Hamilton Journal* declared in its next number, under the heading, 'Lord Durham Triumphant':

The effect of such a verdict, it is acknowledged even by its opponents, will be felt, not only throughout the province but within the walls of St. Stephen's and in the councils of the Cabinet. Truly may it be said, well done the men of Gore! They have taken the lead, as they always do, and hundreds and thousands will take pride in following in their footsteps.[33]

This ebullition of local pride turned out to be literally true. The Hamilton meeting gave a remarkable impetus to that Canadian revolution – a revolution thoroughly British in character, since it worked itself out in a legal and constitutional manner – which won democracy for Canada and laid the foundations of self-government in the British Empire. In the following weeks large and enthusiastic Durham meetings were held in every part of the province. The Hamilton resolutions were frequently accepted as models, and the Hamilton meeting was everywhere presented as the great object of emulation. In a number of places 'Durham Constitutional Clubs' were formed. In this period the most divergent organizations called themselves 'Constitutional', but the supporters of the Report felt that it would secure to them the full substance of the British Constitution.

This province-wide movement did not gather headway without some scenes of violence. On the way back from the

Hamilton meeting, a fight with bludgeons and stones developed over a Durham flag belonging to a delegation from Dundas, who beat off their opponents and saved their banner. A meeting at Davis's Tavern, near Toronto, was broken up by a body of armed men whom Sheriff Jarvis was accused of having brought from Toronto for that purpose. Two men were killed, a number seriously injured, and Francis Hincks narrowly escaped with his life.[34]

The Lieutenant-Governor, Sir George Arthur, the last of the military governors of the old regime, had been deeply offended by the Report. He reported these Durham meetings to Lord John Russell, now Colonial Secretary, in a manner calculated to prejudice the British Government:

> This captivating and exciting cause is influencing all parties. . . . Far more to be lamented than any of the circumstances to which I have referred are the effects of Lord Durham's Report. The bait of 'Responsible Government' has been eagerly taken, and its poison is working most mischievously. . . . That measure recommended by such high authority, is the worst evil that has yet befallen Upper Canada. The impression made throughout the country by Lord Durham's Report is demonstrable in a thousand ways. . . . Many inconsiderate persons by the course they are now pursuing at the 'Responsible Government' meetings promote the designs of the most criminal characters.[35]

Before writing these dispatches, the Lieutenant-Governor had already replied to a committee appointed by the Hamilton meeting that the adoption of Responsible Government as recommended in the Report would 'lead to a state of things inconsistent with the relation of this colony as a dependency of the British Crown'. With a British superiority and patronage, all the more galling to Canadians because its offensiveness was unconscious, he proceeded:

> I consider that the general influence of public opinion on the exercise of the functions of the Sovereign which the constitution of England practically allows ought carefully to be distinguished from the influence which the people of a particular portion of the Empire may safely possess. . . . The necessity of the people of Upper Canada preserving the sympathies and good will of the inhabitants of the neighbouring country has been powerfully recommended by the Report, which formed the subject of

consideration at the public meeting at Hamilton. Need I urge
upon the subjects of the British Crown in Upper Canada the still
more obvious duty and necessity of cultivating the affections of
the sovereign and people, by whose power they are sustained
and to whose protection alone they can look with confidence.[36]

That was Arthur's idea of upholding British connexion, and
he reported it to Russell with satisfaction and pride. Russell
refrained from rebuking him directly, but intimated that he was
to desist from such exhibitions in the future; it was not the
Governor's business to carry on controversies of that nature.[37]
Whatever Russell's attitude on the matter might be, it was not
that of Arthur. He and Thomson had decided to establish a new
system on the lines of Lord Durham's Report, although they
hesitated about committing themselves fully to Durham's bold
theoretical statements. Russell was probably influenced, however, by Arthur's dispatches. If Howe's letters would make him
more confident, these would make him more cautious. We can
never understand Russell's position if we think of his difficulty
as entirely a theoretical one. Like nearly all British statesmen of
these years, he believed that a large proportion of the population of both Canadian provinces was disloyal. With that point
of view he naturally feared what might develop in a crisis if the
full Durham theory were once assented to by the British Government. Yet Durham's Report had convinced him that a new
system must be set up and he was ready to carry out Durham's
suggestions so far as to establish a new order in which the everyday administration of Canada should be conducted through
men who possessed the confidence of the 'inhabitants of the
province' (this is vague, compared with Durham's 'majority of
the Assembly'), and the executive would thus work harmoni-
ously with the legislature. But the Governor and behind him the
British Government were to retain sufficient control – even in
internal affairs – to be able without embarrassment or apparent
tyranny to avert any danger that might develop. So, at the same
time as he warned Poulett Thomson in his dispatch of October
14 against acquiescing in any statement of 'Responsible Government', he expressed his approval of 'the practical views of
colonial government recommended by Lord Durham'. The
establishment of the new system was made easier by Russell's
instructions, October 16, to all governors in British North
America that in the future the members of the Executive Coun-

cil and the principal officials were not to be considered, as in the past, as holding office for life so long as they were not guilty of misconduct (a great bulwark of 'irresponsibility' in the old sense of that term), but were to be subject to removal and substitution 'as often as any sufficient motives of public policy may suggest the expediency of that measure'. His primary instructions to Thomson on the Union, municipal government, education, public works, and the civil list were based directly and specifically on Lord Durham's Report.

These instructions were well suited to Poulett Thomson's outlook and personality. While he was a thorough Liberal and in English politics a Durhamite, and was sympathetic towards the establishment of a more liberal system in Canada, the bent of his mind was practical rather than theoretical. What appealed most to his imagination was that programme of practical measures which Durham had pointed out as being essential to the prosperity of the country. He secured the consent of the Special Council of Lower Canada and both branches of the Legislature of Upper Canada to the Union, established a municipal system in Lower Canada and greatly improved that of the upper province, laid the foundation of important educational improvements, established a land registry office and a rural police in the lower province, outlined a scheme of public works and cleared the way for its inception, revised the customs laws, and established a board of works, a new system of county courts and a stipendiary magistracy; within two years he had put through the whole programme. Nearly all of it had been suggested by Durham and some of it begun by him, but – as Joseph Howe put it – 'it is rare that a statesman so firm, so sagacious and indefatigable follows in the wake of a projector so bold'. His methods were as remarkable as his success. To the Canadian people, accustomed to governors of the old type, he seemed like a beneficent wizard who had come to them out of fairyland. Durham had greatly impressed them, but even Durham was no match for Thomson in the field of administration. Under the Durham system of self-government Canada has developed great statesmen, but it is doubtful if any of them has been as adroit, as resourceful, as successful as the man known in Canadian history as Lord Sydenham.

It was natural that a man with such a task and such a personality should do his own governing rather than leave it to a ministry. Although careful in his public statements, he told his friends that he was the only one who was responsible for the Government and that he would place no responsibility on his ministers. It must be borne in mind that a new order was being inaugurated and that the practical programme which Thomson set himself to carry out was as much a legacy from Lord Durham's Report as was Responsible Government. The programme consisted in the main of the things which Durham considered essential to the successful operation of the new governmental system which he proposed. It may be stated with confidence that no responsible Canadian ministry either would or could, apart from Thomson's controlling hand, have completed that programme and, in that case, Responsible Government would have been crippled from its birth. He was determined to achieve these things, and in the doing of them he did not trouble himself about theories and would not be troubled by others. But when the task was completed and he was longing to hear 'the guns pealing from the rocks of Quebec' – those guns that were never fired – he wrote home to his brother, 'I have got a ministry with an avowed and recognized majority, capable of doing what they think right and not to be upset by my successor'. (Now it was 'what *they* think right'; a few months before, in the midst of his task, he was governing 'as *he* thought right, not as they fancy'.)

He was able to write that with confidence because – theory or no theory – he had gone far towards the establishment in Canada of that British constitutional system which Lord Durham had advocated. In order to effect his legislative programme, he needed a parliamentary majority. With remarkable ability he succeeded in securing that in the first Union Parliament. The ministry which he formed was not a party ministry, but party government is not essential to Responsible Government, except in the sense that a coalition is really a party for the time being. The Canadian political situation at that time was badly broken up, largely because of the Union, and Sydenham created a temporary party which would afford a parliamentary majority to his coalition ministry made up of moderate men selected from various groups. Although he would never agree to any theory of ministerial responsibility, he accustomed the Canadian people to the practice of a ministry realizing a dependence upon a parliamentary majority, and he familiarized them with the methods by which such ministries ruled in Great Britain. He taught them to look to 'government measures' for legislation, as Lord Durham had suggested; he reorganized his Executive Council, again in accordance with Lord Durham's Report, into a Cabinet made up of heads of departments; and he established the rule that its members must sit in Parliament. He thus set up what may be called the machinery of Responsible Government.

Having run ahead to indicate Poulett Thomson's attitude, we return to observe that of the 'Durhamites', who by the time of his arrival constituted a large majority of the people of Upper Canada and were rapidly securing support from the French-Canadians of Lower Canada. They had decided that the test for their new Governor was to be whether he would 'build upon the foundation laid by Lord Durham'. At first they were not a little puzzled. They welcomed Russell's office-holding dispatch as a step in the direction of Responsible Government. The *Toronto Mirror* took the position that they should oppose the Union unless they received a clear promise of Responsible Government as recommended by Lord Durham's Report. But the *Examiner* persuaded them that the Union should be supported because once it was effected they would have sufficient political power to force the acceptance of Responsible Government no matter what the Governor or the British Government thought of it. Hincks, writing to Lafontaine a little later said: 'I know you think we shall never get Responsible Government, that the Ministry are deceiving us. Granted. But we will make them give it whether they like it or not.'[38] The *Hamilton Express* accepted the Russell dispatches as instalments of Responsible Government and urged the people to wait patiently for the remainder which was sure to follow.

Thomson's policy split the Upper Canada Tories. When the Union project was approved by the last session of the Upper Canada Assembly the die-hards attacked the Governor and his supporters bitterly. One of their poetical effusions took the form of 'An Epistle from Beelzebub to His Friend, Governor Pow' and contained the lines:

> *The pill gilt by Durham, they greedily swallowed,*
> *For Mammon by* sic chiels *has ever been hallowed.*
> *Believe me, all Tartarus chuckles not less*
> *Than Yankee allies at your glorious success.*
>
> .   .   .   .
>
> *The sentence on Canada soon shall be passed*
> *And Hell and democracy triumph at last.*[39]

Thomson let the heathen rage and continued on his way. By the spring of 1840 the Union Bill was ready for the British Parliament, and, what was even more important, the British Parliament was ready for it. The Government was no longer dependent on the Radicals for a majority, for Peel was prepared to accept the Union. So Durham, the violent opponent and *bête noire* of the Tories all his life, saw, in his last illness, this feature of his Report triumph on account of Tory statesmanship. Peel had been converted by the Report to the extent, at least, that the Union appeared to be better than any other policy that could be thought of, and Peel was a statesman, never a factious leader of opposition. Wellington, on equally conscientious grounds, was opposed to the Union and quarrelled with Peel so openly that for some time the two Tory leaders were not on speaking terms. But Wellington was not willing to ask the Lords to throw out the Bill after it had been passed by the Commons.

The Union Act differed in two important respects from the recommendations of Lord Durham's Report. Where the Report had provided for a representation of the two provinces in the united legislature in proportion to their population, the Act assigned to them an equal representation. This was an injustice to the French-Canadians, the population of Lower Canada being larger than that of the Upper Province. Durham had been confident that his recommendation would ensure an English-speaking majority and at the same time do justice to the French. But Upper Canada had wanted a considerably larger representation than its sister province, the suggestions varying from mild to gross injustice, and Thomson had had to fight hard to maintain even an equal representation. In this respect at least Durham and Thomson were the friends of the French-Canadians.

Again, Lord Durham had recommended that the establishment of an adequate system of municipal government should be provided for, either by the Act of Union or by separate legislation passed by the British Parliament at the same time. Thomson had included this in the draft of the Union Bill which he had sent home, and was astonished to learn that the bill had been passed without it and no other provision made for it. 'It is with the deepest mortification,' he wrote to Russell, 'that I find the whole system for the establishment of local government omitted from the bill. . . . I should have been far less surprised to find the Union Bill abandoned altogether by the Government than this most essential part of it withdrawn.' After referring to the strong recommendation of Lord Durham's Report in this respect, he reminded the Government that it was hopeless to expect a Canadian Parliament to pass such a measure. 'Lord Durham has given the reply which certainly appeared last year to be conclusive to His Majesty's Government, and the correctness of which I can now confirm. "It is in vain to expect that this sacrifice of power will be voluntarily made by any representative body." '[40] When Russell replied that Peel and Stanley, on whose Tory support they depended for the passing of the measure, had objected to these clauses, Poulett Thomson, now Lord Sydenham, buckled on his armour, established a municipal system in Lower Canada through his Special Council before the Union Act went into effect, and then achieved what both Durham and he had regarded as impossible by steering a municipal bill through the Union Legislature.

In the elections for the first Legislature of United Canada, the Reform candidates throughout Upper Canada appealed to the electors on the recommendations of Lord Durham's Report. That was the first and only plank of their platform. It was the Report, the whole Report, and nothing but the Report. Excitement ran high and the wonder is that there was not more violence. The old Compact lost its last fight for life. In his appeal to the electors of Terrebonne, Lafontaine had, several months before the election, taken common ground with the Upper Canada Reformers on the Responsible Government part of the Report, and urged his fellow countrymen to test all candidates on that question. As for the Union, they should accept it, but seek a modification of those terms which were particularly unfair to them. The following is the core of his new appeal:

In a word, to the great question of the day; Responsible Government. . . . This is the leading feature of the British constitution. Lord Durham in recognizing the necessity of its application to local affairs in the colonies struck at the root of the evil and suggested the efficacious remedy. . . . For my part I have no hesitation in declaring that I am in favour of this British principle of Responsible Government. I see in its operation the only guarantee we can have of a good and effective government. The colonists must possess the management of their own affairs. All their efforts must be devoted towards this object.

On the eve of the meeting of Parliament, Robert Baldwin, already a member of Sydenham's coalition ministry, knowing that a large majority of those elected to the house were in favour of Responsible Government and feeling that a union of Upper and Lower Canada Liberals could be effected on behalf of that principle, suggested to the Governor that the Ministry be reorganized on that basis. But Sydenham was mainly interested in solidifying the Union and putting through his legislative programme. He knew that the combination which he had formed could be relied upon to support him in these objects, and he was confident that the combination proposed by Baldwin could not; he knew how little cohesion Baldwin's so-called 'party' had at that time, apart from Responsible Government; and he would not commit himself to Responsible Government in any case. So he asked for Baldwin's resignation and went ahead. If Baldwin had been able to muster a majority *against Sydenham*, he could have made things interesting, but when Parliament met he discovered that the greater number of the Upper Canada members elected on Lord Durham's Report were too much attracted by Sydenham's programme to oppose him; many features of that programme were laid down in Lord Durham's Report as essential concomitants of the establishment of Responsible Government. When Sydenham had completed his programme, then came the time for Responsible Government on its theoretical side (on its practical, much of it was already in operation). In June the ministers were challenged to say whether they would resign if they lost the support of the majority of the House, and Draper, on behalf of himself and his colleagues, replied that they would. Two months later at the end of the session, September 3, 1841, Baldwin moved his series of Responsible Government resolutions. S. B. Harrison, unquestionably at Sydenham's suggestion, moved in amendment another series, which differed slightly from Baldwin's. Sydenham avoided a few particularly embarrassing phrases; and the Ministry had the satisfaction of offering to Parliament its own statement, rather than receiving dictation from Baldwin. Harrison's resolutions were carried by an overwhelming majority. Their more material statements were that the provincial parliament existed 'for the exercise of a constitutional influence over the executive departments of their government', as well as 'for legislation upon all matters of internal government'; and that 'the chief advisers of the representative of the sovereign, constituting a provincial administration under him, ought to be men possessed of the confidence of the representatives of the people'.[41]

Thus was fulfilled, in the main, a prediction which Charles Buller had made to Lady Durham a year earlier: 'It will be but a few months too before we shall have an aid more powerful than that of reasoning in explaining and enforcing what Ld. Durham really meant by "Responsible Government": we shall have the Parliament of United Canada enforcing the adoption of his policy and demonstrating the soundness of his views.'[42]

When Sydenham died, a month after the Harrison resolutions, the leading advocates of Responsible Government – Baldwin, Hincks, Howe, the *Toronto Mirror*, the *Toronto Examiner*, the *Hamilton Journal* – all stated that Responsible Government was secured. They did not realize fully the possibilities of later disputes in regard to interpretation and detail. But certainly the substance of Responsible Government was secured. There was a ministry, consisting of heads of departments, who conducted a legislative programme by means of 'government measures', whose members were pledged to resign when they lost the support of the majority of the people's representatives in Parliament; and Parliament had declared that henceforth the Governor should carry on the government through a ministry controlled and supported in that manner. The British Government had not yet given its consent to the theoretical implication of this; and Lord Durham's other recommendation (necessary to the completion of *self-government*) that the British Government should not support a Governor who placed himself in conflict with a Canadian Parliament had not yet been tested. But the course of events under the next two Governors convinced British statesmen that, having gone so far, they would have to give way to the full Durham system. Then with Howick (the third Earl Grey), Lord Durham's brother-in-law, and Lord Elgin, Lord Durham's son-in-law, there came into power a Colonial Secretary and a Governor fully prepared to act in harmony with Lord Durham's proposals in theory and practice alike.

✿ ✿ ✿

List of Abbreviations

D.P. Durham Papers, Public Archives of Canada, Ottawa.

Howick MSS Papers of the second Earl Grey, Howick Hall, County of Northumberland, England.

Lambton MSS Papers of the first Earl of Durham, Lambton Castle, Durham County, England.

Q Q Series – Correspondence of the Governor, Lieutenants-Governor and others to Colonial Office to 1841. (Now largely designated as CO42, Public Archives of Canada, Ottawa.)

Notes

CHAPTER I: The Canadian Situation
(pp. 15-41)

[1] *Lord Durham's Report*, iii. 83.

[2] Ontario Archives, *Macaulay Papers*, Dec. 3, 1835.

[3] Aileen Dunham, *Political Unrest in Upper Canada, 1815-1836*, pp. 167-8.

[4] Where the term is employed in this sense I have capitalized it throughout.

[5] See especially Neilson Papers, Mackenzie to Neilson, Feb. 22, 1836, and *Correspondent and Advocate*, Feb. 25, 1836.

[6] Upper Canada Sundries, Mar. 4, 1836. Printed in the newspapers of that month.

[7] The mayor was at that time elected by the councillors, who were elected by the citizens.

[8] I have not mentioned the so-called debate on Responsible Government, Apr. 11, 1836, because it is simply an incident in a struggle which cannot be described in detail here. This debate was on an amendment moved by Peter Perry to the effect that it 'was one of the brightest features of the British constitution that the head of the Government is assisted in *all* its affairs by the advice of *known and responsible* councillors and officers who possess the confidence of the people'. A careful perusal of the verbatim report will yield the same conclusions as I have stated above in regard to the whole controversy between Head and the Reformers.

[9] *Speeches, Messages, and Replies of Sir F. B. Head*, pp. 59-60.

[10] *Buffalo Journal*, Dec. 6, 1837.

[11] Canadian Archives, Neilson Papers.

CHAPTER II: Preparing for Canada
(pp. 41-61)

[1] Howick MSS., Jan. 15, 1838.

[2] Lambton MSS., 'Tuesday' (Jan. 16).

[3] *Ibid.*, Jan. 15, 1838. Given in Reid, ii. 149-150.

[4] *Morning Chronicle*, Feb. 7, 1838.

[5] *D.P.* 1, i. 211 seq., 561 seq., 564 seq.; 6, i. 323 seq., 284 seq., 303 seq., 450 seq., 465 seq., 486 seq.; G. 38: 660.

[6] *D.P.* 6, i. 466 seq.; Strachan to Gillespie, Mar. 2, 1838. Enclosed in Gillespie to Durham, Apr. 19.

[7] *D.P.* 6, i. 413-36.

[8] There is one possible exception to this. Several letters to Durham signed 'Veritas' stated part of the French case in rather high-flown language and warned him against the Canada merchants.

[9] *D.P.* 6, i. 326.

[10] *D.P.* 6, i. 454.

[11] *D.P.*, Lord Durham's engagement book.

[12] Lambton MSS. (copy), Ellice to Lafontaine, Mar. 21.

[13] Roebuck, *The Colonies of England*, pp. 190-2.

[14] *Ibid.*, pp. 193-217. There is a copy among the Durham Papers in the Canadian Archives, *D.P.* 6, iii. 578 seq.

[15] Charles Buller's *Sketch of Lord Durham's Mission* (1840) in the possession of Dr. Doughty, printed in Lucas, iii. 336 seq., and in *Report of Canadian Archives*, 1923, pp. 341 seq. In later references to this document the pagination will be given as in Canadian Archives Report.

[16] *D.P.* 1, i. 564.

[17] Buller, *Sketch*, p. 358.

[18] *Ibid.*, p. 343.

[19] Buller, *Sketch*, p. 342.

[20] *Morning Chronicle*, Apr. 4, 1838.

[21] *Recollections*, v. 82.

[22] *Illustrated London News*, Dec. 25, 1843.

[23] *Examiner*, Dec. 2, 1848.

[24] Garnett, *Life of Wakefield*, p. 20.

[25] *Ibid.*, p. 92.

[26] *Ibid.*, pp. 132-44.

[27] Lambton MSS., Kennedy to Durham, May 31, 1834, July 10, Aug. 8, 20, 1838, and three undated letters; Parkes to Durham, Jan. 5, 1836.

[28] Lambton MSS.

[29] This is evidenced by a number of letters about Turton written by others as well as his own letters to Lord Durham. *D.P.* 6, i. 3, 5, 96, ii. 590, iii. 20, 31; Lambton MSS., Kennedy to Durham, n.d., July 10, 1838; Lady Durham to Lady Grey, June 27, 1838.

[30] Lambton MSS., Kennedy to Durham, n.d.

[31] *D.P.* 6, iii. 31, Turton to Hobhouse, Jan. 1, 1839; Buller's *Sketch*, p. 342. This is confirmed, so far as Hobhouse is concerned, on the

authority of Ellice, by Melbourne to Durham (Lambton MSS.), Apr. 10, 1838. Hobhouse was not quite candid about this matter in his *Recollections* (v. 172, 173), where he shifted the issue to what he advised *after* Lord Melbourne objected, but his daughter, Lady Dorchester, in a foot-note, gave the facts precisely as they are stated above.

[32] Lambton MSS., April 9, 10, 1838.

[33] From the North.

[34] Lambton MSS.

[35] Buller's *Sketch* (1840), pp. 342-3. Lambton MSS., Lady Durham to Lady Grey, July 30, 1838: 'I always understood and Mr. Ellice admits as much that although Lambton yielded as to his appointment by the Govt. at home, he considered himself at liberty to do what he pleased on his *own* responsibility when he arrived here.' For a similar statement by Durham see Q. 246, pt. 2: 312-14 (also in *D.P.* 2, i. 200), Durham, to Glenelg, No. 30, July 30, 1838.

[36] Lambton MSS., Ellice to Durham, July 4, 1838. This is supported by the language of Melbourne and Glenelg to Durham quoted pp. 64-5 *infra*.

[37] Buller's *Sketch*, p. 343.

CHAPTER III: A Good Beginning
(pp. 62-79)

[1] Lady Durham's Journal, 8-12; Buller's *Sketch*, pp. 343-4; Lady Durham to Lady Grey, May 10, 22.

[2] *Le Canadien*, May 23, 1838.

[3] According to Buller this letter was carefully prepared by Durham and handed over to Buller for the latter's signature (*Sketch*, p. 345). The letter is in Q. 246: 62-4 and is printed in the contemporary newspapers and in Kingsford, x. 125.

[4] *Le Canadien*, June 1, 1838.

[5] *Montreal Transcript*, June 2, 5, 1838.

[6] *D.P.* 4, i, 225, and contemporary newspapers; *ibid.* 2, i. 28-34; 4, i. 148, 162, 178, 181, 193; and Q. 246: 77 seq.

[7] Q. 246: 102 seq.; *D.P.* 2, i. 46 seq., June 5, 1838.

[8] Q. 246: 101, June 5, 1838.

[9] Q. 246: 175; *D.P.* 2, i. 100, Poinsett to Macomb, June 12.

[10] Q. 246: 107 seq. See also *D.P.* 2, i. 89, printed in full in *Can. Arch. Report for 1923*, pp. 314-15.

[11] Q. 250: 148-53.

[12] *Ibid*. 246: 164-7.

[13] Q. 246: 164 seq., 119 seq.

[14] Lady Durham's Journal, 14.

[15] Lambton MSS., Lady Durham to Lady Grey, June 11, 1838.

[16] *Ibid*., May 1, 1838.

[17] *Ibid*., May 4, 1838.

[18] *Ibid*., May 4, 1838.

[19] *Ibid*.

[20] *D.P*. 6, i. 589 seq., June 7, 1838.

[21] Lambton MSS. Parts in Reid, ii. 195-8 and Bradshaw, p. 172.

[22] *D.P*. 3, i. 770 seq. The draft of the dispatch, as also of a supplementary one of June 30 (*Ibid*. 3, i. 1037), is in Buller's hand. The commission and the two dispatches are in Appendix B of *Lord Durham's Report* and are printed in full in Lucas, iii. 29-33.

[23] Buller, *Sketch*, p. 350.

[24] See Richardson, *Eight Years*, pp. 33 seq.

[25] Q. 245: 4, Colborne to Glenelg, May 2, 1838.

[26] Q. 253: 175 seq., Gillespie and Moffat to Glenelg, Jan. 9, 1838.

[27] G. 38: 470, Glenelg to Durham, Apr. 21, 1838, enclosing G. 38: 296-307, Glenelg to Colborne, Mar. 19, 1838; *D.P*. I, i. 371 seq., 392 seq.

[28] *D.P*. 6, i. 631 seq., 643 seq., Buller to Durham, June 21, 25, 1838; Bradshaw, pp. 145-6.

[29] Q. 246: 205 seq. Printed in *Ordinances of the Special Council*, 1838, ii. 7, and in *Annual Register*, 1838, Public Documents, pp. 304-8; *Quebec Gazette*, June 28, 1838.

[30] Lambton MSS. (copy), June 28, 1838. Given in full in Reid, ii. 205.

[31] *Ibid*.; Q. 246: 204-5; *D.P*. 2, i. 112.

[32] Brodeur MSS., Durham to Paget, July 3. Quotation from *Royal Gazette of Bermuda*, July 31; *D.P*. 1, ii. 734 seq. (with enclosures); Q. 253: 266.

[33] *Cours d'Histoire*, iv. 251-2.

[34] Buller, *Sketch*, p. 352.

[35] *Quebec Gazette*, June 15, 1838.

[36] Lambton MSS., Lady Durham to Lady Grey, June 24, June 5, 1838.

[37] *Ibid*., June 5, July 4; Lady Durham's Journal, 15.

[38] Lady Durham's Journal, 14.

CHAPTER IV: The Clouds Gather
(pp. 80-108)

1 Correspondence in possession of Dr. Doughty, July 8, 1838.

2 Lambton MSS., Lady Durham to Lady Grey, July 9, 1838.

3 *D.P.* 6, i. 829, July 13.

4 Lambton MSS., July 14, 1838.

5 Q. 246: 282, July 16.

6 Lady Durham's Journal, 26, 28.

7 *Sketch*, p. 354.

8 *D.P.* 6, i. 973, July 31, 1838.

9 Lambton MSS.

10 Lady Durham's Journal, 27.

11 *Ibid.*, 29.

12 *Ibid.*, 30-1.

13 *Toronto Mirror*, July 21, 1838.

14 He actually arrived at 11 o'clock.

15 Kingsford, x. 121-3.

16 Richardson, *Eight Years*, p. 37.

17 *D.P.* 6, i. 907.

18 Charles Grey to Lord Grey, July 24, 1838. Correspondence in possession of Dr. Doughty.

19 Lambton MSS.

20 *D.P.* 1, ii. 92, July 4.

21 *D.P.* 2, i. 193, July 30.

22 Lambton MSS.

23 *Ibid.*

24 *D.P.* 2, i. 271-96. The original in Durham's hand.

25 It need hardly be added that the dispatch was marked 'Secret', and that the passages referred to were suppressed when it was printed later in the *Parliamentary Papers*.

26 *Montreal Transcript*, Aug. 23, 1838.

27 *D.P.* 6, ii. 1 seq., Aug. 1, 1838.

28 *D.P.*, Aug. 23, 1838. The two letters are printed in full in *Canadian Archives Report for 1923*, pp. 326-37.

[29] This is followed closely in *Lord Durham's Report*, ii. 279-80.

[30] *Ibid*. ii. 280.

[31] *Ibid*. ii. 281.

[32] I find it difficult to follow Baldwin's historical statements. Before the date of this letter one finds little advocacy of Responsible Government in this sense of the term. The term was employed as I have indicated, but in a much more general sense. If there was such a movement as early as 1820, it was a mere groping after the principle enunciated here. It was *not* 'introduced into the address in reply to the speech from the throne in 1828 or 1829' (see *Journals of the House of Assembly of Upper Canada*). It was not the issue between the Reformers and Head nor the subject of an appeal to the Home Government in 1835 (see *ibid*. and p. 21 seq. *ante*). While Baldwin correctly described the phrasing of the address carried by the Assembly by 53 votes to 2, the implication that it embodied the adoption of the principles expressed in this letter was a piece of special pleading that was hardly worthy of him (see p. 22 *ante*). He was driving hard for his great idea, and historical accuracy fell by the wayside.

[33] Strangely as this statement may read to both Englishmen and Canadians today, and much as one distrusts such sweeping generalizations, it seems to be literally true.

[34] Letter by Wakefield to the *Spectator*, Nov. 25, 1838, in reply to an earlier letter by Roebuck dealing with the former's trip to Saratoga. Wakefield stated also in his letter that after he had had many conversations with Lafontaine and the other French leaders, he came to the conclusion that their policies were mistaken and decided to seek out Papineau and bring his influence to bear on the situation. Lafontaine in his letter to the press in the following January gave him the lie direct. He met Wakefield for the first time on July 10 (in Montreal), and on that occasion the latter asked him for a letter to Papineau, informing him that he had left Quebec with the purpose of seeking out Papineau, which he immediately did. Wakefield also stated that he had reported nothing which Lafontaine said to him to any one connected with the mission. Lafontaine stated that the first time he met Buller the latter had mentioned as one reason for the interview a statement which Wakefield had told him had been made to him by Lafontaine.

[35] *D.P.* 3, i. 203, 930, 1023.

[36] Duncombe, i. 250-3.

[37] Lambton MSS., Lady Durham to Lady Grey; Lady Durham's Journal, pp. 39-40.

[38] *D.P.* 6, ii. III.

[39] This is not a reference to the disallowance of the ordinance, of which Durham knew nothing at this time. He considered that the Ministers had betrayed him on the Turton question.

[40] The debates on Turton and the constitution of the Councils.

41 This is not a spontaneous utterance of Buller's feeling. This paragraph stands in the draft in Wakefield's hand.

42 *D.P.* 6, ii. 134 seq.

CHAPTER V: The Storm Breaks
(pp. 109-150)

1 See pp. 68-75 *ante,* for the content of the ordinance and the circumstances of its promulgation.

2 *D.P.* 1, ii. 386.

3 Sir William Follett's speech when he suggested this amendment makes that quite clear. See *Hansard.*

4 *Times,* Aug. 29, 1838.

5 Lambton MSS., Lady Durham to Lady Grey, Sept. 13, 1838; *Quebec Gazette,* Sept. 10, 1838.

6 Lady Durham's Journal, 40-2.

7 Buller's *Sketch,* p. 359.

8 Lord Durham's recommendation of Responsible Government exactly meets this difficulty. This letter provides further evidence that that solution had not yet occurred to the British Government.

9 Lambton MSS. There is an extract (the part relating to the ordinance) in *D.P.* 1, ii. 231.

10 *D.P.* 1, ii. 232.

11 Lady Durham's Journal, 42. The account is saturated with personal feeling, but when checked by other sources, Lady Durham is found to be remarkably accurate in her statement of facts and, in view of what followed, the probabilities are all in favour of this statement.

12 *D.P.* 3, ii. 694.

13 Lady Durham's Journal, 43-4; Duncombe, ii. 256.

14 *Cobourg Star,* Oct. 3, 1838.

15 *Quebec Mercury,* Oct. 18, 1838.

16 *D.P.* 6, ii. 201.

17 Edward Ellice Jr., Lord Durham's ex-private secretary and son of 'Bear' Ellice.

18 *D.P.* 3, ii. 701.

19 *Ibid.,* 705.

20 *Montreal Herald,* Oct. 4, 1838.

[21] Q. 247: 222-4, Sept. 29, 1838.

[22] Duncombe, ii. 257.

[23] I am indebted for this view originally to Professor Egerton's Oxford lectures. My research has confirmed and strengthened it.

[24] *D.P.* 3, ii. 748, 846, 877; 6, ii. 228.

[25] Lambton MSS., Aug. 16, 1838.

[26] Lady Durham's Journal, 43; Lambton MSS., Lady Durham to Lady Grey, Oct. 11, 1838.

[27] *Ibid.*, Lambton MSS., Lady Durham to Lady Grey, Oct. 11, 1838; *D.P.* 6, ii. 220, Thom to Buller, Sept. 27, 1838.

[28] *D.P.* 6, ii. 347.

[29] Lambton MSS., Oct. 2, 1838.

[30] *D.P.* 6, iii. 251.

[31] Papers in possession of Dr. Doughty.

[32] *Quebec Gazette*, Oct. 10, 1838.

[33] *Annual Register*, 1838, pp. 312-17; Reid, ii. 275-85.

[34] Howick MSS., Lord Grey to Charles Grey, Nov. 29, 1838.

[35] *Melbourne Papers*, p. 438.

[36] Lambton MSS., Nov. 29, 1838.

[37] *Ibid.*, Dec. 5, 1838.

[38] *Morning Chronicle*, Nov. 7, 1838.

[39] For details the reader is referred to Buller's *Sketch*, Note A; *Can. Arch. Report for 1923*, pp. 367-9.

[40] Canadian Archives, Lower Canada Sundries, Sept. 20, 1838; Letter Books of Civil Secretary, Sept. 22, 1838.

[41] *Le Canadien*, Oct. 17, 22, Nov. 2, 1838.

[42] See pp. 40-1 *ante*.

[43] See article by Professor R. G. Trotter on 'Durham and the Idea of a Federal Union of British North America', in *Report of Canadian Historical Association, 1925*, for the details of this paper and a full account of the whole subject.

[44] I have identified the handwriting of the pencilled notes on the margin of this plan of Lord Durham's in the Canadian Archives as that of John Beverley Robinson. Roebuck's plan and this one modelled after it are in *D.P.* 6, iii. 578-673. The paper submitted to Sir John Harvey is in Delancey-Robinson Papers. There is practically no difference in content between the latter and the plan which was

criticized by Robinson, but the wording is different here and there and some points are more fully explained.

[45] These amendments are indicated by *D.P.* 3, ii. 675 (Durham to Robinson, Sept. 16, 1838), and the erasures and changes in the document at the Canadian Archives, all of which are in accordance with Robinson's marginal comments.

[46] *D.P.* 6, ii. 98, Thom to Durham, Aug. 17, 1838.

[47] Buller's *Sketch*, p. 358; *D.P.* 3, ii. 675. See Bradshaw, pp. 319-20, for a letter to *The Observer* (published Dec. 24, 1838) giving another description of Durham's revised plan. The supporting authority is of a very doubtful character.

[48] Lady Durham's Journal, 39.

[49] *D.P.* 3, ii. 378, Aug. 16, 1838.

[50] *D.P.* 3, ii. 562, Sept. 4, 1838.

[51] *D.P.* 3, ii. 378; *Lord Durham's Report*, ii. 322-3.

[52] *D.P.* 6, ii. 220, Sept. 27, 1838.

[53] *Montreal Courier*, Oct. 3, 1838.

[54] Richardson, *Eight Years*, p. 227.

[55] *D.P.* 3, ii. 815.

[56] Lower Canada Sundries, Oct. 22, 1838.

[57] *Edinburgh Review*, Apr. 1847 (review of Head's 'Emigrant'). 'Time, and the honest co-operation of the various parties, would be required to aid the action of a federal constitution; and time is not allowed, in the present state of Lower Canada, nor co-operation to be expected . . . The only efficacious government would be that formed by a legislative union' (*Lord Durham's Report*, ii. 307).

[58] Richardson stated that Peter McGill told him – eight years after the event – of a conversation with Buller after Durham had sailed in which he was informed that Lord Durham had abandoned his former intention in favour of a legislative union. The preference must be given to Buller's statement, quoted above, especially as in the article referred to he would have been glad to prove the contrary and place Head in the wrong. But Buller probably said something to McGill which indicated a changing, if not a changed mind, on Durham's part. Such conversions are not usually sudden ones, and we shall see that the question was not finally settled until some time after Durham's return to England.

[59] Q. 248: 154, Oct. 20, 1838.

[60] *D.P.* 3, ii. 902, 935, Oct. 24, Nov. 16, 1838.

[61] *D.P.* 4, i. 837, Oct. 19; *ibid.* 6, ii. 443 [Oct. 20].

[62] *D.P.* 6, ii. 435.

[63] See his dispatch to Glenelg, Q. 247: 222, where he said something very like that.

[64] Lady Durham's Journal, 51; Buller's *Sketch*, p. 363.

[65] Duncombe, ii. 265. Quoted in Reid, ii. 304-5.

[66] Buller, *Sketch*, p. 363.

[67] Lady Durham's Journal, 52-4. Quoted in part in Reid, ii. 303-4.

[68] [End of Chapter Note.] For a letter from Buller to Mill dealing with Lord Durham's resignation, which was secured by the Canadian Archives after this book was set up in page form, see Canadian Archives Report for 1928 (published in 1929).

CHAPTER VI: Return to England
(pp. 150-167)

[1] *Melbourne Papers*, p. 434, Oct. 21, 1838.

[2] Sir George Trevelyan, *Life and Letters of Macaulay*, i. 543-4.

[3] Bradshaw, p. 230.

[4] See pp. 138-9, *ante*.

[5] What a remarkable prophecy this would have been if Mill had written 'Imperial' instead of 'English'.

[6] The reference, of course, is to the Reform Bill.

[7] Fawcett, p. 202, Nov. 27, 1838.

[8] *D.P.* 6, ii. 466 seq., 477 seq., Lambton MSS.

[9] Lambton MSS., Nov. 29, 1838.

[10] *Ibid.*, Nov. 29, 1838.

[11] Quoted in *Montreal Gazette*, Jan. 12, 1839.

[12] *Morning Chronicle*, Dec. 6, 1838, and other contemporary newspapers. Parts are quoted in *Annual Register*, 1838; Reid, ii. 308-9; Bradshaw, pp. 232-3.

[13] *D.P.* 6, ii. 503 seq., Dec. 3, 1838.

[14] *Morning Chronicle*, Dec. 8, 1838 (from *Exeter Post*).

[15] Greville, pt. 2, i. 141-2.

[16] *Ibid.* i. 141 (Dec. 6, 1838).

[17] *Melbourne Papers*, p. 440, Melbourne to Russell, Dec. 4, 1838.

[18] See p. 138, *ante*.

[19] *Melbourne Papers*, pp. 440-1, Melbourne to Russell, Dec. 8, 1838.

20 *Ibid.*, p. 442, Melbourne to Russell, Dec. 11, 1838.

21 Lambton MSS., Dec. 21, 1838.

22 See pp. 119-20, *ante*.

23 Lambton MSS., Lady Durham to Lady Grey, 'Monday', 'Friday', 'Tuesday', [Jan. 10, 14, 18, 1839].

24 Pierce, *Memoirs of Charles Sumner* ii. 58.

25 Molesworth was converted and did yeoman service in support of Durham's ideas, but he was an exception among the Radical leaders. Even at this time he did not agree with them that colonies were good things to lose.

26 *D.P.* 6, iii. 414.

27 *Morning Chronicle,* Dec. 14, 15, 1838.

28 Buller, *Sketch*, pp. 363-4.

29 Lady Durham's Journal, p. 48, Lambton MSS., Dec. 21, 1838, Jan. 26, 1839.

30 Although Lady Durham uses the plural, the work that kept him busy must have been the writing of the main report, as he had nothing to do with 'getting up' the reports of the sub-commissioners which were printed as appendices.

31 Lambton MSS. Lady Durham to Charles Grey, Jan. 25, 1839.

32 *Ibid.*

33 Ellice wrote a microscopic hand and took little pains to form his letters. These two words 'many minds' represent what I must acknowledge to be a guess.

34 Lambton MSS., Ellice to Durham, 'Tuesday evening'.

35 *Ibid.*, 'Sunday' [Jan. 20 or Jan. 27, 1839].

36 *Melbourne Papers*, pp. 442-4, Melbourne to Russell, Dec. 11, 23, 1838.

37 *Girlhood of Queen Victoria*, ii. 110 seq.

CHAPTER VII: Lord Durham's Report
(pp. 167-185)

0 These quotations have been selected more or less at random from the shelves of my own library. Similar statements are so frequent in modern historical literature that further search would be a waste of time.

1 The above statement does not stand or fall with the answer to the question whether or not William IV dismissed the first Melbourne Ministry. I believe that he did. But there can be no doubt that such

action was considered constitutional at the time. The only objection taken was to the *manner* in which it was believed that the dismissal had been made.

[3] For the divergences between the views of Robert Baldwin and the recommendations of Lord Durham see pp. 95-6, *ante*.

[4] See E. M. Wrong, *Charles Buller and Responsible Government*, p. 19, where the similarity is indicated. Compare with Durham's words quoted above those of Buller in the 'Buller-Macarthur Constitution', Article XV, given in Sweetman, *Australian Constitutional Development*, p. 147.

[5] See particularly *Report*, pp. 310-12.

[6] *Report*, ii. 263.

[7] See Lucas, i. 232-9.

[8] Lower Canada had practically no municipal government at the time, and although Upper Canada had incorporated cities and elective township councils, the latter had very few powers and rural municipal expenditure was largely in the hands of the Legislature.

CHAPTER VIII: Immediate Reception of the Report
(pp. 186-218)

[0] *Morning Chronicle*, Feb. 16; *Times*, Feb. 13, 1839.

[2] Manuscript account of the Haliburton family by Miss Georgina Haliburton, quoted in Chittick, *Thomas Chandler Haliburton*, p. 242.

[3] *Times*, Feb. 18-26, 1839, letters signed 'A Colonist'. Also published in pamphlet form.

[4] One hesitates to use the term 'Family Compact' in relation to John Beverley Robinson, who certainly stands clear of any nepotism. The term was and is an unfair one, but for nearly a hundred years it has served as a proper name for a certain political group and as such the historian is bound to employ it. In that sense it may continue to be employed without its earlier opprobrium. The case is similar to that of many of our historical designations for political parties and religious denominations.

[5] C. W. Robinson, *Life of Sir John Beverley Robinson*, pp. 277-8.

[6] Q. 425: 42 seq.

[7] Draft in Robinson Papers (Ont. Arch. Pk. 23 E. 24, No. 18).

[8] *D.P.* 6, iii. 149, Feb. 8, 1839.

[9] *Ibid.* 6, iii. 156, Feb. 11, 1839.

[10] Printed in full in *Canadian Archives Report of 1923*, pp. 338 seq.

[11] Lambton MSS., Aug. 1, 1839.

[12] Lady Durham's Journal, 60-1; Buller's *Sketch*, 365; *D.P.* 6, iii. 396, 397.

[13] See Shortt, *Lord Sydenham*, pp. 135-41.

[14] Sweetman, *Australian Constitutional Development*, pp. 191-2.

[15] *D.P.* 6, iii. 410.

[16] Chittick, *Thomas Chandler Haliburton*, pp. 276-86, on which this paragraph is directly and entirely based.

[17] The letters are given in Egerton and Grant, pp. 190-252; Kennedy, *Documents*, pp. 480-514; J. A. Chisholm, *Speeches and Letters of Joseph Howe*, i. 221-66.

[18] *D.P.* 6, iii. 323.

[19] Lambton MSS., April 11, 1839; *D.P.* 6, iii. 300, April 12, 1839.

[20] Lafontaine Papers (Canadian Archives), Hincks to Lafontaine, Apr. 12, 30, May 4, Sept. 9, Nov. 14, 1839.

[21] Beginning 'The colonial Governor must, in this case . . .'. See Egerton and Grant, *Selected Speeches and Despatches,* p. 178, and Kennedy, *Constitutional Documents,* p. 472.

[22] The Legislative Council Report is given in Egerton and Grant, pp. 173-188 and in Kennedy's *Documents,* pp. 470-8. That of the Assembly may be found in the official documents (dispatches and journals) and in a reprint in pamphlet form, which is accessible in some of the better historical libraries.

[23] Q. 419: 21 seq., 61.

[24] *Christian Guardian,* Apr. 10, 1839.

[25] Quoted in *Toronto Mirror,* July 19, 1839.

[26] See Merritt Papers (Canadian Archives) and Merritt Papers (Ontario Archives).

[27] Strachan Papers (Ontario Archives), E. 21, Pk. 85, No. 7, July 25, 1839.

[28] Perrault Papers (Can. Arch.), Apr. 2, 1839.

[29] *Upper Canada Register,* June 7; *Niagara Reporter,* June 7; *Toronto Mirror,* June 14; *Cobourg Star,* June 19, 1839.

[30] *Cobourg Star,* July 10, 1839.

[31] *Hamilton Journal,* July 26, 1839.

[32] Q. 425; 470 seq.; 419: 89-91.

[33] *Hamilton Journal,* Aug. 2, 1839.

[34] *Toronto Mirror,* Aug. 2, Oct. 18; *Cobourg Star,* Oct. 23, 1839; Q. 424: 383 seq.

[35] Q. 419: 27 seq., 46 seq., Aug. 21, Sept. 27, 1839.

[36] G. 44: 19-35.

[37] G. 44. 57-8.

[38] Lafontaine Papers, June 17, 1840.

[39] *Cobourg Star,* Jan. 22, 1840.

[40] Q. 273: 276 seq., Sept. 16, 1840; Kennedy, *Documents of the Canadian Constitution,* pp. 155 seq.

[41] See Kennedy, *Documents,* pp. 564-5.

[42] *D.P.* 6, iii. 513 seq., Aug. 27, 1840.

Notes on Persons Mentioned in the Text

Lord Chandos, Tory peer, author of the famous "Chandos Clause" of 1831 which, against Durham's judgement, was added to the Reform Bill.

Thomas Denman, distinguished Whig lawyer and M.P.; one of the defence counsel in the trial of Queen Caroline.

Lord Duncannon, Lord Privy Seal in the second Melbourne government.

Edward Ellice, Whig M.P. and member of Durham's entourage in the early 1830's; Secretary for War in the Grey and first Melbourne governments.

Lord Glenelg, Secretary for War and Colonies in the second Melbourne government.

Lord Gosford, Governor of Lower Canada, 1835-38.

J. C. Hobhouse, Radical colleague of Durham in the Reform Movement; President of the Board of Control in the second Melbourne government.

Lord Howick, later third Earl Grey; Secretary for War in the second Melbourne government.

Joseph Hume, Radical M.P.

Lord Lansdowne, Lord President of the Council in the second Melbourne government.

R. E. Leader, Radical M.P.

Lord Lyndhurst, ex-chancellor and leading Tory in the House of Lords.

Harriet Martineau, popular publicist and advocate of reform.

Sir William Molesworth, Radical M.P. and advocate of colonial separation.

Joseph Parkes, Radical Birmingham lawyer and friend of Durham.

Sir Robert Peel, Tory leader in the House of Commons.

Francis Place, influential Radical leader in London.

J. A. Roebuck, Radical M.P. and friend of the Canadian Reformers.

Lord John Russell, Home Secretary in the second Melbourne government and Whig leader in the House of Commons.

Poulett Thomson, a political adherent of Durham; President of the Board of Trade in the second Melbourne government; later Lord Sydenham.

Henry Warburton, Radical M.P.

SUGGESTIONS FOR FURTHER READING

A selection from LORD DURHAM's *Report on the Affairs of British North America* is available in paperback form in the Carleton Library (Toronto, 1963). The complete Report is contained in an edition prepared by SIR CHARLES LUCAS (Oxford, 3 vols., 1912). A comprehensive bibliography of works relating to the Canadas in the 1830's can be found in the original edition of NEW's *Lord Durham* (Oxford, 1929). Two works especially, which describe political conditions in Upper Canada, should be mentioned: AILEEN DUNHAM *Political Unrest in Upper Canada, 1815-36* (London, 1927; reprinted in the Carleton Library, Toronto, 1963) and W. STEWART WALLACE, *The Family Compact* (Toronto, 1915). E. M. WRONG, *Charles Buller and Responsible Government* (Oxford, 1926) is a useful study of the Colonial Reformer who was Durham's principal political adviser. Attention should also be drawn to the *Report of the Public Archives, 1923* (Ottawa, 1924), which provides a calendar of the Durham Papers at the Public Archives of Canada, and reprints several documents and dispatches.

Among items published since the appearance of New's biography which bear on the period of Durham's mission to Canada are the following: WILLIAM SMITH, *Political Leaders of Upper Canada* (Toronto, 1931); D. G. CREIGHTON, *The Commercial Empire of the St. Lawrence, 1760-1850* (New Haven and Toronto, 1937; reprinted as *The Empire of the St. Lawrence*, Toronto, 1956); *Canadian Historical Review*, XX (June, 1939), containing articles by LORD TWEEDSMUIR, CHESTER NEW, GEORGE W. BROWN, D.C. HARVEY, and CHESTER MARTIN, commemorating the centenary of the Report; L'ABBE ARTHUR MAHEUX, "Durham et la Nationalité Canadienne-Française," *Annual Report* of the Canadian Historical Association, 1943, pp. 19-24; H. T. MANNING, *The Revolt of French Canada, 1800-1835* (Toronto, 1962); and G. M. CRAIG, *Upper Canada: The Formative Years, 1784-1841* (Toronto, 1963).

NOTE ON THE AUTHOR

Chester William New, though born in Montreal, spent most of his life in Hamilton, Ontario. He studied at the University of Toronto, taking his B.A. in 1903, followed by a B.D. from McMaster in 1907 and, after graduate work in England and Germany, by a PH.D. from Chicago in 1913. He joined the staff of McMaster University in 1920 and served as Head of its History Department for almost thirty years before retiring in 1951. The products of his academic career included many hundreds of enthusiastically affectionate students, a series of Rhodes Scholars, and a small number of major historical works of the highest quality.

His *Lord Durham* (Oxford, 1929) won for him the gold medal of the Royal Empire Society and the acclaim of scholars on both sides of the Atlantic. A full-scale biography of Lord Brougham became his second principal undertaking, a project which grew directly out of his *Lord Durham*. It was after thirty years of work on this subject, and just as the page proofs of the first volume had been corrected, that he died in 1960 at the age of seventy-eight. The book was published posthumously by Oxford University Press with the title, *The Life of Lord Brougham to 1830* (1961).

Professor New was a member of the Athenaeum Club and Fellow both of the Royal Society of Canada and of the Royal Historical Society. He served for some time on the editorial board of the *Journal of Modern History* and was elected President of the Canadian Historical Association in 1936.

THE CARLETON LIBRARY